GACE Middle Grades
015 Social Science

Teacher Certification Exam

By: Sharon Wynne, M.S.
Southern Connecticut State University

"And, while there's no reason yet to panic, I think it's only prudent that we make preparations to panic."

XAMonline, INC.
Boston

SOCIAL STUDIES

To obtain permission(s) to use the material from this work for any purpose including workshops or seminars, please submit a written request to:

XAMonline, Inc.
21 Orient Ave.
Melrose, MA 02176
Toll Free 1-800-509-4128
Email: info@xamonline.com
Web www.xamonline.com
Fax: 1-781-662-9268

Library of Congress Cataloging-in-Publication Data
Wynne, Sharon A.
GACE: Middle Grades Social Science 015   Teacher Certification / Sharon A. Wynne.
ISBN: 978-1-58197-546-8
1. Middle Grades Social Science 015 2. Study Guides. 3. GACE 4. Teachers' Certification & Licensure
5. Careers

Managing Editor	Dr. Harte Weiner, Ph. D.
Copy Editor	Ira Glasser, B.A.
Associate Editor	Kerrie Forbes, B.A.

Disclaimer:

The opinions expressed in this publication are the sole works of XAMonline and were created independently from the National Education Association, Educational Testing Service, or any State Department of Education, National Evaluation Systems or other testing affiliates. Between the time of publication and printing, state specific standards as well as testing formats and website information may change that is not included in part or in whole within this product. Sample test questions are developed by XAMonline and reflect similar content as on real tests; however, they are not former tests. XAMonline assembles content that aligns with state standards but makes no claims nor guarantees teacher candidates a passing score. Numerical scores are determined by testing companies such as NES or ETS and then are compared with individual state standards. A passing score varies from state to state.

Printed in the United States of America   œ-1

GACE: Middle Grades Social Science 015
ISBN: 978-1-58197-686-1

Table of Contents

Great Study and Testing Tips!

What to study in order to prepare for the subject assessments is the focus of this study guide but equally important is *how* you study.

You can increase your chances of truly mastering the information by taking some simple, but effective steps.

Study Tips:

1. <u>Some foods aid the learning process</u>. Foods such as milk, nuts, seeds, rice, and oats help your study efforts by releasing natural memory enhancers called CCKs (*cholecystokinin*) composed of *tryptopha*n, *choline*, and *phenylalanine*. All of these chemicals enhance the neurotransmitters associated with memory. Before studying, try a light, protein-rich meal of eggs, turkey, and fish. All of these foods release the memory enhancing chemicals. The better the connections, the more you comprehend.

Likewise, before you take a test, stick to a light snack of energy boosting and relaxing foods. A glass of milk, a piece of fruit, or some peanuts all release various memory-boosting chemicals and help you to relax and focus on the subject at hand.

2. <u>Learn to take great notes</u>. A by-product of our modern culture is that we have grown accustomed to getting our information in short doses (i.e. TV news sound bites or USA Today style newspaper articles.)

Consequently, we've subconsciously trained ourselves to assimilate information better in <u>neat little packages</u>. If your notes are scrawled all over the paper, it fragments the flow of the information. Strive for clarity. Newspapers use a standard format to achieve clarity. Your notes can be much clearer through use of proper formatting. A very effective format is called the <u>*"Cornell Method."*</u>

Take a sheet of loose-leaf lined notebook paper and draw a line all the way down the paper about 1-2" from the left-hand edge.

Draw another line across the width of the paper about 1-2" up from the bottom. Repeat this process on the reverse side of the page.

Look at the highly effective result. You have ample room for notes, a left hand margin for special emphasis items or inserting supplementary data from the textbook, a large area at the bottom for a brief summary, and a little rectangular space for just about anything you want.

3. Get the concept then the details. Too often we focus on the details and don't gather an understanding of the concept. However, if you simply memorize only dates, places, or names, you may well miss the whole point of the subject.

A key way to understand things is to put them in your own words. If you are working from a textbook, automatically summarize each paragraph in your mind. If you are outlining text, don't simply copy the author's words.

Rephrase them in your own words. You remember your own thoughts and words much better than someone else's, and subconsciously tend to associate the important details to the core concepts.

4. Ask Why? Pull apart written material paragraph by paragraph and don't forget the captions under the illustrations.

Example: If the heading is "Stream Erosion", flip it around to read "Why do streams erode?" Then answer the questions.

If you train your mind to think in a series of questions and answers, not only will you learn more, but it also helps to lessen the test anxiety because you are used to answering questions.

5. Read for reinforcement and future needs. Even if you only have 10 minutes, put your notes or a book in your hand. Your mind is similar to a computer; you have to input data in order to have it processed. *By reading, you are creating the neural connections for future retrieval.* The more times you read something, the more you reinforce the learning of ideas.

Even if you don't fully understand something on the first pass, *your mind stores much of the material for later recall.*

6. Relax to learn so go into exile. Our bodies respond to an inner clock called biorhythms. Burning the midnight oil works well for some people, but not everyone.

If possible, set aside a particular place to study that is free of distractions. Shut off the television, cell phone, pager and exile your friends and family during your study period.

If you really are bothered by silence, try background music. Light classical music at a low volume has been shown to aid in concentration over other types. Music that evokes pleasant emotions without lyrics are highly suggested. Try just about anything by Mozart. It relaxes you.

7. <u>Use arrows not highlighters</u>. At best, it's difficult to read a page full of yellow, pink, blue, and green streaks. Try staring at a neon sign for a while and you'll soon see that the horde of colors obscure the message.

A quick note, a brief dash of color, an underline, and an arrow pointing to a particular passage is much clearer than a horde of highlighted words.

8. <u>Budget your study time</u>. Although you shouldn't ignore any of the material, *allocate your available study time in the same ratio that topics may appear on the test.*

Testing Tips:

1. Get smart, play dumb. Don't read anything into the question. Don't make an assumption that the test writer is looking for something else than what is asked. Stick to the question as written and don't read extra things into it.

2. Read the question and all the choices *twice* before answering the question. You may miss something by not carefully reading, and then re-reading both the question and the answers.

If you really don't have a clue as to the right answer, leave it blank on the first time through. Go on to the other questions, as they may provide a clue as to how to answer the skipped questions.

If later on, you still can't answer the skipped ones . . . *Guess.* The only penalty for guessing is that you *might* get it wrong. Only one thing is certain; if you don't put anything down, you will get it wrong!

3. Turn the question into a statement. Look at the way the questions are worded. The syntax of the question usually provides a clue. Does it seem more familiar as a statement rather than as a question? Does it sound strange?

By turning a question into a statement, you may be able to spot if an answer sounds right, and it may also trigger memories of material you have read.

4. Look for hidden clues. It's actually very difficult to compose multiple-foil (choice) questions without giving away part of the answer in the options presented.

In most multiple-choice questions you can often readily eliminate one or two of the potential answers. This leaves you with only two real possibilities and automatically your odds go to Fifty-Fifty for very little work.

5. Trust your instincts. For every fact that you have read, you subconsciously retain something of that knowledge. On questions that you aren't really certain about, go with your basic instincts. **Your first impression on how to answer a question is usually correct.**

6. Mark your answers directly on the test booklet. Don't bother trying to fill in the optical scan sheet on the first pass through the test.

Be careful not to miss-mark your answers when you transcribe them to the scan sheet.

7. Watch the clock! You have a set amount of time to answer the questions. Don't get bogged down trying to answer a single question at the expense of 10 questions you can more readily answer.

DOMAIN I.   U.S. HISTORY

COMPETENCY 1.0   UNDERSTAND NATIVE AMERICAN CULTURES AND
                    THE EUROPEAN SETTLEMENT OF NORTH
                    AMERICA.

Skill 1.1   Demonstrate knowledge of how early Native American cultures
               developed in North America, analyze why Native American
               groups occupied the areas they did, and demonstrate
               familiarity with basic features of different Native American
               cultures

Though not greatly differing from each other in degree of civilization, the native peoples north of present-day Mexico varied widely in customs, housing, dress, and religion. Among the native peoples of North America there were at least 200 languages and 1500 dialects. Each of the hundreds of tribes was somewhat influenced by its neighbors. Communication between tribes that spoke different languages was conducted primarily through a very elaborate system of sign language. Several groups of tribes can be distinguished.

The Woods Peoples occupied the area from the Atlantic to the Western plains and prairies. They cultivated corn and tobacco, fished and hunted.

The Plains Peoples, who populated the area from the Mississippi River to the Rocky Mountains, were largely wandering and warlike, hunting buffalo and other game for food. After the arrival of Europeans and the re-introduction of the horse they became great horsemen.

The Southwestern Tribes of New Mexico and Arizona included Pueblos, who lived in villages constructed of *adobe* (sun-dried brick), cliff dwellers, and nomadic tribes. These tribes had the most advanced civilizations.

The California Tribes were separated from the influence of other tribes by the mountains. They lived primarily on acorns, seeds and fish, and were probably the least advanced civilizations.

The Northwest Coast Peoples of Washington, British Columbia and Southern Alaska were not acquainted with farming, but built large wooden houses and traveled in huge cedar canoes.

The Plateau Peoples, who lived between the plains and the Pacific coast, were simple people who lived in underground houses or brush huts and subsisted primarily on fish.

The native peoples of America, like other peoples of the same stage of development, believed that all objects, both animate and inanimate, were endowed with certain spiritual powers. They believed a soul inhabited every living thing. Certain birds and animals were considered more powerful and intelligent than humans and capable of influence for good or evil. These people were intensely religious, and lived every aspect of their lives as their religion prescribed.

Most of the tribes were divided into clans of close blood relations, whose *totem* was a particular animal from which they were often believed to have descended. The sun and the four principal directions were often objects of worship. The *shaman*, a sort of priest, was often the *medicine-man* of a tribe. Sickness was often supposed to be the result of displeasing some spirit and was treated with incantations and prayer. Many of the traditional stories resemble those of other peoples in providing answers to primordial questions and guidance for life. The highest virtue was self-control. Hiding emotions and enduring pain or torture unflinchingly was required of each. Honesty was also a primary virtue, and promises were always honored no matter what the personal cost.

For the most part, these communities did not have any strict form of government. Each individual was responsible for governing him or herself, particularly with regard to the rights of other members of the community. The chiefs generally carried out the will of the tribe. Each tribe was a discrete unit, with its own land. Boundaries of tribal territories were determined by treaties with neighbors. There was an organized confederation among certain tribes, often called a nation. For example, the Iroquois confederation was often referred to as "The Five Nations" (later "The Six Nations").

Customs varied from tribe to tribe. One consistent cultural element was the smoking of the calumet, a stone pipe, at the beginning and end of a war. In Native American communities, no individual owned land. The plots of land that were cultivated were, however, respected. Wealth was sometimes an honor, but generosity was more highly valued. Agriculture was quite advanced and irrigation was practiced in some locations. Most tribes practiced unique styles of basket work, pottery and weaving, either in terms of shape or decoration.

Skill 1.2   Demonstrate knowledge of reasons for and obstacles to European exploration and settlement of North America.

During the Age of Exploration, a major goal was a route to the East by sailing west across the Atlantic Ocean.

Of course, everyone knows that Columbus' first trans-Atlantic voyage was to try to prove his theory or idea that Asia could be reached by sailing west. To a certain extent, his idea was true. It could be done but only after figuring how to go around or across or through the landmass in between. Soon after Spain dispatched explorers and her famed conquistadors to gather the wealth for the Spanish monarchs and their coffers, the British were searching valiantly for the "Northwest Passage." This was a land-sea route across North America and the open sea to the wealth of Asia. It was not until after the Lewis and Clark Expedition when Captains Meriwether Lewis and William Clark proved conclusively that there simply was no Northwest Passage – it did not exist.

However, this did not deter exploration and settlement. Spain, France, and England (along with some participation by the Dutch) led the way with expanding Western European civilization in the New World. These nations had strong monarchial governments and were struggling for dominance and power in Europe. With the defeat of Spain's mighty Armada in 1588, England became undisputed mistress of the seas. Spain lost its power and influence in Europe and it was left to France and England to carry on the rivalry, leading to eventual British control in Asia as well.

Spain's influence was in Florida, the Gulf Coast from Texas all the way west to California, south to the tip of South America, and some of the islands of the West Indies. French control centered from New Orleans north to what is now northern Canada including the entire Mississippi Valley, the St. Lawrence Valley, the Great Lakes, and the land that constituted the Louisiana Territory. A few West Indies islands were also part of France's empire. England settled the eastern seaboard of North America, including parts of Canada and from Maine to Georgia. Some West Indies islands also came under British control. The Dutch had New Amsterdam for a period but later ceded it into British hands. One interesting aspect was with each of these three nations, especially England, the land claims extended partly or all the way across the continent, regardless of the fact that the others claimed the same land. The wars for dominance and control of power and influence in Europe would undoubtedly and eventually extend to the Americas, especially North America.

Skill 1.3 **Recognize the goals and accomplishments of major Spanish, French, Dutch, and English explorations led by Vasco Núñez de Balboa, Juan Ponce de León, Christopher Columbus, Jacques Cartier, Henry Hudson, and John Cabot,**

In the century and a half after 1520, European nations began to reap the benefits of the age of exploration and discovery. They began a period of economic and colonial expansion that spread European civilization throughout the world. Europeans invaded the Far East and unknown areas to the West, and pillaging, trading, colonizing, and introducing Christianity to the native peoples. Capitalism spread to an extent that essentially dominated the economic activities of the nations. Considering the rate of expansion of overseas trade, the great increase in the volume and variety of goods transported, and the resulting increase in the wealth of European nations, it seems appropriate to speak of a "commercial revolution." Several factors fueled this desire for expansion, including: the desire for knowledge, the desire to convert the heathen natives to Christianity, the lust for gold and silver, and the capitalist desire to reap the benefits of trade.

In the early years of expansion, the most active peoples were the Spanish, the Portuguese, and the Dutch. In fact, in 1494, the Pope divided the planet between Spain and Portugal. The French and English did not become active players in the competition for foreign colonies and domination until the 17th century. By 1600 foreign trade was becoming more important to both nations. The English East India Company was typical of the way this expansion was occurring. This was a chartered company, rather than a government effort, that became the agency of expansion.

Portugal made the start under the encouragement, support, and financing of Prince Henry the Navigator. The better known explorers who sailed under the flag of Portugal included Cabral, Diaz, and Vasco da Gama, who successfully sailed all the way from Portugal, around the southern tip of Africa, to Calcutta, India.

Christopher Columbus, sailing for **Spain**, is credited with the discovery of America although he never set foot on its soil. Ferdinand Magellan is credited with the first circumnavigation of the earth. Other Spanish explorers made their marks in parts of what are now the United States, Mexico, and South America.

For **France**, claims to various parts of North America were the result of the efforts of such men as Verrazano, Champlain, Cartier, LaSalle, Father Marquette and Joliet. **Dutch** claims were based on the work of one Henry Hudson. **England** gained its stake in North America with explorers John Cabot, John Hawkins, Sir Francis Drake, and the half-brothers Sir Walter Raleigh and Sir Humphrey Gilbert.

Actually, the first Europeans to explore the New World were Norsemen led by Eric the Red and later, his son Leif the Lucky. However, before any of these, the ancestors of today's Native Americans and Latin American Indians crossed the Bering Strait from Asia to Alaska, eventually settling in all parts of the Americas.

Skill 1.4 Identify key events in the foundation of different European settlements

Competition for trade monopolies in the East led to a struggle between the English and the Dutch. England's first Navigation Act (1651) was directed against the Dutch. There was rivalry with Spain for control of various areas on the part of the Dutch and the English. This was superseded by the *Anglo-Dutch Wars*. There were a number of issues in this conflict: slave trade of Africa, Atlantic fisheries, North American settlements, and trade. The Dutch East India Company had shut off the Spice Islands from the English. The final result was an English trading post in the Spice Islands.

England and France had stood together to evict the Dutch from the North American mainland. Numerous changes were occurring, however, within England, eventually bringing William of Orange to the throne. William and Louis XIV of France were bitter enemies, and this opinion turned the view that England's true enemy was France. This resulted in the Anglo-French Conflict. Both nations had adopted mercantilist policies. Both countries had competing colonies and trading interests in the New World, Asia and the West Indian islands. On the North American mainland, English settlements essentially controlled the Atlantic coast from Maine to Georgia. These areas were well populated and provided fish, tobacco, and trade. Although less densely populated, the French had claims of a large area of land. The Louisiana Territory was under French control. Competition between England and France for land, sugar, and furs was intense. The English colonies were barred from westward expansion by French territory, which was being protected by a strong line of military defenses. India, which was densely populated and in possession of a strong culture, was also highly prized by both nations. By 1689 the English had established outposts at Bombay, Madras, and Calcutta. The French had come to India somewhat later and established their outposts in two areas near Calcutta and Madras. Both nations saw these outposts as entry points for greater penetration of India, and were the loci of the conflicts that ensued.

The first struggle was *The War of the League of Augsburg,* which occurred in Acadia. The Treaty of Ryswick restored the previous division of territory. The second was *The War of the Spanish Succession*. English and Dutch sea power prevailed over French and Spanish. The Treaty of Utrecht gave England clear possession of Acadia (New Scotland), Newfoundland, Hudson Bay, and St. Kitts in the West Indies. The third conflict was *The War of the Austrian Succession*. This was a resumption of the hostilities between England and Spain. It merged into the European War. France and England were at odds again in North America and in India. The treaty of Aix-la-Chapelle restored pre-war territorial holdings. The French had, however, strengthened their positions in the Louisiana territory. The issue of control of the Ohio Valley led to the French and Indian Wars. Spain tried to intervene on behalf of France, but it was too late. The war in India, at about the same time, ended with the British dominating the east coast of India. Both of these struggles came to be incorporated into the Seven Years' War in Europe. The Treaty of Paris (1763) restored peace at a very high cost to France. The treaty essentially ended France's claim to be an imperial power.

When the American colonies declared independence thirteen years later, the assistance of the French was critical to the success of the colonies. With the decline of French power, England was able to expand her empire and consolidate her interests.

Skill 1.5 Examine interactions among different groups of Europeans and Native Americans and recognize how early European settlers adapted or failed to adapt to the physical environments in which they lived and traveled

In the non-settled areas of interior North America were the French fur traders. They made friends with welcoming tribes of Indians, spending the winters with them getting the furs needed for trade. In the spring, they would return to Montreal in time to take advantage of trading their furs for the products brought by the cargo ships from France, which usually arrived at about the same time. Most of the wealth for New France and its "Mother Country" was from the fur trade, which provided a livelihood for many, many people. Manufacturers and workmen back in France, ship-owners and merchants, as well as the fur traders and their Indian allies all benefited from this alliance. However, the freedom of roaming and trapping in the interior was a strong enticement for the younger, stronger men. This resulted in the French not strengthening the areas settled along the St. Lawrence.

Into the 18th century, the rivalry with the British was getting stronger and stronger. New France was united under a single government and enjoyed the support of many Indian allies. The French traders were very diligent in not destroying the forests and driving away game upon which the Indians depended for life. It was difficult for the French to defend all of their settlements as they were scattered over half of the continent. However, by the early 1750s in Western Europe, France was the most powerful nation. Its armies were superior to all others and its navy was giving the British stiff competition for control of the seas. The stage was set for confrontation in both Europe and America.

Spanish settlement had its beginnings in the Caribbean with the establishment of colonies on Hispaniola (at Santo Domingo which became the capital of the West Indies), Puerto Rico, and Cuba. There were a number of reasons for Spanish involvement in the Americas, to name just a few:

• The spirit of adventure;
• The desire for land;
• Expansion of Spanish power, influence, and empire;
• The desire for great wealth; and
• Expansion of Roman Catholic influence and conversion of native peoples.

The first permanent settlement in what is now the United States was in 1565 at St. Augustine, Florida. A second permanent settlement was in the southwestern United States at Santa Fe, New Mexico in 1609. At the peak of Spanish power, the area in the United States claimed, settled, and controlled by Spain included Florida and all land west of the Mississippi River--quite a piece of choice real estate.

Of course, France and England also lay claim to the same areas. Nonetheless, ranches and missions were built and the Indians who came in contact with the Spaniards were introduced to animals, plants, and seeds from the Old World that they had never seen before. Animals brought in included: horses, cattle, donkeys, pigs, sheep, goats and poultry.

Spain's control over her New World colonies lasted more than 300 years – longer than those of England and France. To this day, Spanish influence remains in names of places, art, architecture, music, literature, law, and cuisine. The Spanish settlements in North America were not commercial enterprises but were for protection and defense of the trading and wealth from their colonies in Mexico and South America. The Russians hunting seals came down the Pacific coast, the English moved into Florida and west into and beyond the Appalachians, and the French traders and trappers were making their way from Louisiana and other parts of New France into Spanish territory. The Spanish never realized or understood that self-sustaining economic development and colonial trade was so important. Consequently, the Spanish settlements in the U.S. never really prospered.

Before 1763, when England was rapidly on the way to becoming the most powerful of the three major Western European powers, its thirteen colonies, located between the Atlantic and the Appalachians, physically occupied the least amount of land. Moreover, it is interesting that even before the Spanish Armada was defeated, two Englishmen, Sir Humphrey Gilbert and his half-brother Sir Walter Raleigh were unsuccessful in their attempts to build successful permanent colonies in the New World. Nonetheless, the thirteen English colonies were successful and, by the time they had gained their independence from Britain, were more than able to govern themselves. They had a rich historical heritage of law, tradition, and documents leading the way to constitutional government conducted according to laws and customs. The settlers in the British colonies highly valued individual freedom, democratic government, and getting ahead through hard work.

Skill 1.6 **Compare and contrast life in the New England, mid-Atlantic, and Southern colonies - including the experiences of landowners, farmers, artisans, women, indentured servants, and slaves, and analyze how the physical geography of each colony helped determine the economic activities that were practiced there**

The English colonies, with only a few exceptions, were considered commercial ventures to make a profit for the crown or the company or whoever financed its beginnings. One was strictly a philanthropic enterprise and three others were primarily for religious reasons but the other nine were started for economic reasons. Settlers in these unique colonies came for different reasons:

- Religious Freedom
- Political Freedom
- Economic Prosperity
- Land Ownership

The colonies were divided generally into the three regions of New England, Middle Atlantic, and Southern. The culture of each was distinct and affected attitudes, ideas towards politics, religion, and economic activities. The geography of each region also contributed to its unique characteristics.

The New England colonies consisted of Massachusetts, Rhode Island, Connecticut, and New Hampshire. Life in these colonies was centered on the towns. What farming was done was by each family on its own plot of land but a short summer growing season and limited amount of good soil gave rise to other economic activities such as manufacturing, fishing, shipbuilding, and trade. The vast majority of the settlers shared similar English and Scottish origins. Towns were carefully planned and each one was laid out in the same way. The form of government was the town meeting where all adult males met to make the laws. The legislative body, the General Court, consisted of upper and lower houses.

The Middle or Middle Atlantic colonies included New York, New Jersey, Pennsylvania, Delaware, and Maryland. New York and New Jersey were at one time the Dutch colony of New Netherlands and Delaware at one time was New Sweden. These five colonies, from their beginnings were considered "melting pots" with settlers from many different nations and backgrounds. The main economic activity was farming with the settlers scattered over the countryside cultivating rather large farms. The Indians were not as much of a threat as in New England so they did not have to settle in small farming villages. The soil was very fertile, the land was gently rolling, and a milder climate provided a longer growing season.

These farms produced a large surplus of food, not only for the colonists themselves but also for sale. This colonial region became known as the "breadbasket" of the New World. The New York and Philadelphia seaports were constantly filled with ships being loaded with meat, flour, and other foodstuffs for the West Indies and England. There were other economic activities such as shipbuilding, iron mines, and factories producing paper, glass, and textiles. The legislative body in Pennsylvania was unicameral or consisted of one house. In the other four colonies, the legislative body had two houses. The units of local government were in counties and towns.

The Southern colonies were Virginia, North and South Carolina, and Georgia. Virginia was the first permanent successful English colony and Georgia was the last. The year 1619 was a very important year in the history of Virginia and the United States with three very significant events. First, sixty women were sent to Virginia to marry and establish families. Second, twenty Africans, the first of thousands, arrived; and third, most importantly, the Virginia colonists were granted the right to self-government and they began by electing their own representatives to the House of Burgesses, their own legislative body.

The major economic activity in this region was farming. Here the soil was very fertile and the climate was very mild with an even longer growing season. The large plantations eventually requiring large numbers of slaves were found in the coastal or tidewater areas. Although the wealthy slave-owning planters set the pattern of life in this region, most of the people lived inland away from coastal areas. They were small farmers and very few, it any, owned slaves.

The settlers in these four colonies came from diverse backgrounds and cultures. Virginia was colonized mostly by people from England while Georgia was started as a haven for debtors from English prisons. Pioneers from Virginia settled in North Carolina while South Carolina welcomed people from England and Scotland, French Protestants, Germans, and emigrants from islands in the West Indies. Products from farms and plantations included rice, tobacco, indigo, cotton, some corn and wheat. Other economic activities included lumber and naval stores (tar, pitch, rosin, and turpentine) from the pine forests and fur trade on the frontier. Cities such as Savannah and Charleston were important seaports and trading centers.

In the colonies, the daily life of the colonists differed greatly between the coastal settlements and those inland. The Southern planters and the people living in the coastal cities and towns had a way of life similar to that in towns in England. This influence was seen and heard in the way people dressed and talked; the architectural styles of houses and public buildings, and the social divisions or levels of society. Both the planters and city dwellers enjoyed an active social life and had strong emotional ties to England.

On the other hand, life inland on the frontier had marked differences. All facets of daily living – clothing, food, home, economic, and social activities – were all connected to what was needed to sustain life and survive in the wilderness. Everything was produced practically themselves. They were self-sufficient and extremely individualistic and independent. There were little, if any, levels of society or class distinctions as they considered themselves to be the equal to all others, regardless of station in life. The roots of equality, independence, individual rights and freedoms were extremely strong and well developed. People were not judged by their fancy dress, expensive house, eloquent language, or titles following their names.

COMPETENCY 2.0   UNDERSTAND THE CAUSES, EVENTS, AND OUTCOMES OF THE AMERICAN REVOLUTION AND THE DEVELOPMENT OF THE U.S. CONSTITUTION.

Skill 2.1   Recognize major causes of conflict between the colonies and the British government

In 1763, Spain, France, and Great Britain met to draw up the Treaty of Paris. Great Britain got most of India and all of North America east of the Mississippi River, except for New Orleans. From Spain, Britain received control of Florida and returned Cuba and the islands of the Philippines, taken during the war. France lost nearly all of its possessions in America. India and was allowed to keep four islands: Guadeloupe, Martinique, Haiti on Hispaniola, and Miquelon and St. Pierre. France gave Spain New Orleans and the vast territory of Louisiana, west of the Mississippi River. Britain was now the most powerful nation – period.

Where did all of this leave the British colonies? Their colonial militias had fought with the British and they too benefited. These militias and their officers gained much experience in fighting, something that would be very valuable later. The thirteen colonies began to realize that cooperating with each other was the only way to defend themselves. They did not really understand the importance of unity until the war for independence and setting up a national government, but a start had been made. At the onset of the war in 1754, Benjamin Franklin proposed to the thirteen colonies that they unite permanently, so they could protect themselves from the British. This was after the French and their Indian allies had defeated Major George Washington and his militia at **Fort Necessity**. The entire northern frontier of the British colonies was left vulnerable and open to attack.

Delegates from seven of the thirteen colonies met at Albany, New York, along with the representatives from the **Iroquois Confederation** and British officials. Franklin's proposal, known as the Albany Plan of Union called for a crown appointed President and the establishment of an assembly made up of representatives of the colonies. This plan was totally rejected by the colonists, along with a similar proposal from the British. They simply did not want each of the colonies to lose its right to act independently. However, the seed of self-governance was planted.

The **War for Independence** occurred due to a number of changes – the two most important ones being economic and political. By the end of the French and Indian War in 1763, Britain's American colonies were 13 out of a total of 33 scattered around the earth. Like all other countries, Britain strove for having a strong economy and a favorable balance of trade. To have that delicate balance a nation needs wealth, self-sufficiency, and a powerful army and navy. The overseas colonies would provide raw materials for the industries in the Mother Country, be a market for the finished products by buying them and assist her in becoming powerful and strong (as in the case of Great Britain). By having a strong merchant fleet, it would be a school for training the Royal Navy and provide bases of operation for the Royal Navy.

The foregoing explained the major reason for British encouragement and support of colonization, especially in North America. Thus, between 1607 and 1763, at various times and for various reasons, the British Parliament enacted different laws to assist the government in getting and keeping this trade balance. One series of laws required that most of the manufacturing be done only in England, such as: prohibition of exporting any wool or woolen cloth from the colonies and banning the manufacture of beaver hats or iron products. The colonists were not concerned as they lacked money and highly skilled labor to set up any industries anyway.

The **Navigation Acts** of 1651 put restrictions on shipping and trade within the British Empire by requiring that they were allowed only on British ships. This increased the strength of the British merchant fleet and greatly benefited the American colonists. Since they were British citizens, they could have their own vessels, building and operating them as well. By the end of the war in 1763, the shipyards in the colonies were building one third of the merchant ships under the British flag. There were quite a number of wealthy, American, colonial merchants.

The Navigation Act of 1660 restricted the shipment and sale of colonial products to England only. In 1663 another Navigation Act stipulated that the colonies had to buy manufactured products only from England and that any European goods going to the colonies had to go through England first. These acts were a protection from enemy ships and pirates and from competition from European rivals.

The New England and Middle Atlantic colonies at first felt threatened by these laws. The colonies started to produce many of the products that were produced in Britain. They soon found new markets for their goods and began a "triangular trade." Colonial vessels started the first part of the triangle by sailing for Africa loaded with kegs of rum from colonial distilleries. On Africa's West Coast, the rum was traded for either gold or slaves. The second part of the triangle was from Africa to the West Indies where slaves were traded for molasses, sugar, or money. The third part of the triangle was home, bringing sugar or molasses (to make more rum), gold, and silver.

The major concern of the British government was that the trade violated the **1733 Molasses Act**. Planters had wanted the colonists to buy all of their molasses in the British West Indies but these islands could give the traders only about one eighth of the amount of molasses needed for distilling the rum. The colonists were forced to buy the rest of what they needed from the French, Dutch, and Spanish islands, thus evading the law by not paying the high duty on the molasses bought from these islands. If Britain had enforced the Molasses Act, economic and financial chaos and ruin would have occurred. Nevertheless, for this act and all the other mercantile laws, the government followed the policy of "salutary neglect," deliberately failing to enforce the laws.

In 1763, after the war, money was needed to pay the British war debt, for the defense of the empire, and to pay for the governing of 33 colonies scattered around the earth. The British then decided to adopt a new colonial policy and pass laws in order to raise revenue. It was reasoned that the colonists were subjects of the king and since the king and his ministers had spent a great deal of money defending and protecting them (this especially for the American colonists), therefore, it was only right and fair that the colonists should help pay the costs of their defense. The earlier laws passed had been for the purposes of regulating production and trade which generally put money into colonial pockets. These new laws would take some of that rather hard-earned money out of their pockets and it would be done, in colonial eyes, unjustly and illegally.

Before 1763, except for trade and supplying raw materials, the colonies had been left pretty much autonomous. England looked on them merely as part of an economic or commercial empire. Since little consideration was given as to how they were to conduct their daily affairs, the colonists became very independent, self-reliant, and extremely skillful at handling those daily affairs. This, in turn, gave rise to leadership, initiative, achievement, and vast experience. In fact, there was a far greater degree of independence and self-government in the British colonies in America than could be found in Britain or the major countries on the Continent or any other colonies anywhere.

There were a number of reasons for this:

1. The religious and scriptural teachings of previous centuries put forth the worth of the individual and equality in God's sight. Keep in mind that freedom of worship and from religious persecution were major reasons to live in the New World.

2. European Protestants, especially Calvinists, believed and taught the idea that government originates from those governed, that rulers are required to protect individual rights and that the governed have the right and privilege to choose their rulers.

3. Trading companies put into practice the principle that their members had the right to make the decisions and shape the policies affecting their lives.

4. The colonists believed and supported the idea that a person's property should not be taken without his consent, based on that treasured English document, the Magna Carta, and English common law.

5. From about 1700 to 1750, population increases in America came about through immigration and generations of descendants of the original settlers. The immigrants were mainly Scots and Irish, who hated the English; Germans, who cared nothing about England; and black slaves, who knew nothing about England. The descendants of the original settlers had never been out of America at any time.

6. In America, as new towns and counties were formed, the practice of representation in government began. Representatives to the colonial legislative assemblies were elected from the district in which they lived, chosen by qualified property-owning male voters, and representing the interests of the political district from which they were elected. One thing to remember: each of the 13 colonies had a royal governor appointed by the king representing his interests in the colonies. Nevertheless, the colonial legislative assemblies controlled the purse strings having the power to vote on all issues involving money to be spent by the colonial governments.

Contrary to this was the governmental set-up in England. Members of Parliament were not elected to represent their own districts. They were considered representative of classes, not individuals. If some members of a professional or commercial class or some landed interests were able to elect representatives, then those classes or special interests were represented. It had nothing at all to do with numbers or territories. Some large population centers had no direct representation at all, yet the people there considered themselves represented by men elected from their particular class or interest somewhere else. Consequently, it was extremely difficult for the English to understand why the American merchants and landowners claimed they were not represented because they themselves did not vote for a Member of Parliament.

The colonists' protest of "no taxation without representation" was meaningless to the English. Parliament represented the entire nation, was completely unlimited in legislation, and had become supreme; the colonists were incensed at the English attitude of "of course you have representation--everyone does." The colonists considered their colonial legislative assemblies equal to Parliament, which was, of course, totally unacceptable in England. There were two different environments: the older traditional British system in England, and the new and different ideas and ways of government in America. In a new country, a new environment has little or no tradition, institutions, or vested interests. New ideas and traditions grew extremely fast pushing aside what was left of the old ideas and old traditions. By 1763, Britain had changed its perception of its American colonies to their being a "territorial" empire. The stage was set and the conditions were right for a showdown.

In 1763, Parliament decided to have a standing army in North America to reinforce British control. In 1765, the **Quartering Act** was passed requiring the colonists to provide supplies and living quarters for the British troops. In addition, efforts by the British were made to keep the peace by establishing good relations with the Indians. Consequently, a proclamation was issued which prohibited any American colonists from making any settlements west of the Appalachians until provided for through treaties with the Indians.

The Sugar Act of 1764 required efficient collection of taxes on any molasses that were brought into the colonies. It also gave British officials free license to conduct searches of the premises of anyone suspected of violating the law. The colonists were taxed on newspapers, legal documents, and other printed matter under the **Stamp Act of 1765**. Although a stamp tax was already in use in England, the colonists would have none of it and after the ensuing uproar of rioting and mob violence, Parliament repealed the tax.

Of course, great exultation, jubilance, and wild joy resulted when news of the repeal reached America. However, what no one noticed was the small, quiet **Declaratory Act** attached to the repeal. This act plainly and unequivocally stated that Parliament still had the right to make all laws for the colonies. It denied their right to be taxed only by their own colonial legislatures – a very crucial, important piece of legislation but virtually overlooked and unnoticed at the time. Other acts leading up to armed conflict included the **Townshend Acts** passed in 1767 taxing lead, paint, paper, and tea brought into the colonies. This increased anger and tension resulting in the British sending troops to New York City and Boston.

In Boston, mob violence provoked retaliation by the troops thus bringing about the deaths of five people and the wounding of eight others. The so-called **Boston Massacre** shocked Americans and British alike. Subsequently, in 1770, Parliament voted to repeal all the provisions of the Townshend Acts with the exception of the tea tax. In 1773, the tax on tea sold by the British East India Company was substantially reduced, fueling colonial anger once more. This gave the company an unfair trade advantage and forcibly reminded the colonists of the British right to tax them. Merchants refused to sell the tea; colonists refused to buy and drink it; and a shipload of it was dumped into Boston Harbor – a most violent Tea Party.

In 1774, the passage of the **Quebec Act** extended the limits of that Canadian colony's boundary southward to include territory located north of the Ohio River. However, the punishment for Boston's Tea Party came in the same year with the Intolerable Acts. Boston's port was closed; the royal governor of the colony of Massachusetts was given increased power, and the colonists were compelled to house and feed the British soldiers. The propaganda activities of the patriot organizations **Sons of Liberty** and **Committees of Correspondence** kept the opposition and resistance before everyone. Delegates from twelve colonies met in Philadelphia September 5, 1774, in the First Continental Congress. They definitely opposed acts of lawlessness and wanted some form of peaceful settlement with Britain. They maintained American loyalty to Britain and affirmed Parliament's power over colonial foreign affairs.

They insisted on repeal of the **Intolerable Acts** and demanded ending all trade with Britain until this took place. The reply from King George III, the last king of America, was an insistence of two options: colonial submission to British rule or be crushed. With the start of the Revolutionary War April 19, 1775, the Second Continental Congress began meeting in Philadelphia May 10 that year to conduct the business of war and government for the next six years.

One historian explained that the British were interested only in raising money to pay war debts, regulate the trade and commerce of the colonies, and look after business and financial interests between the Mother Country and the rest of her empire. The establishment of overseas colonies was first, and foremost, a commercial enterprise, not a political one. The political aspect was secondary and assumed. The British took it for granted that Parliament was supreme, was recognized so by the colonists, and were very resentful of the colonial challenge to Parliament's authority. They were contemptuously indifferent to politics in America and had no wish to exert any control over it. As resistance and disobedience swelled and increased in America, the British increased their efforts to punish them and put them in their place.

The British had been extremely lax and totally inconsistent in enforcement of the mercantile or trade laws passed in the years before 1754. The government itself was not particularly stable. Actions against the colonies occurred in anger and the British attitude was one of a moral superiority – that they knew how to manage America better than the Americans did themselves. This of course points to a lack of sufficient knowledge of conditions and opinions in America. The colonists had been left on their own for nearly 150 years and by the time the Revolutionary War began, they were quite adept at self-government and adequately handling the affairs of their daily lives. The Americans equated ownership of land or property with the right to vote. Property was considered the foundation of life and liberty and, in the colonial mind and tradition, these went together.

Therefore when an indirect tax on tea was made, the British felt that since it wasn't a direct tax, there should be no objection to it. The colonists viewed any tax, direct or indirect, as an attack on their property. They felt that as a representative body, the British Parliament should protect British citizens, including the colonists, from arbitrary taxation. Since they felt they were not represented in Parliament, they had no protection. So, war began. August 23, 1775, George III declared that the colonies were in rebellion and warned them to stop or else.

By 1776, the colonists and their representatives in the Second Continental Congress realized that things were past the point of no return. The Declaration of Independence was drafted and declared July 4, 1776. George Washington labored against tremendous odds to wage a victorious war. The turning point in the Americans' favor occurred in 1777 with the American victory at Saratoga. This victory resulted in French aide to the the Americans against the British. With the aid of Admiral deGrasse and French warships blocking the entrance to Chesapeake Bay, British General Cornwallis was trapped at Yorktown, Virginia. He surrendered in 1781 and the war was over. The Treaty of Paris officially ending the war was signed in 1783.

Skill 2.2   Demonstrate knowledge of key events and important figures of the American Revolution and analyze the military, diplomatic, and geographic factors leading to colonial victory and British defeat

Many Americans wanted war. They urged people to get their guns and fight the British. But the British army was large and well-trained. American leaders knew this would be a desperate fight.

The fighting began almost without warning. Paul Revere's famous ride let the people of **Lexington and Concord** know that the British were coming. The first shots were fired on Lexington Green on April 19, 1775. Neither side claimed victory, but several soldiers on both sides were hurt.

The British focused on Boston and New York in the early part of the war. In the famous Battle of Bunker Hill (June, 1775), the British advanced up a steep hill for two straight days before finally capturing it. The American forces had lost the hill (and its commanding view of Boston) but had proved to themselves that they could fight against the British.

Both sides fought minor skirmishes, but no major battles were fought for several months after that. The following spring, 30,000 British troops arrived in New York harbor. With the amount of reinforcements, the British began winning battle after battle. These included the battles of Brooklyn, White Plains, and several others in and around New York City.

Further north, American attempts to invade Canada ended in defeat. Even the famous seizure of Fort Ticonderoga (May, 1775) ended in a British victory two years later.

The Americans angered the British further by getting together for the Second Continental Congress and issuing the Declaration of Independence, which documented offenses to the American people committed by Britain's King George III. Now that the Americans had declared themselves independent, they had to continue fighting to keep it.

Desperate for some kind of success, American Commander George Washington led his men across the ice-packed Delaware River on Christmas night, 1776, and won a stunning victory against Hessian forces at Trenton, New Jersey. Moving quickly, Washington also beat back the British at Princeton a few days later.

But again, the British proved too strong. In a series of battles in Pennsylvania (including Brandywine and Germantown), the British drove the Americans steadily back from their homes and their families. Under General James Howe, the British occupied Philadelphia in the fall of 1777.

Things looked very bad for America. British troops were seemingly everywhere. They were winning every battle in sight. Then came the Battle of **Saratoga**. It was supposed to be a great British victory, resulting in the seizure of all of New York. British forces, commanded by three generals, would converge on Saratoga and trap the American forces there, forcing them to surrender.

Instead, only one British general, General John Burgoyne, showed up at Saratoga. He fought anyway, but in the end, had to surrender almost his entire army to American General Horatio Gates (October, 1777). This was a stunning development, and the world took notice. In particular, France, always willing to fight against Great Britain, agreed to send money and troops to the Americans.

Even though Saratoga was a great victory, the British still owned a lot of territory in America. George Washington was still fighting for his life in Pennsylvania and New Jersey. Just a few months after Saratoga, Washington and his troops had to endure the terrible winter at Valley Forge, when it was so cold that many soldiers died or deserted.

In the spring of 1778, Washington fought the British to a draw at the Battle of Monmouth. This was considered to be somewhat of a victory. Both sides fought on, in minor battles for the better part of 1779.

Then, the focus turned south. The American success at Saratoga and at several skirmishes after that had convinced the British to focus more on the south, where they were having greater success.

The British had occupied Savannah, Georgia, in December of 1778. The Americans tried to take it back the next year but failed miserably and suffered heavy casualties.

But the American people fought on. In battle after battle in the south, British victories didn't seem to matter. The British won at Charleston and Camden, but the Americans kept retreating but not giving up. Finally, in October of 1780, a breakthrough came at the Battle of Kings Mountain, South Carolina. In just 65 minutes, American forces decidedly defeated the British and captured one-third of the entire southern British army.

The following January, the Continental Army followed up that success with another smashing victory at Cowpens, South Carolina. Now, the Americans had the British on the run. A few months later, the British technically won the Battle of Guilford Courthouse (in North Carolina). However, the British lost even more men. With French reinforcements on the way on land and at sea, the British turned north.

Lord Charles Cornwallis, the British commander in the south, thought that Yorktown, in Virginia, was a good place to hole up and wait for more British troops to arrive. They never did. French ships sailed into Yorktown harbor instead, while the American army advanced. Forced into a battle he didn't want, Cornwallis fought anyway. But the combined might of America and France was too much. On October 19, 1781, Cornwallis surrendered his army to American General George Washington.

A few details remained. Some minor skirmishes took place, mainly between people who hadn't heard that the war was over. British troops left America while the two sides negotiated the terms of a peace treaty. That treaty came in 1783 and was called the **Treaty of Paris**. America had won the war, and more importantly, their independence.

Skill 2.3   Identify important intellectual sources of the Declaration of Independence and analyze the fundamental concepts contained in the Declaration

The Declaration of Independence is an outgrowth of both ancient Greek ideas of democracy and individual rights and the ideas of the European Enlightenment and the Renaissance, especially the ideology of the political thinker **John Locke**. Thomas Jefferson (1743-1826) the principle author of the Declaration borrowed much from Locke's theories and writings. John Locke was one of the most influential political writers of the 17th century. He put great emphasis on human rights and put forth the belief that when governments violate those rights people should rebel. He wrote the book *Two Treatises of Government* in 1690, which had tremendous influence on political thought in the American colonies and helped shape the Declaration of Independence and the U.S. Constitution.

Essentially, Jefferson applied Locke's principles to the contemporary American situation. Jefferson argued that the currently reigning King George III had repeatedly violated the rights of the colonists as subjects of the British Crown. Disdaining the colonial petition for redress of grievances (a right guaranteed by the Declaration of Rights of 1689), the King seemed bent upon establishing an "absolute tyranny" over the colonies. Such disgraceful behavior itself violated the reasons for which government had been instituted. The American colonists were left with no choice, *"it is their right, it is their duty, to throw off such a government, and to provide new guards for their future security"* wrote Thomas Jefferson.

Yet, though his fundamental principles were derived from Locke's, Jefferson was bolder than his intellectual mentor was. Jefferson's view of natural rights was much broader than Locke's and less tied to the idea of property rights and more on personal rights.

For instance, though both Jefferson and Locke believed very strongly in property rights, especially as a guard for individual liberty, the famous line in the Declaration about people being endowed with the inalienable right to "life, liberty and the pursuit of happiness", was originally Locke's idea. It was "life, liberty, and *private property*". Jefferson did not want to tie the idea of rights to any one particular circumstance however. Thus, he changed Locke's original specific reliance on property and substituted the more general idea of human happiness as being a fundamental right that is the duty of a government to protect.

Locke and Jefferson both stressed that the individual citizen's rights are prior to and more important than any obligation to the state. Government is the servant of the people. The officials of government hold their positions at the sufferance of the people. Their job is to ensure that the rights of the people are preserved and protected by that government. The citizen come first, the government comes second. The Declaration thus produced turned out to be one of the most important and historic documents that expounded the inherent rights of all peoples; a document still looked up to as an ideal and an example.

Skill 2.4   Analyze the strengths and weaknesses of the Articles of Confederation and recognize major issues in the debate over the Constitution

Articles of Confederation - This was the first political system under which the newly independent colonies tried to organize themselves. It was drafted after the Declaration of Independence in 1776, was passed by the Continental Congress on November 15, 1777, ratified by the thirteen states, and took effect on March 1, 1781.

The newly independent states were unwilling to give too much power to a national government. They were already fighting Great Britain. They did not want to replace one harsh ruler with another. After many debates, the form of the Articles was accepted. Each state agreed to send delegates to the Congress, and had one vote. The Articles gave Congress the power to declare war, appoint military officers, and coin money. The Congress was also responsible for foreign affairs. The Articles of Confederation limited the powers of the Congress by giving the states final authority. Although Congress could pass laws, at least nine of the thirteen states had to approve a law before it went into effect. Congress could not pass any laws regarding taxes. To get money, Congress had to ask each state for it, no state could be forced to pay.

Thus, the Articles created a loose alliance among the thirteen states. The national government was weak, in part, because it didn't have a strong chief executive to carry out laws passed by the legislature. This weak national government might have worked if the states were able to get along with each other. However, many different disputes arose and there was no way of settling them. Thus, the delegates went to meet again to try to fix the Articles; instead they ended up scrapping them and created a new Constitution that learned from these earlier mistakes.

The central government of the new United States of America consisted of a Congress of two to seven delegates from each state with each state having just one vote. The government under the Articles solved some of the postwar problems but had serious weaknesses. Some of its powers included: borrowing and coining money, directing foreign affairs, declaring war and making peace, building and equipping a navy, regulating weights and measures, asking the states to supply men and money for an army. The delegates to Congress had no real authority as each state carefully and jealously guarded its own interests and limited powers under the Articles. Also, the delegates to Congress were paid by their states and had to vote as directed by their state legislatures. The serious weaknesses were the lack of power: to regulate finances, over interstate trade, over foreign trade, to enforce treaties, and over the military. Something better and more efficient was needed.

In May of 1787, delegates from all states except Rhode Island began meeting in Philadelphia. At first, they met to revise the Articles of Confederation as instructed by Congress. However, they soon realized that much more was needed. Abandoning the instructions, they set out to write a new Constitution, a new document, the foundation of all government in the United States and a model for representative government throughout the world.

The first order of business was the agreement among all the delegates that the convention would be kept secret. No discussion of the convention outside of the meeting room would be allowed. They wanted to be able to discuss, argue, and agree among themselves before presenting the completed document to the American people.

The delegates were afraid that if the people were aware of what was taking place before it was completed the entire country would be plunged into argument and dissension. It would be extremely difficult, if not impossible, to settle differences and come to an agreement. Between the official notes kept and the complete notes of future President James Madison, an accurate picture of the events of the Convention is part of the historical record.

The delegates went to Philadelphia representing different areas and different interests. They all agreed on a strong central government but not one with unlimited powers. They also agreed that no one part of government could control the rest. It would be a republican form of government (sometimes referred to as representative democracy) in which the supreme power was in the hands of the voters who would elect the men who would govern for them.

One of the first serious controversies involved equal representation in Congress. There was vehement disagreement between small states and t the large states. Virginia's Governor Edmund Randolph proposed that state population determine the number of representatives sent to Congress, also known as the Virginia Plan. New Jersey delegate William Paterson countered with what is known as the New Jersey Plan, each state having equal representation.

After much argument and debate, the Great Compromise was devised, known also as the **Connecticut Compromise**, as proposed by Roger Sherman. It was agreed that Congress would have two houses. A Senate would consist of two Senators from each state, giving equal representation in the Senate. The House of Representatives would have its members elected based on each state's population. Both houses could draft bills to debate and vote on with the exception of bills pertaining to money, which must originate in the House of Representatives.

Another controversy involved economic differences between North and South. One issue concerned the counting of the African slaves when determining representation in the House of Representatives. The southern delegates wanted this, but did not want their slaves to determine taxes to be paid. The northern delegates argued the opposite: count the slaves for taxes but not for representation. The resulting agreement was known as the "three-fifths" compromise. Three-fifths of the slaves would be counted for both taxes and determining representation in the House.

The last major compromise, also between North and South, was the **Commerce Compromise**. The economic interests of the northern part of the country were ones of industry and business whereas the south's economic interests were primarily agricultural. The Northern merchants wanted the government to regulate and control commerce with foreign nations and with the states. Of course, Southern planters opposed this idea as they felt that any tariff laws passed would be unfavorable to them. The acceptable compromise to this dispute was that Congress was given the power to regulate commerce with other nations and the states, including levying tariffs on imports. However, Congress did not have the power to levy tariffs on any exports. This increased Southern concern about the effect it would have on the slave trade. The delegates finally agreed that the importation of slaves would continue for 20 more years with no interference from Congress. Any import tax could not exceed 10 dollars per person. After 1808, Congress would be able to decide whether to prohibit or regulate any further importation of slaves.

Of course, when work was completed and the document was presented, nine states needed to approve for it to go into effect. There was no little amount of discussion, arguing, debating, and haranguing. The opposition had three major objections:

1) The states seemed as if they were being asked to surrender too much power to the national government.
2) The voters did not have enough control and influence over the men who would be elected by them to run the government.
3) A lack of a "bill of rights" guaranteeing hard-won individual freedoms and liberties.

Eleven states finally ratified the document and the new national government went into effect. It was no small feat that the delegates were able to produce a workable document that satisfied all opinions, feelings, and viewpoints. The separation of powers of the three branches of government and the built-in system of checks and balances to keep power balanced were a stroke of genius. It provided for the individuals and the states as well as an organized central authority to keep a new inexperienced young nation on track. They created a system of government so flexible that it had continued in its basic form to this day. In 1789, the Electoral College unanimously elected George Washington as the first President and the new nation was on its way.

Skill 2.5 **Identify major principles (e.g., popular sovereignty, federalism), features (e.g., the process of amendment), and functions of the government (e.g., making and enforcing laws, managing conflicts, providing for the defense of the nation, limiting the power of authority, promoting fiscal responsibility) created by the U.S. Constitution**

Legislative – Article I of the Constitution established the legislative or law-making branch of the government called the Congress. It is made up of two houses, the House of Representatives and the Senate. Voters in all states elect the members who serve in each respective House of Congress. The Legislative branch is responsible for making laws, raising and printing money, regulating trade, establishing the postal service and federal courts, approving the President's appointments, declaring war and supporting the armed forces. The Congress also has the power to change the Constitution itself, and to *impeach* (bring charges against) the President. Charges for impeachment are brought by the House of Representatives, and are then tried in the Senate.

Executive – Article II of the Constitution created the Executive branch of the government, headed by the President, who leads the country, recommends new laws, and can veto bills passed by the legislative branch. As the chief of state, the President is responsible for carrying out the laws of the country and the treaties and declarations of war passed by the legislative branch. The President also appoints federal judges and is commander-in-chief of the military when it is called into service. Other members of the Executive branch include the Vice-President (also elected), and various appointed cabinet members (such as ambassadors, presidential advisors, members of the armed forces, and other appointed and civil servants of government agencies, departments and bureaus). Though the President appoints them, they must be approved by the Senate.

Judicial – Article III of the Constitution established the Judicial Branch of government headed by the Supreme Court. The Supreme Court has the power to rule that a law passed by the legislature, or an act of the Executive branch is illegal and unconstitutional. Citizens, businesses, and government officials can in an appeal capacity, ask the Supreme Court to review a decision made in a lower court if someone believes that the ruling by a judge is unconstitutional. The Judicial branch also includes lower federal courts known as federal district courts that have been established by the Congress. These courts try lawbreakers and review cases referred from other courts. Supreme Court justices must also be approved by the Senate.

Powers Delegated to the Federal Government	Powers Reserved For the States:
• To tax. • To borrow and coin money. • To establish postal service. • To grant patents and copyrights. • To regulate interstate & foreign commerce. • To establish courts. • To declare war. • To raise and support the armed forces • To govern territories. • To define and punish felonies and piracy on the high seas. • To fix standards of weights and measures. • To conduct foreign affairs	• To regulate intrastate trade. • To establish local governments. • .To protect general welfare. • To protect life and property. • To ratify amendments. • To conduct elections. • To make state and local laws.

Concurrent Powers of the Federal Government and States.

1. Both Congress and the states may tax.
2. Both may borrow money.
3. Both may charter banks and corporations.
4. Both may establish courts.
5. Both may make and enforce laws.
6. Both may take property for public purposes.
7. Both may spend money to provide for the public welfare.

Implied Powers of the Federal Government.

1. To establish banks or other corporations implied from delegated powers to tax, borrow, and to regulate commerce.
2. To spend money for roads, schools, health, insurance, etc.
3. To establish post roads, to tax to provide for general welfare and defense, and regulate commerce.
4. To create military academies, implied from powers to raise and support an armed force.
5. To locate and generate sources of power and sell surplus implied from powers to dispose of government property, commerce, and war powers.
6 To assist and regulate agriculture implied from power to tax and spend for general welfare and regulate commerce.

Skill 2.6 **Analyze the role of the Bill of Rights in protecting individual liberties and demonstrate knowledge of the rights and responsibilities of U.S. citizenship**

The first amendment guarantees the basic rights of freedoms of religion, speech, press, and assembly.

The next three amendments came out of the colonists' struggle with Great Britain. For example, the third amendment prevents Congress from forcing citizens to keep troops in their homes. Before the Revolution, Great Britain tried to coerce the colonists to house soldiers.

Amendments five through eight protect citizens who are accused of crimes and are brought to trial. Every citizen has the right to due process of law (due process as defined earlier, being that the government must follow the same fair rules for everyone brought to trial.) These rules include the right to a trial by an impartial jury, the right to be defended by a lawyer, and the right to a speedy trial.

The last two amendments limit the powers of the federal government to those that are expressly granted in the Constitution, any rights not expressly mentioned in the Constitution, thus, belong to the states or to the people. In regards to specific guarantees:

Freedom of Religion: Religious freedom has not been seriously threatened in the United States historically. The policy of the government has been guided by the premise of a separation between church and state. When religious practices have been at cross purposes with attitudes prevailing in the nation at particular times, there have been restrictions placed on these practices. Some of these have been restrictions against the practice of polygamy that is supported by certain religious groups. The idea of animal sacrifice that is promoted by some religious beliefs is generally prohibited. The use of mind altering illegal substances that some have used in religious rituals has been restricted. In the United States, all recognized religious institutions are tax-exempt in following the idea of separation of church and state, and therefore, there have been many quasi-religious groups that have in the past tried to take advantage of this fact. All of these issues continue, and most likely will continue to occupy both political and legal considerations for some time to come.

Freedom of Speech, Press, and Assembly: These rights historically have been given wide latitude in their practice. Though there have been instances when one or the other have been limited for various reasons. The classic limitation, for example, in regards to freedom of speech, has been the famous precept that an individual is prohibited from yelling "fire!" in a crowded theatre. This prohibition is an example of the state saying that freedom of speech does not extend to speech that might endanger other people. There is also a prohibition against slander, or the knowingly stating of a deliberately falsehood against one party by another. Also there are many regulations regarding freedom of the press, the most common example are the various laws against libel, (or the printing of a known falsehood). In times of national emergency, various restrictions have been placed on the rights of press, speech and sometimes assembly.

All these ideas found their final expression in the United States Constitution's first ten amendments, known as the Bill of Rights. In 1789, the first Congress passed these first amendments and by December 1791, three-fourths of the states at that time had ratified them. The Bill of Rights protects certain liberties and basic rights. James Madison, who wrote the amendments, said that the Bill of Rights does not give Americans these rights. People, Madison said, already have these rights. They are natural rights that belong to all human beings. The Bill of Rights simply prevents the governments from taking away these rights.

COMPETENCY 3.0 **UNDERSTAND THE GROWTH, DEVELOPMENT, AND EXPANSION OF THE UNITED STATES FROM 1800 THROUGH THE CIVIL WAR.**

Skill 3.1 **Recognize the causes, major events, and consequences of the War of 1812**

United States' unintentional and accidental involvement in what was known as the **War of 1812** came about due to the political and economic struggles between France and Great Britain. Napoleon's goal was complete conquest and control of Europe, including and especially Great Britain. Although British troops were temporarily driven off the mainland of Europe, the navy still controlled the seas, the seas across which France had to bring the products needed. America traded with both nations, especially with France and its colonies. The British decided to destroy the American trade with France, mainly for two reasons: (a) Products and goods from the U.S. gave Napoleon what he needed to keep up his struggle with Britain. He and France was the enemy and it was felt that the Americans were aiding the Mother Country's enemy. (b) Britain felt threatened by the increasing strength and success of the U.S. merchant fleet. They were becoming major competitors with the ship owners and merchants in Britain.

The British issued the **Orders in Council** which was a series of measures prohibiting American ships from entering any French ports, not only in Europe but also in India and the West Indies. At the same time, Napoleon began efforts for a coastal blockade of the British Isles. He issued a series of Orders prohibiting all nations, including the United States, from trading with the British. He threatened seizure of every ship entering French ports after they stopped at any British port or colony, even threatening to seize every ship inspected by British cruisers or that paid any duties to their government. British were stopping American ships and impressing American seamen to service on British ships. Americans were outraged.

In 1807, Congress passed the **Embargo Act,** forbidding American ships from sailing to foreign ports. This could not be completely enforced, and it really hurt business and trade in America and was repealed in 1809. Two additional acts passed by Congress after James Madison became president attempted to regulate trade with other nations and to have Britain and France remove the restrictions they had put on American shipping. The catch was that whichever nation removed restrictions, the U.S. agreed not to trade with the other one. Napoleon was clever and the first to do this, prompting Madison to issue orders prohibiting trade with Britain, ignoring warnings from the British not to do so. Of course, this did not work either, and although Britain eventually rescinded the Orders in Council, war came in June of 1812 and ended Christmas Eve, 1814, with the signing of the Treaty of Ghent.

During the war, Americans were divided over not only whether or not it was necessary to even fight but also over what territories should be fought for and taken. The nation was still young and just not prepared for war. The primary American objective was to conquer Canada but it failed.

Two naval victories and one military victory stand out for the United States. Oliver Perry gained control of Lake Erie and Thomas MacDonough fought on Lake Champlain. Both of these naval battles successfully prevented the British invasion of the United States from Canada. Nevertheless, the troops did land on the Potomac, below Washington, D.C., marched into the city, and burned the public buildings, including the White House.

Andrew Jackson's victory at New Orleans was a great morale booster to Americans, giving them the impression the U.S. had won the war. The battle actually took place after Britain and the United States had reached an agreement and it had no impact on the war's outcome. The peace treaty did little for United States' territorial expansion, but it did bring peace, release prisoners of war, restore all occupied territory, and set up a commission to settle boundary disputes with Canada. Interestingly, the war proved to be a turning point in American history. Since then, European events had profoundly shaped U.S. policies, especially foreign policies.

Skill 3.2 **Locate major physical and human features of the United States, recognize physical barriers that hindered and physical gateways that facilitated territorial expansion, demonstrate knowledge of major territorial acquisitions and analyze the causes and effects of westward expansion**

The continental United States is bordered by the Pacific Ocean on the west and the Atlantic Ocean on the east. The western part of the country is divided into two main sections by the Rocky Mountains. These mountains extend from New Mexico in the south through the Canadian border on the north. The western portion of the country contains forested and mountainous areas in the Pacific Northwest and Northern California, including Mt. St. Helens, an active volcano in the Cascade Range. Dryer, warmer regions are in the south, including the Mojave Desert in the Southwest. The Great Salt Lake is located in Utah, at the foot of the Wasatch Mountains – an extension of the Rockies.

The Rocky Mountains slope down in the east to the Great Plains, a large, flat and grassy region drained by the Mississippi River, the nation's largest river, and one of the largest rivers in the world. The Great Plains give way in the east to hilly, forested regions. The Appalachian Mountain chain runs along the eastern coast of the U.S. Along the border with Canada between Minnesota and New York are the Great Lakes: Lake Huron, Lake Ontario, Lake Michigan, Lake Erie and Lake Superior. Alaska is located in northwestern North America and contains Mt. McKinley, also called Denali, which is the highest mountain on the continent. Hawaii is a series of volcanic islands in the South Pacific

The **Industrial Revolution** had spread from Great Britain to the United States. Before 1800, most manufacturing activities were done in small shops or in homes. However, starting in the early 1800s, factories with contemporary machines were built making it easier to produce goods faster. The eastern part of the country became a major industrial area although some developed in the West. At about the same time, improvements began to be made in building roads, railroads, canals, and steamboats. The increased ease of travel facilitated westward expansion and boosted the economy with faster and cheaper shipment of goods and products, covering larger areas. An example of one of the innovations include the Erie Canal connecting the interior and Great Lakes with the Hudson River and the coastal port of New York.

Westward expansion occurred for a number of reasons, most important being economic. Cotton had become important to most of the people who lived in the South. The effects of the Industrial Revolution, which began in England, were now being felt in the United States. With the invention of power-driven machines, the demand for cotton fiber greatly increased for the yarn needed in spinning and weaving. Eli Whitney's cotton gin made the separation of the seeds from the cotton much more efficient and faster. This, in turn, this increased the demand, and more and more farmers became involved in the raising and selling of cotton.

The innovations and developments of better methods of long-distance transportation moved the cotton in greater quantities to textile mills in England as well as the areas of New England and Middle Atlantic States in the U.S. As prices increased along with increased demand, southern farmers began expanding by clearing increasingly more land to grow more cotton. Movement, settlement, and farming headed west to utilize the fertile soils. This, in turn, demanded increased need for a large supply of cheap labor. The system of slavery expanded, both in numbers and in the movement to lands "west" of the South.

Cotton farmers and slave owners were not the only ones heading west. Many in other fields of economic endeavor began migrating: trappers, miners, merchants, ranchers, and others were all seeking their fortunes. The **Lewis and Clark Expedition** stimulated the westward push. Fur companies hired men, known as "Mountain Men", to go westward, searching for the animal pelts to supply the market and meet the demands of the East and Europe. These men explored and discovered the many passes and trails that would eventually be used by settlers in their trek to the west. The California gold rush also had a very large influence on the movement west.

There were also religious reasons for westward expansion. Increased settlement was encouraged by missionaries who traveled west with the fur traders. They sent word back east for more settlers and the results were tremendous. By the 1840s, the population increases in Oregon country alone were at a rate of about a thousand people a year. People of many different religions and cultures as well as Southerners with black slaves made their way west which leads to a third reason: political.

It was the belief of many that the United States was destined to control all of the land between the two oceans. One newspaper editor termed it, "Manifest Destiny." This mass migration westward put the U.S. government on a collision course with the Indians, Great Britain, Spain, and Mexico. The fur traders and missionaries ran up against the Indians in the northwest and the claims of Great Britain for the Oregon country.

The U.S. and Britain had shared the Oregon country. By the 1840s, with the increase in the free and slave populations and the demand of the settlers for control and government by the U.S., the conflict had to be resolved. In a treaty signed by both nations in 1846, a peaceful resolution occurred with Britain giving up its claims south of the 49th parallel, which is still the straight border along the Northern United States.

In the American southwest, the results were exactly the opposite. Spain had claimed this area since the 1540s, had spread northward from Mexico City. In the 1700s, Spain had established missions, forts, villages, towns, and very large ranches. After the purchase of the Louisiana Territory in 1803, Americans began moving into Spanish territory. A few hundred American families moved in what is now Texas and were allowed to live there, but had to agree to become loyal subjects to Spain. In 1821, Mexico successfully revolted against Spanish rule, won independence, and chose to be more tolerant towards the American settlers and traders. The Mexican government encouraged and allowed extensive trade and settlement, especially in Texas. Many of the new settlers were southerners and brought with them their slaves. Slavery was outlawed in Mexico and therefore technically illegal in Texas, although the Mexican government rather looked the other way.

With the influx of so many Americans and the liberal policies of the Mexican government, there came to be concern over the possible growth and development of an American state within Mexico. Settlement restrictions, cancellation of land grants, the forbidding of slavery and increased military activity brought everything to a head. The order of events included the fight for Texan independence, the brief Republic of Texas, eventual annexation of Texas, statehood, and finally war with Mexico. The Texas controversy was not the sole reason for war. Since American settlers had begun pouring into the Southwest, the cultural differences played a prominent part. Language, religion, law, customs, and government were totally different and opposite between the two groups. A clash was bound to occur.

People were exposed to works of literature, art, newspapers, drama, live entertainment, and political rallies. With better communication and travel, more information was desired about previously unknown areas of the country, especially the West. The discovery of gold and other mineral wealth resulted in a literal surge of settlers and even more interest.

Skill 3.3 Demonstrate knowledge of the Middle Passage and the institution of slavery in the United States

The drafting , ratification and implementation of the Constitution united 13 different, independent states into a Union under one central government. The two crucial compromises of the convention delegates concerning slaves pacified Southerners, especially the slave owners, but the issue of slavery was not settled. From then on, **sectionalism** became stronger and more apparent each year, putting the entire country on a collision course.

Slavery in the English colonies began in 1619 when 20 Africans arrived in the colony of Virginia at Jamestown. From then on, slavery had a foothold, especially in the agricultural South, where a large amount of slave labor was needed for the extensive plantations. Free men refused to work for wages on the plantations when land was available for settling on the frontier. Therefore, slave labor was the only recourse left. If it had been profitable to use slaves in New England and the Middle Colonies, then without doubt slavery would have been more widespread. However, it came down to whether or not slavery was profitable. It was in the South, but not in the other two colonial regions.

It is interesting that the West was involved in the controversy as well as the North and South. By 1860, the country was made up of these three major regions. The people in all three sections or regions had a number of beliefs and institutions in common. Of course, there were major differences with each region having its own unique characteristics. The basic problem was their development along very different lines.

The section of the North was industrial with towns and factories growing and increasing at a very fast rate. The South had become agricultural, eventually becoming increasingly dependent on one crop – cotton. In the West, restless pioneers moved into new frontiers seeking land, wealth, and opportunity. Many were from the South and were slave owners, bringing their slaves with them. So, between these three different parts of the country the view on: tariffs, public lands, internal improvements at federal expense, banking and currency, and the issue of slavery were decidedly, totally different. This time in U.S. history was a period of compromises, their breakdowns, desperate attempts to restore and retain harmony among the three sections, short-lived intervals of the uneasy balance of interests, and ever-increasing conflict.

At the Constitutional Convention, one of the slavery compromises concerned counting slaves for deciding the number of representatives for the House and the amount of taxes to be paid. Southerners pushed for counting the slaves for representation but not for taxes. The Northerners pushed for the opposite. The resulting compromise, sometimes referred to as the "three-fifths compromise," was that both groups agreed that three-fifths of the slaves would be counted for both taxes and representation.

The other compromise over slavery was part of the disputes over how much regulation the central government would control over commercial activities such as trade with other nations and the slave trade. It was agreed that Congress would regulate commerce with other nations including taxing imports. Southerners were worried about taxing slaves and the possibility of Congress prohibiting the slave trade altogether. The agreement reached allowed the states to continue importation of slaves for the next 20 years until 1808, at which time Congress would make the decision as to the future of the slave trade.   During the 20-year period, no more than $10 per person could be levied on slaves coming into the country.

These two "slavery' compromises were a necessary concession to have Southern support and approval for the new Constitution and government. Many Americans felt that the system of slavery would eventually die out in the U.S., but by 1808, cotton was becoming increasingly important in the primarily agricultural South. The institution of slavery had become firmly entrenched in Southern culture. It is also evident that as early as the Constitutional Convention, active anti-slavery feelings and opinions were very strong, leading to extremely active groups and societies.

Democracy is loosely defined as "rule by the people," either directly or through representatives. Associated with democracy are freedom, equality, and opportunity. The basic concept of democracy existed in the 13 English colonies with the practice of independent self-government. The right of qualified persons to vote, hold office and actively participate in his or her own government is sometimes referred to as "political" democracy. "Social" and "economic" democracy pertain to the idea that all have the opportunity to get an education, choose their own careers, and live as free men everyday all equal in the eyes of the law to everyone.

These three concepts of democracy were basic reasons why people came to the New World. The practices of these concepts continued through the colonial and revolutionary periods and were extremely influential in shaping the new central government under the Constitution. As the nation extended its borders into the lands west of the Mississippi, thousands of settlers started to enter the new territories. They brought with them ideas and concepts and adapted them to the development of the unique characteristics of the region. Equality for everyone, as stated in the Declaration of Independence, did not yet apply to minority groups, black Americans, American Indians, or women. Voting rights and the right to hold public office were restricted in varying degrees in each state. All of these factors decidedly affected the political, economic, and social life of the country and these were focused in the attitudes towards slavery in three sections of the country.

The first serious clash between North and South occurred during 1819-1820 when James Monroe was in office as President and it concerned Missouri's admittance to the Union. In 1819, the U.S. consisted of 21 states: 11 free states and 10 slave states. The Missouri Territory allowed slavery and if admitted would cause an imbalance in the number of U.S. Senators. Alabama had already been admitted as a slave state and that had balanced the Senate with the North and South each having 22 senators. The first Missouri Compromise resolved the conflict by approving the admission of Maine as a free state along with Missouri as a slave state. The balance of power in the Senate continued with the same number of free and slave states.

An additional provision of this compromise was that with the admission of Missouri, slavery would not be allowed in the rest of the Louisiana Purchase territory north of latitude 36 degrees 30'. This was acceptable to the Southern Congressmen since it was not profitable to grow cotton on land north of this latitude line anyway. It was thought that the crisis had been resolved but in the next year, it was discovered that in its state constitution, Missouri discriminated against the free blacks. Anti-slavery supporters in Congress went into an uproar, determined to exclude Missouri from the Union. Henry Clay, known as the Great Compromiser, then proposed a second Missouri Compromise, which was acceptable to everyone.

His proposal stated that the Constitution of the United States guaranteed protections and privileges to citizens of states and Missouri's proposed constitution could not deny these to any of its citizens. The acceptance in 1820 of this second compromise opened the way for Missouri's statehood--a temporary reprieve only.

Skill 3.4 Analyze the effects of technological developments on life in the United States

Westward expansion occurred for a number of reasons, most important being economic. Cotton had become most important to most of the people who lived in the southern states. The effects of the Industrial Revolution were now being felt in the United States. With the invention of power-driven machines, the demand for cotton fiber greatly increased for the yarn needed in spinning and weaving. **Eli Whitney's cotton gin** made the separation of the seeds from the cotton much more efficient and faster. This, in turn, increased the demand and more and more farmers became involved in the raising and selling of cotton.

Robert Fulton's "**Clermont**," the first commercially successful steamboat, led the way in the fastest way to ship goods, making it the most important way to do so. Later, steam-powered railroads soon became the biggest rival of the steamboat as a means of shipping, eventually being the most important transportation method opening the West. With expansion into the interior of the country, the United States became the leading agricultural nation in the world. The hardy pioneer farmers produced a vast surplus and an emphasis went to producing products with a high-sale value. These implements, such as the cotton gin and reaper, improved production. Travel and shipping were greatly assisted in areas not yet touched by railroad or, by improved or new roads, such as the **National Road** in the East and in the West the **Oregon and Santa Fe Trails**.

The telegraph changed the way Americans communicated, creating the possibility of nearly instantaneous communication, something that would have been unthinkable to the Founding Fathers. Telegraph lines soon snaked across the country, dotting the skyline for mile after mile and making it possible for those who used it to communicate with others in the blink of an eye.

No invention changed the landscape and potential of America more than the steam locomotive. Transportation of goods, mail, and people could occur in just a few days, as opposed to a few weeks, which was the norm for stagecoach travel. The building of the railroad created several hundred new jobs and several thousand new business opportunities, as more and more Americans moved west. Other modes of transportation suffered as a result, with the canal system being the primary victim. The railroad—with its speedy travel and its pollution— was here to stay.

Skill 3.5   Demonstrate knowledge of the major reform movements of the first half of the nineteenth century identifying key reform figures and analyze the effects of reform movements on U.S. society

Many **social reform movements** began in the United States including education, women's rights, labor and working conditions, temperance, prisons and insane asylums. But the most intense and controversial movement was the abolitionists' efforts to end slavery. This was an effort that alienated and split the country, hardening Southern defense of slavery, and leading to four years of a bloody, civil war. The **abolitionist movement** had political fallout, affecting admittance of states into the Union and the government's continued efforts to keep a balance between total numbers of free and slave states. Congressional legislation after 1820 reflected this.

Religion has always been a factor in American life. Many early settlers came to America in search of religious freedom. Religion, particularly Christianity, was an essential element of the value and belief structure shared by the Founding Fathers. Yet the Constitution prescribes a separation of Church and State.

The **First Great Awakening** was a religious movement within American Protestantism in the 1730s and 1740s. This was primarily a movement among Puritans seeking a return to strict interpretation of morality and values as well as emphasizing the importance and power of personal religious or spiritual experience. Many historians believe the First Great Awakening unified the people of the original colonies and supported the independence of the colonists.

The **Second Great Awakening** (the Great Revival) was a broad movement within American Protestantism that led to several kinds of activities that were distinguished by region and denominational tradition. Generally, the Second Great Awakening, which began in the 1820s, was a time of recognition that an "awakened religion" must weed out sin on both personal and social levels. It inspired a wave of social activism. In New England, the Congregationalists established missionary societies to evangelize the West. Publication and education societies arose, most notably the American Bible Society.

This social activism gave rise to the temperance movement, prison reform efforts, and help for the handicapped and mentally ill. This period was particularly notable for the abolitionist movement. In the Appalachian region, the camp meeting was used to revive religion. The camp meeting became a primary method of evangelizing new territory.

The **Third Great Awakening** (the Missionary Awakening) gave rise to the Social Gospel Movement. This period (1858 to 1908) resulted in a massive growth in membership of all major Protestant denominations through their missionary activities. This movement was partly a response to claims that the Bible was fallible. Many churches attempted to reconcile or change biblical teaching to fit scientific theories and discoveries. Colleges associated with Protestant churches began to appear rapidly throughout the nation. Socially and politically, the Third Great Awakening was the most expansive and profound. Coinciding with many changes in production and labor, it won battles against child labor and stopped the exploitation of women in factories. Compulsory elementary education for children came from this movement, as did the establishment of a set work day. Much was also done to protect and rescue children from abandonment and abuse, to improve the care of the sick, to prohibit the use of alcohol and tobacco, as well as numerous other "social ills."

Skilled laborers organized into a labor union called the **American Federation of Labor (AFL)**, in an effort to fight for better working conditions and wages for its members and the right to collectively bargain. Farmers joined organizations such as the National Grange and Farmers Alliances. Farmers were producing more food than people could afford to buy. This was the result of (1) new farmlands rapidly opening on the plains and prairies, and (2) development and availability of new farm machinery and newer and better methods of farming. American **women** began actively campaigning for the right to vote. Elizabeth Cady Stanton and Susan B. Anthony in 1869 founded the organization called National Women Suffrage Association the same year the Wyoming Territory gave women the right to vote. Soon after, a few states followed by giving women the right to vote, limited to local elections only.

Governmental reform began with the passage of the Civil Service Act, also known as the Pendleton Act. It created the Civil Service Commission, a federal agency responsible for giving jobs based on merit rather than as political rewards or favors. Another successful reform was the adoption of the secret ballot in voting, as were such measures as the direct primary, referendum, and recall. Additionally, U.S. Senators were now elected directly from the people rather than by their state legislatures (the 17th Amendment). Following the success of reforms made at the national level, the progressives were successful in gaining reforms in government at state and local levels.

Following is just a partial list of well-known Americans who contributed their leadership and talents in various fields and reforms:

Women's Suffrage
Lucretia Mott
Elizabeth Cady Stanton

Education For Women
Emma Hart Willard
Catharine Esther Beecher
Mary Lyon

First Woman Doctor
Dr. Elizabeth Blackwell

First Female Minister
Antoinette Louisa Blackwell

Reforms in Prisons and Insane Asylums
Dorothea Lynde Dix

Peace Movements
Elihu Burritt
William Ladd

Utopian Society
Robert Owen

Public Education
Horace Mann   Caleb Mills   Henry Barnard
John Swett   Calvin E. Stowe

Abolitionist Movement / Underground Railroad
Benjamin Lundy   David Walker   William Lloyd Garrison
Isaac Hooper   Theodore Weld   Arthur and Lewis Tappan
Frederick Douglass   Harriet Tubman   James G. Birney
Henry Highland Garnet   James Forten   Robert Purvis
Harriet Beecher Stowe   Wendell Phillips   John Brown

Famous Writers
Louisa Mae Alcott   Washington Irving   James Fenimore Cooper
Henry David Thoreau   Walt Whitman   Ralph Waldo Emerson
Herman Melville   Richard Henry Dana   Nathaniel Hawthorne
Edgar Allan Poe   Henry Wadsworth Longfellow
John Greenleaf Whittier,   Oliver Wendell Holmes

Explorers
John C. Fremont
Zebulon Pike
Kit Carson

American Statesmen
Henry Clay   Daniel Webster
Stephen Douglas   John C. Calhoun

Inventors
Robert Fulton
Cyrus McCormick
Eli Whitney

American Dictionary and Spellers
Noah Webster

Skill 3.6   Analyze the growth of sectionalism, examine efforts to resolve North-South divisions and demonstrate knowledge of the immediate causes of the Civil War

The first serious clash between North and South occurred during 1819-1820 when James Monroe was in office as President and it concerned Missouri's admittance to the Union. In 1819, the U.S. consisted of 21 states: 11 free states and 10 slave states. The Missouri Territory allowed slavery and if admitted would cause an imbalance in the number of U.S. Senators. Alabama had already been admitted as a slave state and that had balanced the Senate with the North and South each having 22 senators. The first Missouri Compromise resolved the conflict by approving the admission of Maine as a free state along with Missouri as a slave state. The balance of power in the Senate continued with the same number of free and slave states.

An additional provision of this compromise was that with the admission of Missouri, slavery would not be allowed in the rest of the Louisiana Purchase territory north of latitude 36 degrees 30'. This was acceptable to the Southern Congressmen since it was not profitable to grow cotton on land north of this latitude line anyway. It was thought that the crisis had been resolved, but in the next year it was discovered that in the Missouri State constitution, free blacks were discriminated against. Anti-slavery supporters in Congress went into an uproar, determined to exclude Missouri from the Union. Henry Clay, known as the Great Compromiser, then proposed a second Missouri Compromise, which was acceptable to everyone.

His proposal stated that the Constitution of the United States guaranteed protections and privileges to citizens of states and Missouri's proposed constitution could not deny these to any of its citizens. The acceptance in 1820 of this second compromise opened the way for Missouri's statehood – a temporary reprieve only.

The issue of tariffs also was a divisive factor during this period, especially between 1829 and 1833. The Embargo Act of 1807 and the War of 1812 had completely cut America off from the source of manufactured goods, so it was necessary to build factories to produce what was needed. After 1815, Great Britain proceeded to get rid of its industrial rivals by unloading its goods in America. To protect and encourage its own industries and their products, Congress passed the Tariff of 1816, which required high duties to be levied on manufactured goods coming into the United States. Southern leaders, such as John C. Calhoun of South Carolina, supported the tariff with the assumption that the South would develop its own industries.

For a brief period after 1815, the nation enjoyed the "Era of Good Feelings." People were moving into the West; industry and agriculture were growing; a feeling of national pride united Americans in their efforts and determination to strengthen the country. However, over-speculation in stocks and lands for quick profits backfired. Cotton prices were rising; many Southerners bought land for cultivation at inflated prices. Manufacturers in the industrial North purchased land to build more plants and factories as an attempt to have a part of this prosperity. Settlers in the West rushed to buy land to reap the benefits of the increasing prices of meat and grain. To have the money for all of these economic activities, all of these groups were borrowing heavily from the banks. The banks themselves encouraged this by giving loans on insubstantial security.

In late 1818, the Bank of the United States and its branches stopped renewal of personal mortgages and required state banks to immediately pay their bank notes in gold, silver, or in national bank notes. The state banks were unable to do this so they closed their doors and were unable to do any business at all. Since mortgages could not be renewed, people lost all their properties and foreclosures were rampant throughout the country. At the same time, as all of this was occurring, cotton prices collapsed in the English market. Its high price had caused the British manufacturers to seek cheaper cotton from India for their textile mills. With the fall of cotton prices, the demand for American manufactured goods declined, revealing how fragile the economic prosperity had been.

Congress passed a higher tariff in 1824 favoring the financial interests of the manufacturers in New England and the Middle Atlantic States. In addition, this tariff was closely tied to the presidential election of that year. Before becoming law, Calhoun had proposed the high tariffs in an effort to get Eastern business interests to vote with the agricultural interests in the South (who were against it).

Supporters of candidate Andrew Jackson sided with whichever side served their best interests. Jackson himself would not be involved in any of this scheming.

To Calhoun's surprise, the bill became law. This is due mainly to the political maneuvering of Martin van Buren and Daniel Webster. By the time the higher 1828 tariff was passed, feelings were extremely bitter in the South, who believed that the New England manufacturers greatly benefited from it. Vice-President Calhoun, also speaking for his home state of South Carolina, promptly declared that if any state felt that a federal law was unconstitutional, that state could nullify it. In 1832, Congress took the action of lowering the tariffs to a degree but not enough to please South Carolina, which promptly declared the tariff null and void, threatening to secede from the Union.

In 1833, Congress lowered the tariffs again, this time at a level acceptable to South Carolina. Although President Jackson believed in states' rights, he also firmly believed in and determined to keep the preservation of the Union. A constitutional crisis had been averted but sectional divisions were getting deeper and more pronounced. The abolition movement was growing rapidly, becoming an important issue in the North.

The slavery issue was at the root of every problem, crisis, event, decision, and struggle from then on. The next crisis involved the issue concerning Texas. By 1836, Texas was an independent republic with its own constitution. During its fight for independence, Americans were sympathetic to and supportive of the Texans and some recruited volunteers who crossed into Texas to help the struggle. Problems arose when the state petitioned Congress for statehood. Texas wanted to allow slavery but Northerners in Congress opposed admission to the Union because it would disrupt the balance between free and slave states and give Southerners in Congress increased influence. Others believed that granting statehood to Texas would lead to a war with Mexico. Mexico had refused to recognize Texas independence. For the time being, statehood was put on hold.

The slavery issue flared again, but it was not done away with until the end of the Civil War. It was obvious that the newly acquired territory would be divided up into territories and later become states. Factions of Northerners advocated prohibition of slavery and Southerners favored slavery. A third faction arose supporting the doctrine of "popular sovereignty" which stated that people living in territories and states should be allowed to decide for themselves whether or not slavery should be permitted. In 1849, California applied for admittance to the Union and the furor continued.

The result was the **Compromise of 1850**, a series of laws designed to be the final solution to the issue. Concessions made to the North included the admission of California as a free state and the abolition of slave trading in Washington, D.C. The laws also provided for the creation of the New Mexico and Utah territories.

As a concession to Southerners, the residents there would decide whether to permit slavery when these two territories became states. In addition, Congress authorized implementation of stricter measures to capture runaway slaves.

A few years later, Congress started to address the new territories between Missouri and present-day Idaho. Again, heated debate over permitting slavery in these areas flared up. Those opposed to slavery used the Missouri Compromise to prove their point showing that the land being considered for territories was part of the area the Compromise had designated as banned to slavery. On May 25, 1854, Congress passed the infamous **Kansas-Nebraska Act,** which nullified the provision creating the territories of Kansas and Nebraska. This provided the people of these two territories the ability to decide for themselves whether or not to permit slavery there. Feelings were so deep and divided that any further attempts to compromise would end with little, if any, success. Political and social turmoil swirled everywhere. Kansas became known as "Bleeding Kansas" because of the extreme violence and bloodshed throughout the territory because two governments existed there, one pro-slavery and the other anti-slavery.

The Supreme Court in 1857 handed down a decision guaranteed to cause explosions throughout the country. **Dred Scott** was a slave whose owner had taken him from a slave state, Missouri, then to a free state, Illinois, into the Minnesota Territory, free under the provisions of the Missouri Compromise, then finally back to slave state Missouri. Abolitionists pursued the dilemma by presenting a court case, stating that since Scott had lived in a free state and free territory, he was in actuality a free man. Two lower courts had ruled before the Supreme Court became involved, one ruling in favor and one against. The Supreme Court decided that residing in a free state and free territory did not make Scott a free man because Scott (and all other slaves) was neither a U.S. citizen nor a state citizen of Missouri. Therefore, he did not have the right to sue in state or federal courts. The Court went a step further and ruled that the old Missouri Compromise was now unconstitutional because Congress did not have the power to prohibit slavery in the Territories.

Anti-slavery supporters were stunned. They had just recently formed the new Republican Party, and one of its platforms was keeping slavery out of the Territories. Now, according to the Dred Scott decision, this basic party principle was unconstitutional. The only way to ban slavery in new areas was by a Constitutional Amendment, requiring ratification by three-fourths of all states. At this time, this was out of the question because the supporters would be unable to get a majority due to Southern opposition.

In 1858, Abraham Lincoln and Stephen A. Douglas were running for the office of U.S. Senator from Illinois. They participated in a series of debates, which directly affected the outcome of the 1860 Presidential election. Lincoln, a Republican, was not an abolitionist but he believed that slavery was morally wrong and he firmly believed in and supported the Republican Party principle that slavery must not be allowed to extend any further.

On the other hand, Douglas, a Democrat, was up for re-election and knew that if he won this race, he had a good chance of becoming President in 1860. He coined the doctrine of "popular sovereignty" and was responsible for supporting the inflammatory **Kansas-Nebraska Act**, and helped its passage through Congress. In the course of the debates, Lincoln challenged Douglas to show that popular sovereignty reconciled with the Dred Scott decision. Either way he answered Lincoln, Douglas would lose crucial support from one group or the other. If he supported the Dred Scott decision, Southerners would support him but he would lose Northern support. If he stayed with popular sovereignty, Northern support would be his but Southern support would be lost. His reply to Lincoln, stating that Territorial legislatures could exclude slavery by refusing to pass laws supporting it, gave him enough support and approval to be re-elected to the Senate. But it cost him the Democratic nomination for President in 1860.

In 1859, **Abolitionist John Brown** and his followers seized the federal arsenal at Harper's Ferry in what is now West Virginia. His purpose was to take the guns stored in the arsenal, give them to slaves nearby, and lead them in a widespread rebellion. He and his men were captured by Colonel Robert E. Lee of the United States Army and after a trial with a guilty verdict, he was hanged. Most Southerners felt that the majority of Northerners approved of Brown's actions but in actuality, most of them were stunned and shocked. Southern newspapers took great pains to quote a small but well-known minority of abolitionists who applauded and supported Brown's actions. This merely served to widen the gap between the two sections.

The final straw came with the election of Lincoln to the Presidency the next year. Due to a split in the Democratic Party, there were four candidates from four political parties. Lincoln received a minority of the popular vote and a majority of electoral votes. In response, the Southern states, one by one, voted to secede from the Union, as they had promised they would do if Lincoln and the Republicans were victorious. The die was cast.

Skill 3.7   Recognize major events, key figures, and important developments of the Civil War and analyze the effects of the war on the North and the South

It is ironic that South Carolina was the first state to secede from the Union and the first shots of the war were fired on Fort Sumter in Charleston Harbor. Both sides quickly prepared for war. The North had more in its favor: a larger population; superiority in finances and transportation facilities; manufacturing, agricultural, and natural resources. The North possessed most of the nation's gold, had about 92% of all industries, and almost all known supplies of copper, coal, iron, and various other minerals. Most of the nation's railroads were in the North and mid-West, men and supplies could be moved wherever needed; food could be transported from the farms of the mid-West to workers in the East and to soldiers on the battlefields. Trade with nations overseas could go on as usual due to control of the navy and the merchant fleet. The Northern states numbered 24 and included western (California and Oregon) and border (Maryland, Delaware, Kentucky, Missouri, and West Virginia) states.

The Southern states numbered 11 and included South Carolina, Georgia, Florida, Alabama, Mississippi, Louisiana, Texas, Virginia, North Carolina, Tennessee, and Arkansas, made up the Confederacy. Although outnumbered in population, the South was completely confident of victory. They knew that all they had to do was fight a defensive war and protect their own territory. The North had to invade and defeat an area almost the size of Western Europe. They figured the North would get tired of the struggle and give up. Another advantage of the South was that a number of its best officers had graduated from the U.S. Military Academy at West Point and had had long years of army experience. Many had exercised varying degrees of command in the Indian Wars and the war with Mexico. Men from the South were conditioned to living outdoors and were more familiar with horses and firearms than men from northeastern cities. Since cotton was such an important crop, Southerners felt that British and French textile mills were so dependent on raw cotton that they would be forced to help the Confederacy in the war.

The South had specific reasons and goals for fighting the war, more so than the North. The major aim of the Confederacy never wavered: to win independence, the right to govern themselves as they wished, and to preserve slavery. The Northerners were not as clear in their reasons for conducting war. At the beginning, most believed, along with Lincoln, that preservation of the Union was paramount. Only a few extremely fanatical abolitionists looked on the war as a way to end slavery. However, by war's end, more and more northerners had come to believe that freeing the slaves was just as important as restoring the Union.

The war strategies for both sides were relatively clear and simple. The South planned a defensive war, wearing down the North until it agreed to peace on Southern terms. The only exception was to gain control of Washington, D.C., go north through the Shenandoah Valley into Maryland and Pennsylvania in order to drive a wedge between the Northeast and mid-West, interrupt the lines of communication, and end the war quickly. The North had three basic strategies:

1. Blockade the Confederate coastline in order to cripple the South;
2. Seize control of the Mississippi River and interior railroad lines to split the Confederacy in two; and
3. Seize the Confederate capital of Richmond, Virginia, driving southward joining up with Union forces coming east from the Mississippi Valley.

The South won decisively until the Battle of Gettysburg, July 1 - 3, 1863. Until Gettysburg, Lincoln's commanders, McDowell and McClellan, were less than desirable, Burnside and Hooker, were not what was needed. General Robert E. Lee, on the other hand, had many able officers, "Stonewall" Jackson and J.E.B. Stuart depended on heavily by him. Jackson died at Chancellorsville and was replaced by Longstreet. Lee decided to invade the North and depended on Stuart and his cavalry to keep him informed of the location of Union troops and their strengths.

Four things worked against Lee at Gettysburg:

1) The Union troops gained the best positions and the best ground first, making it easier to make a stand there.

2) Lee's move into Northern territory put him and his army a long way from food and supply lines. They were more or less on their own.

3) Lee thought that his Army of Northern Virginia was invincible and could fight and win under any conditions or circumstances.

4) Stuart and his men did not arrive at Gettysburg until the end of the second day of fighting and by then, it was too little too late. He and the men had had to detour around Union soldiers and he was delayed getting the information Lee needed.

Consequently, he made the mistake of failing to listen to Longstreet and following the strategy of regrouping back into Southern territory to the supply lines. Lee felt that regrouping was retreating and almost an admission of defeat.

He was convinced the army would be victorious. Longstreet was concerned about the Union troops occupying the best positions and felt that regrouping to a better position would be an advantage. He was also very concerned about the distance from supply lines.

It was not the intention of either side to fight there, but the fighting began when a Confederate brigade, that was looking for shoes, stumbled into a Union cavalry unit. The third and last day Lee launched the final attempt to break Union lines. General George Pickett sent his division of three brigades under Generals Garnet, Kemper, and Armistead against Union troops on Cemetery Ridge under command of General Winfield Scott Hancock. Union lines held, and Lee and the defeated Army of Northern Virginia made their way back to Virginia. Although Lincoln's commander George Meade successfully turned back a Confederate charge, he and the Union troops failed to pursue Lee and the Confederates. This battle was the turning point for the North. After this, Lee never again had the troop strength to launch a major offensive.

The day after Gettysburg, on July 4, Vicksburg, Mississippi surrendered to Union General Ulysses Grant, thus severing the western Confederacy from the eastern part. In September 1863, the Confederacy won its last important victory at Chickamauga. In November, the Union victory at Chattanooga made it possible for Union troops to go into Alabama and Georgia, and split the eastern Confederacy in two. Lincoln gave Grant command of all Northern armies in March of 1864. Grant led his armies into battles in Virginia while Phil Sheridan and his cavalry did as much damage as possible. In a skirmish at a place called Yellow Tavern, Virginia, Sheridan's and Stuart's forces met, with Stuart being fatally wounded.

The Union won the Battle of Mobile Bay, and in May 1864, William Tecumseh Sherman began his march to successfully demolish Atlanta, then on to Savannah. He and his troops turned northward through the Carolinas to meet Grant in Virginia. On April 9, 1865, Lee formally surrendered to Grant at the Appomattox Courthouse, Virginia.

The Civil War took more American lives than any other war in history. The South lost one-third of its soldiers in battle, whereas the North lost about one-sixth. More than half of the total deaths were caused by disease and the horrendous conditions of field hospitals. Both sides paid a tremendous economic price but the South suffered more severely from direct damages. Destruction was pervasive with towns, farms, trade, and industry. Lives and homes of men, women, children were destroyed, and an entire Southern way of life was lost. The South had no voice in the political, social, and cultural affairs of the nation, lessening to a great degree the influence of the more traditional Southern ideals. The Northern Yankee Protestant ideals of hard work, education, and economic freedom became the standard of the United States and helped influence the development of the nation into a modern, industrial power.

COMPETENCY 4.0   UNDERSTAND THE GROWTH AND TRANSFORMATION OF U.S. SOCIETY FROM RECONSTRUCTION THROUGH THE 1920S.

Skill 4.1   Identify and analyze major challenges, events, and outcomes of the Reconstruction period

The effects of the Civil War were tremendous. It changed the methods of waging war and has been called the first modern war. It introduced weapons and tactics that, when improved later, were used extensively in wars of the late 1800s and early 1900s. Civil War soldiers were the first to fight in trenches, under a unified command, wage defenses called "major cordon defenses" (a strategy of advance on all fronts). They were also the first to use repeat and breech loading weapons. Observation balloons were first used during the war along with submarines, ironclad ships, and mines. Telegraphy and railroads were put to use first in the Civil War. It was considered a modern war because of the vast destruction and was "total war," involving the use of all resources of the opposing sides. There was no *way* it could have ended other than total defeat and unconditional surrender of one side or the other.

By executive proclamation and constitutional amendment, slavery was officially unconstitutional, although deep prejudice and racism remained, still raising its ugly head today. Also, the Union was preserved and the states were finally truly united. **Sectionalism**, especially in the area of politics, remained strong for another 100 years but not to the degree and with the violence as existed before 1861. It has been noted that the Civil War may have been American democracy's greatest failure for, from 1861 to 1865, basic to democracy, fell to human passion. Nevertheless, democracy survived. The victory of the North established that no state has the right to end or leave the Union. Because of this unity, the U.S. became a major global power. Lincoln never proposed to punish the South. Instead, he was most concerned with restoring the South to the Union in a program that was flexible and practical rather than rigid and unbending. In fact he never really felt that the states had succeeded in leaving the Union but that they had left the 'family circle' for a short time. His plans consisted of two major steps:

- All Southerners taking an oath of allegiance to the Union who promised to accept all federal laws and proclamations dealing with slavery would receive a full pardon. The only ones excluded from this were men who had resigned from civil and military positions in the federal government to serve in the Confederacy, those who were part of the Confederate government, in the Confederate army above the rank of lieutenant, and Confederates who were guilty of mistreating prisoners of war and blacks.

- Each state would be able to write a new constitution, elect new officials, and return to the Union fully equal to all other states on certain conditions: a minimum number of persons (at least 10% of those who were qualified voters in their states before secession from the Union who had voted in the 1860 election) must take an oath of allegiance.

While the war dragged on to its bloody and destructive conclusion, Lincoln was very concerned and anxious to get the states restored to the Union. He showed flexibility in his thinking as he made changes to his Reconstruction program to make it as easy and painless as possible. Congress had final approval of many actions. It would be interesting to know how differently things might have turned out if Lincoln had lived to see some or all of his kind policies supported by fellow moderates, put into action. Unfortunately, it didn't turn out that way. After Andrew Johnson became President and the Radical Republicans gained control of Congress. The harsh measures of Radical Reconstruction were implemented.

The economic and social chaos in the South after the war was unbelievable. Starvation and disease were rampant, especially in the cities. The U.S. Army provided some relief of food and clothing for both white and blacks but the major responsibility fell to the **Freedmen's Bureau.** Though the bureau agents to a certain extent helped southern whites, their main responsibility was to the freed slaves. They were to assist the freedmen to become self-supporting and protect them from being taken advantage of by others. Northerners looked on it as a real, honest effort to help the South out of the chaos it was in. Most white Southerners charged the bureau with causing racial friction, deliberately encouraging the freedmen to consider former owners as enemies.

As a result, as southern leaders began to be able to restore life as it had once been, they adopted a set of laws known as "black codes", containing many of the provisions of the prewar "slave codes." There were certain improvements in the lives of freedmen, but the codes denied the freedmen their basic civil rights. In short, except for the condition of freedom and a few civil rights, white Southerners made every effort to keep the freedmen inferior.

Federal troops were stationed throughout the South and protected Republicans who took control of Southern governments. Bitterly resentful, white Southerners fought the new political system by joining a secret society called the **Ku Klux Klan (KKK)**, using intimidation and violence to keep black Americans from voting and getting equality. However, before being allowed to rejoin the Union, the Confederate states were required to agree to all federal laws. Between 1866 and 1870, all of them had returned to the Union, but Northern interest in Reconstruction was fading. **Reconstruction** officially ended when the last Federal troops left the South in 1877. It can be said that Reconstruction had a limited success as it set up public school systems and expanded legal rights of black Americans. Nevertheless, white supremacy came to be in control again and its bitter fruitage is still with us today.

First organized in the Reconstruction South, the KKK was a loose group made up mainly of former Confederate soldiers who opposed the Reconstruction government and espoused a doctrine of white supremacy. KKK members intimidated and sometimes killed their proclaimed enemies. The first KKK was never completely organized, despite having nominal leadership. In 1871, President Grant took action to use federal troops to halt the activities of the KKK, and actively prosecuted them in federal court. Klan activity waned, and the organization disappeared

Lincoln and Johnson had considered the conflict of Civil War as a "rebellion of individuals". Congressional Radicals, such as Charles Sumner in the Senate, considered the Southern states as complete political organizations and were now in the same position as any unorganized Territory and should be treated as such. Radical House leader Thaddeus Stevens did not consider the Confederate States as Territories, but rather as conquered provinces and thus should be treated that way. President Johnson refused to work with Congressional moderates, insisting on having his own way. As a result the Radicals gained control of both houses of Congress and when Johnson opposed their harsh measures they came within one vote of impeaching him. **General Grant** was elected President in 1868, serving two scandal-ridden terms. He was himself an honest, upright person but he greatly lacked political experience and his greatest weakness was a blind loyalty to his friends. He absolutely refused to believe that his friends were not honest and stubbornly would not admit to their using him to further their own interests. One of the sad results of the war was the rapid growth of business and industry with large corporations controlled by unscrupulous men. However, after 1877, some degree of normalcy returned and there was time for rebuilding, expansion, and growth.

There was a marked degree of industrialization before and during the Civil War, but at war's end, American industry was small. After the war, dramatic changes took place. Machines replaced hand labor, extensive nationwide railroad service made possible the wider distribution of goods, invention of new products made available in large quantities, and large amounts of money from bankers and investors for expansion of business operations. American life was definitely affected by this phenomenal industrial growth. Cities became the centers of this new business activity resulting in mass population movements there and tremendous growth. This new boom in business resulted in huge fortunes for some Americans and extreme poverty for many others. The discontent this caused resulted in a number of new reform movements from which came measures controlling the power and size of big business and helping the poor.

Of course, industry before, during, and after the Civil War was centered mainly in the North, especially the tremendous industrial growth after. The late 1800s and early 1900s saw the increasing buildup of military strength and the U.S. becoming a world power.

The rise of the Redeemer governments marked the beginning of the **Jim Crow** laws and official segregation. Blacks were allowed to vote, but the South found ways to make it difficult for them to do so, such as literacy tests and poll taxes. Reconstruction, which had set as its goal the reunification of the south with the north and the granting of civil rights to freed slaves was a limited success, at best, and in the eyes of blacks was considered a failure.

Segregation laws were foreshadowed in the **Black Codes**, strict laws proposed by some southern states during the Reconstruction Period that sought to essentially recreate the conditions of pre-war servitude. Under these codes, blacks were to remain subservient to their white employers, and were subject to fines and beatings if they failed to work. Freedmen, as newly freed slaves were called, were afforded some civil rights protection during the Reconstruction period, however beginning around 1876, so called Redeemer governments began to take office in southern states after the removal of Federal troops that had supported Reconstruction goals. Redeemer state legislatures began passing segregation laws which came to be known as Jim Crow laws.

The **Jim Crow laws** varied from state to state, but the most significant of them required separate facilities for blacks and whites. School systems libraries, ticket windows, waiting rooms, seating areas on trains and, later, other public transportation, are examples of such services. Restaurant owners were permitted or sometimes required to provide separate entrances and tables and counters for blacks and whites, so that the two races not see one another while dining. Public parks and playgrounds were constructed for each race. Landlords were not allowed to mix black and white tenants in apartment houses in some states. The Jim Crow laws were given credibility in 1896 when the Supreme Court handed down its decision in the case *Plessy vs. Ferguson.* In 1890, Louisiana had passed a law requiring separate train cars for blacks and whites. To challenge this law, in 1892 Homer Plessy, a man who had a black great grandparent and so was considered legally "black" in that state, purchased a ticket in the white section and took his seat. Upon informing the conductor that he was black, he was told to move to the black car. He refused and was arrested. His case was eventually elevated to the Supreme Court.

The Court ruled against Plessy, thereby ensuring that the Jim Crow laws would continue to proliferate and be enforced. The Court held that segregating races was not unconstitutional as long as the facilities for each were identical. This became known as the "separate but equal" principle. In practice, facilities were seldom equal. Black schools were not funded at the same level, for instance. Streets and parks in black neighborhoods were not maintained.

The **13th Amendment** abolished slavery and involuntary servitude, except as punishment for crime. The amendment was proposed on January 31, 1865. It was declared ratified by the necessary number of states on December 18, 1865.

Abraham Lincoln's **Emancipation Proclamation** freed slaves held in states that were considered to be in rebellion. The 13th Amendment freed slaves in states and territories controlled by the Union. The Supreme Court has ruled that this amendment does not bar mandatory military service.

The **14th Amendment** provides for Due Process and Equal Protection under the law. It was proposed on June 13, 1866 and ratified on July 28, 1868. The drafters of the Amendment took a broad view of national citizenship. The law requires that states provide equal protection under the law to all persons (not just all citizens). This amendment also came to be interpreted as overturning the Dred Scott case (which said that blacks were not and could not become citizens of the U.S.). The full potential of interpretation of this amendment was not realized until the 1950s and 1960s, when it became the basis of ending segregation in the Supreme Court case *Brown v. Board of Education*. This amendment includes the stipulation that all children born on American soil, with very few exceptions, are U.S. citizens. There have been recommendations that this guarantee of citizenship be limited to exclude the children of illegal immigrants and tourists, but this has not yet occurred. There is no provision in this amendment for loss of citizenship.

The **15th Amendment** grants voting rights regardless of race, color or previous condition of servitude. It was ratified on February 3, 1870.

All three of these Constitutional Amendments were part of the Reconstruction effort to create stability and rule of law to provide, protect, and enforce the rights of former slaves throughout the nation.

Skill 4.2   Recognize the expansion of settlement in the trans-Mississippi West after the Civil War and analyze the causes and effects of westward expansion on settlers, Native American peoples, and U.S. society

The time from 1830 to 1914 is characterized by the extraordinary growth and spread of patriotic pride in a nation along with intense, widespread imperialism. Loyalty to one's nation included national pride; extension and maintenance of sovereign political boundaries; unification of smaller states with common language, history, and culture into a more powerful nation; or smaller national groups who, as part of a larger multi-cultural empire, wished to separate into smaller, political, cultural nations.

It was the belief of many that the United States was destined to control all of the land between the two oceans or as one newspaper editor termed it, "**Manifest Destiny.**" **Westward expansion** occurred for a number of reasons, most important being economic. Cotton had become most important to most of the people who lived in the southern states. The effects of the Industrial Revolution, which began in England, were now being felt in the United States. With the invention of power-driven machines, the demand for cotton fiber greatly increased for the yarn needed in spinning and weaving. Eli Whitney's **cotton gin** made the separation of the seeds from the cotton much more efficient and faster. This, in turn, increased the demand and more and more farmers became involved in the raising and selling of cotton.

The innovations and developments of better methods of long-distance transportation moved the cotton in greater quantities to textile mills in England as well as the areas of New England and Middle Atlantic States in the U.S. As prices increased along with increased demand, southern farmers began expanding by clearing increasingly more land to grow more cotton. Movement, settlement, and farming headed west to utilize the fertile soils. This, in turn, increased need for a large supply of cheap labor. The system of slavery expanded, both in numbers and in the movement to lands "west" of the South.

Many, in other fields of economic endeavor, began the migration: trappers, miners, merchants, ranchers, and others were all seeking their fortunes. The Lewis and Clark expedition stimulated the westward push. Fur companies hired men, known as "**Mountain Men**", to go westward, searching for the animal pelts to supply the market and meet the demands of the East and Europe. These men in their own way explored and discovered the many passes and trails that would eventually be used by settlers in their trek to the west. The **California gold rush** also had a very large influence on the movement west. Increased settlement was encouraged by missionaries who traveled west with the fur traders. They sent word back east for more settlers and the results were tremendous. By the 1840s, the population increases in the Oregon country alone were at a rate of about a thousand people a year. People of many different religions and cultures as well as Southerners with black slaves made their way west which leads to a third reason: political.

This mass migration westward put the U.S. government on a collision course with the Indians, Great Britain, Spain, and Mexico. The fur traders and missionaries ran up against the Indians in the northwest and the claims of Great Britain for the Oregon country. The U.S. and Britain had shared the Oregon country but by the 1840s, with the increases in the free and slave populations and the demand of the settlers for control and government by the U.S., the conflict had to be resolved. In a treaty, signed in 1846, by both nations, a peaceful resolution occurred with Britain giving up its claims south of the 49th parallel.

In the American southwest, the results were exactly the opposite. Spain had claimed this area since the 1540s, had spread northward from Mexico City, and, in the 1700s, had established missions, forts, villages, towns, and very large ranches. After the purchase of the Louisiana Territory in 1803, Americans began moving into Spanish territory. A few hundred American families in what is now Texas were allowed to live there but had to agree to become loyal subjects to Spain.

Also refer to Skill 4.5.

Skill 4.3   Recognize the causes and effects of immigration from 1870 to 1910; demonstrate knowledge of the growth of industry and the evolving roles of business, labor, banking, and government in the U.S. economy; and use the basic economic concepts of opportunity cost, price incentives, specialization, voluntary exchange, productivity, and trade to analyze historical events of the period

Between 1870 and 1916, more than 25 million immigrants came into the United States adding to the phenomenal population growth already taking place. This tremendous growth aided business and industry in two ways: (1) The number of consumers increased creating a greater demand for products thus enlarging the markets for the products, and (2) with increased production and expanding business, more workers were available for newly created jobs. The completion of the nation's transcontinental railroad in 1869 contributed greatly to the nation's economic and industrial growth. Some examples of the benefits of using the railroads include raw materials were shipped quickly by the mining companies and finished products were sent to all parts of the country. Many wealthy industrialists and railroad owners saw tremendous profits steadily increasing due to this improved method of transportation.

As businesses grew, methods of sales and promotion were developed. Salespersons went to all parts of the country promoting the various products, opening large department stores in growing cities which offered a variety of products at reasonable and affordable prices. People who lived too far from the cities could not shop there, but had the advantage of using a mail order services, buying what they needed from catalogs furnished by the companies. The developments in communication, such as the telephone and telegraph, increased the efficiency and prosperity of big business.

Investments in corporate stocks and bonds resulted from business prosperity. Individuals began investing heavily in order to share in the profits. Their investments made available the needed capital for companies to expand their operations. From this, banks increased in number throughout the country and made loans to businesses and significant contributions to economic growth. At the same time, during the 1880s, government made little effort to regulate these businesses. This gave rise to monopolies where larger businesses eliminated their smaller competitors and assumed complete control of their market.

Once the Industrial Revolution occurred, the economic growth and expansion led to the formation of trusts. These were monopolies that were controlling large industrial groups of companies. Even though they represented a concentration of power in the hands of a few people, they contributed to the growth of the nation with large efficient corporations. But there were many unfair business practices with smaller businesses being forced out of business. This led to the enactment of the **Sherman Anti-Trust Act** which made trusts or any combination that existed to restrain trade illegal. The government dissolved the huge trusts, like John D. Rockefeller's Standard Oil, over the following decades. The economy continued to grow and prosper in the years approaching World War I.

Monopolies had some good effects on the economy. Out of them grew the large, efficient corporations, which made important contributions to the growth of the nation's economy. Also, the monopolies enabled businesses to keep their sales steady and avoid sharp fluctuations in price and production. At the same time, the downside of monopolies was the unfair business practices of the business leaders. Some acquired so much power that they took unfair advantage of others. Those who had little or no competition would require their suppliers to supply goods at a low cost, sell the finished products at high prices, and reduce the quality of the product to save money.

Skilled laborers organized into a labor union called the **American Federation of Labor (AFL)**, in an effort to fight for better working conditions and wages for its members and the right to collectively bargain. Farmers joined organizations such as the National Grange and Farmers Alliances. Farmers were producing more food than people could afford to buy. This was the result of (1) new farmlands rapidly opening on the plains and prairies, and (2) development and availability of new farm machinery and newer and better methods of farming. American **women** began actively campaigning for the right to vote. Elizabeth Cady Stanton and Susan B. Anthony in 1869 founded the organization called National Women Suffrage Association the same year the Wyoming Territory gave women the right to vote. Soon after, a few states followed by giving women the right to vote, limited to local elections only.

The World War I years resulted in a wartime economy with heavy reliance on the banking system to assist with finances. After the war, the European nations were devastated and the U.S. helped with lending money to rebuild the war-torn nations. The United States emerged from its isolationist stance during the war, but tried to stay out of European affairs. There were changes in the social structure of the economy with the formation of unions and women's rights. The 1920s, or "Roaring Twenties," represented an era of prosperity. During this period there was increased urbanization as people left the farms to move to the cities for jobs. There was massive investment in building, the expansion of the auto industry, and excessive stock market investment. Most of this investment represented buying on margin.

Margin buying allowed people to control huge amount of stock with a minimal cash outlay. This was one of the main reasons for the stock market crash and eventually the **Great Depression**. The massive unemployment of the depression years led the government to focus on policies that they hoped would relieve the misery and stimulate the economy. The government enacted the **National Recovery Act** with its variety of alphabet agencies to try to stimulate the economy and provide jobs. With the outbreak of World War II and the U.S. entry into the war, the Depression ended. The United States emerged from World War II as a world power, along with Russia.

Skill 4.4   Demonstrate knowledge of the women's-suffrage movement culminating in the passage of the Nineteenth Amendment

It might sound hard to believe, but women in America have been voting for only 87 years. That's right, women have been allowed to vote since 1920. The Nineteenth Amendment to the Constitution gave women the right to vote.

Why did this happen? Isn't America the land where "all men are created equal"? Well, yes and no. Since men have run the country and were in charge of passing the laws since our country began, they believed that women's place was in the home and not in politics. This belief extended to voting. Additionally, in the colonial period only land-owners were allowed to vote, and women were not allowed to own land. The men who made the laws believed that their wives and daughters and mothers were not informed enough about the men running for office to decide for themselves whom to vote for. So, women could not vote.

In fact, it wasn't entirely clear in the early days of the United States whether women could vote. So, state legislatures passed laws barring women's suffrage. In 1807, the Wyoming Territory, allowed women to vote, but only in state and local elections. It took awhile, but some states followed. However, these women were not allowed to vote for president, Congress, in national elections.

The first serious movement to give women the right to vote was started in the early 1840s. It ended in 1848 with a national convention in Seneca Falls, New York. The leaders of this movement were Elizabeth Cady Stanton, Lucretia Mott, and Susan B. Anthony. At the convention, they drafted a Declaration of Sentiments and Resolutions, which said that "all men and women are created equal."

But women still could not vote. And it wasn't just in America. Women were denied the right to vote anywhere in the world. New Zealand, in 1893, became the first country in the world to grant women the right to vote in national elections. Great Britain had, in 1869, given unmarried women the right to vote in local elections.

(Again, it was thought that a woman's place was in the home, not in politics. Having the right to vote was thought to be equal to having the right to run for political office.)

In 1866, Stanton and Anthony formed the Equal Rights Association, which wanted equal rights for all people, men and women, white and black.

In 1872, more than a hundred women tried to vote in New Jersey. They were allowed to fill out ballots, but their ballots were ignored. Susan B. Anthony was arrested for trying to vote for president. She was convicted and ordered to pay a $1,000 fine.

In 1884, Belva Lockwood ran for president on the National Equal Rights Party ticket. She got more than 4,000 votes in a total of six states. Lockwood was the first woman lawyer to argue cases before the Supreme Court.

Women did get elected to local offices. In 1887, the town of Argonia, Kansas, elected America's first woman mayor, Susanna Salter. Many states by this time had allowed women to vote in local and even state elections. But voting in national elections was another matter. It was a lot more difficult to convince an entire nation of people to do something.

In 1918, Canada and the United Kingdom granted women the right to vote. But American men held out, for the most part. Many men in American wanted women to vote. There just were not enough of them. But the more women had parades and rallies and speeches and magazines calling for the right to vote, the more the lawmakers began to listen. Public opinion in America and worldwide was decidedly in favor of granting women the right to vote.

Finally, the Nineteenth Amendment was introduced in Congress in 1919. One year later, it was passed. Women had won the right to vote.

Skill 4.5 **Recognize how William McKinley and Theodore Roosevelt expanded the role of the United States in the world through involvement in the Spanish-American War and the construction of the Panama Canal**

By the 1880s, Secretary of State James G. Blaine pushed for expanding U.S. trade and influence to Central and South America. In the 1890s, President Grover Cleveland invoked the **Monroe Doctrine** to intercede in Latin American affairs when it looked like Great Britain was going to exert its influence and power in the Western Hemisphere. In the Pacific, the United States lent its support to American sugar planters who overthrew the **Kingdom of Hawaii** and eventually annexed it as U.S. territory.

During the 1890s, Spain controlled such overseas possessions as Puerto Rico, the Philippines, and Cuba. Cubans rebelled against Spanish rule and the U.S. government found itself besieged by demands from Americans to assist the Cubans in their revolt. The event that proved a turning point was the **Spanish-American War** in 1898 that used the explosion of the USS Maine as a pretext for the United States to invade Cuba, when the underlying reason was the ambition for empire and economic gain. Two months later, Congress declared war on Spain and the U.S. quickly defeated them. The war with Spain also triggered the dispatch of the fleet under Admiral George Dewey to the Philippines, followed up by sending the American Army. Victory over the Spanish proved fruitful for American territorial ambitions. Although Congress passed legislation renouncing claims to annex Cuba, in a rare moment of idealism, the United States gained control of the island of **Puerto Rico**, a permanent deep-water naval harbor at Guantanamo Bay, Cuba, the Philippines and various other Pacific islands formerly possessed by Spain. The decision to occupy the **Philippines**, rather than grant it immediate independence, led to a guerrilla war, the "Philippines Insurrection," which lasted until 1902. U.S. rule over the Philippines lasted until 1942, but unlike the guerrilla war years, American rule was relatively benign. The peace treaty gave the U.S. possession of **Puerto Rico, the Philippines, Guam and Hawaii**, which was annexed during the war.

This success enlarged and expanded the U.S. role in foreign affairs. Under the administration of Theodore Roosevelt, the U.S. armed forces were built up, and greatly increased its strength. Roosevelt's foreign policy was summed up in the slogan of "Speak softly and carry a big stick" – backing up the efforts in diplomacy with a strong military. During the years before the outbreak of World War I, evidence of U.S. emergence as a world power could be seen in a number of actions.

Using the Monroe Doctrine of non-involvement of Europe in the affairs of the Western Hemisphere, President Roosevelt forced Italy, Germany, and Great Britain to remove their blockade of Venezuela; gained the rights to construct the **Panama Canal** by threatening force; assumed the finances of the Dominican Republic to stabilize it and prevent any intervention by Europeans; and in 1916 under President Woodrow Wilson, to keep order, U.S. troops were sent to the Dominican Republic.

The **Panic of 1893** was a sharp decline in the United States economy that resulted in several bank failures, widespread unemployment and a drop in farm crop prices. The panic was partly due to a run on the gold supply when people began exchanging U.S. silver notes for gold. The federal reserve of gold soon reached its minimum level and no more notes could be redeemed. The price of silver fell and thousands of companies went bankrupt, including several major railroads. High unemployment continued for over five years following the panic. The economy and the practice of using silver and gold to back U.S. Treasury notes became central issues in the 1896 presidential election, which was won by William McKinley. McKinley's election restored confidence, and the economy began to recover.

Skill 4.6 Analyze the causes, domestic effects, and consequences of U.S. involvement in World War I

Many causes attributed to the World War I. Some included the surge of nationalism, the increasing strength of military capabilities, massive colonization for raw materials needed for industrialization and manufacturing, and military and diplomatic alliances. The spark which started the conflagration was the assassination of Austrian Archduke Francis Ferdinand and his wife in Sarajevo.

In Europe, war broke out in 1914, involved nearly 30 nations, and ended in 1918. One of the major causes of the war was the tremendous surge of **nationalism** during the 1800s and early 1900s. People of the same nationality or ethnic group sharing a common history, language or culture began uniting or demanding the right of unification, especially in the empires of Eastern Europe, such as Russian, Ottoman, and Austro-Hungarian Empires. Getting stronger and more intense were the beliefs of these peoples in loyalty to common political, social, and economic goals considered to be before any loyalty to the controlling nation or empire.

Emotions ran high and minor disputes magnified into major ones and sometimes quickly led to threats of war. Especially sensitive to these conditions was the area of the states on the Balkan Peninsula. Along with the imperialistic colonization for industrial raw materials, military build-up (especially by Germany), and diplomatic and military alliances, the conditions for one tiny spark to set off the explosion were in place. In July 1914, a Serbian national assassinated the Austrian heir to the throne and his wife and war began a few weeks later. There were a few attempts to keep war from starting, but these efforts were futile.

In 1916, Wilson was reelected to a second term based on the slogan proclaiming his efforts at keeping America out of the war. For a few months after, he put forth most of his efforts to stopping the war but German submarines began unlimited warfare against American merchant shipping. The development of the German *unterseeboat,* or **U-boat,** allowed them to efficiently attack merchant ships that were supplying their European enemies from Canada and the US. In 1915, a German U-boat sunk the passenger liner **RMS Lusitania**, killing over 1,000 civilians including over 100 Americans. This attack outraged the American public and turned public opinion against Germany. The attack on the Lusitania became a rallying point for those advocating US involvement in the European conflict.

Great Britain intercepted and decoded a secret message from Germany to Mexico urging Mexico to go to war against the U.S. The publishing of the **Zimmerman Telegram,** along with continued German destruction of American ships resulted in the eventual entry of the U.S. into the conflict, the first time the country prepared to fight in a conflict not on American soil.

Though unprepared for war, governmental efforts and activities resulted in massive defense mobilization with America's economy directed to the war effort.

Some ten months before the war ended, President Wilson had proposed a program called the **Fourteen Points** as a method of bringing the war to an end with an equitable peace settlement. Within these Points, five set out general ideals; eight pertained to and immediate resolution to territorial and political problems; and the fourteenth established an organization of nations to help keep world peace, the League of Nations.

When Germany agreed in 1918 to an armistice, it assumed that the peace settlement would be drawn up on the basis of these Fourteen Points. However, the peace conference in Versailles ignored these points and Wilson had to be content with efforts at establishing the **League of Nations**. Italy, France, and Great Britain, having suffered and sacrificed far more in the war than America, wanted retribution. The treaty severely punished the Central Powers, taking away arms and territories and required the payment of reparations. Germany was punished more than the others and, according to one clause in the treaty, was forced to assume the responsibility for causing the war.

Pre-war empires lost tremendous amounts of territories as well as the wealth of natural resources in them. New, independent nations were formed and some predominately ethnic areas came under control of nations of different cultural backgrounds. Some national boundary changes overlapped and created tensions and hard feelings as well as political and economic confusion. The wishes and desires of every national or cultural group could not possibly be realized and satisfied, resulting in disappointments for both; those who were victorious and those who were defeated. Germany received harsher terms than expected from the treaty which weakened its post-war government and, along with the world-wide depression of the 1930s, set the stage for the rise of Adolf Hitler and his Nationalist Socialist Party and World War II.

World War I saw the introduction of new types of warfare. The use of tanks, airplanes, machine guns, submarines, poisonous gas, and flame throwers got their first use in World War I. Fighting on the Western front was characterized by a series of trenches that were used throughout the war until 1918. U.S. involvement in the war did not occur until 1917. When it began in 1914, President Woodrow Wilson declared U.S. neutrality and most Americans were opposed to any involvement anyway.

President Wilson lost in his efforts to get the U.S. Senate to approve the Peace Treaty of Versailles. The Senate at the time reflected American public opinion and its rejection of the treaty was a rejection of Wilson. The approval of the treaty would have made the U.S. a member of the League of Nations but Americans had just come off a bloody war to ensure that democracy would exist throughout the world.

Skill 4.7   Demonstrate knowledge of major cultural developments and individual contributions of the 1920s and analyze their effects on U.S. society

Also Refer to Skill 5.1.

As African Americans left the rural South and migrated to the North in search of opportunity, many settled in Harlem in New York City. By the 1920s Harlem had become a center of life and activity for persons of color. The music, art, and literature of this community gave birth to a cultural movement known as **the Harlem Renaissance**. The artistic expressions that emerged from this community in the 1920s and 1930s celebrated the black experience, black traditions, and the voices of black America. Major writers and works of this movement included: Langston Hughes (*The Weary Blues*), Nella Larsen (*Passing*), Zora Neale Hurston (*Their Eyes Were Watching God*), Claude McKay, Countee Cullen, and Jean Toomer.

Many refer to the decade of the 1920s as **The Jazz Age**. The decade was a time of optimism and exploration of new boundaries. It was a clear movement in many ways away from conventionalism. Jazz music, uniquely American, was the country's popular music at the time. The jazz musical style perfectly typified the mood of society. Jazz is essentially free-flowing improvisation on a simple theme with a four-beat rhythm. Jazz originated in the poor districts of New Orleans as an outgrowth of the Blues. The leading jazz musicians of the time included: Buddy Bolden, Joseph "King" Oliver, Duke Ellington, Louis Armstrong, and Jelly Roll Morton.

As jazz grew in popularity and intricacy, it gave birth to Swing music and the era of Big Band Jazz by the late 1920s and early 1930s. Some of the most notable musicians of the Big Band era were: Bing Crosby, Frank Sinatra, Don Redman, Fletcher Henderson, Count Basie, Benny Goodman, Billie Holiday, Ella Fitzgerald, and The Dorsey Brothers among others.

In painting and sculpture, the new direction of the decade was **realism**. In the early years of the twentieth century, American artists had developed several realist styles, some of which were influenced by modernism, others that reacted against it. Several groups of artists of this period are particularly notable.

1. *The Eight or The Ashcan School* developed around the work and style of Robert Henri. Their subjects were everyday urban life that was presented without adornment or glamour.

2. *The American Scene Painters* produced a tight, detailed style of painting that focused on images of American life that were understandable to all. In the Midwest, a school within this group was called *regionalism*. One of the leading artists of regionalism was Grant Wood, best known for *American Gothic*.

3. Other important realists of the day were Edward Hopper and Georgia O'Keeffe.

Although the British patent for the **radio** was awarded in 1896, it was not until WWI that the equipment and capability of the use of radio was recognized. The first radio program was broadcast August 31, 1920. The first entertainment broadcasts began in 1922 from England. One of the first developments in the twentieth century was the use of commercial AM radio stations for aircraft navigation. In addition, radio was used to communicate orders and information between army and navy units on both sides of the war during WWI. Broadcasting became practical in the 1920s. Radio receivers were introduced on a wide scale.

The relative economic boom of the 1920s made it possible for many households to own a radio. The beginning of broadcasting and the proliferation of receivers revolutionized communication. The news was transmitted into every home with a radio. In addition, news and information could be transmitted very quickly. Rather than the newsreels at movie theaters or awaiting the printing of stories sent to newspapers by mail, the news was now immediate. With the beginning of entertainment broadcasting, people were able to remain in their homes to be entertained. Rather than obtaining filtered information, people were able to hear the actual speeches and information that became news. By the time of the Stock Market Crash in 1929, approximately 40% of households had a radio.

Another innovation of the 1920s was the introduction of **mass production**. This is the production of large quantities of standardized products on production lines. The method became very popular when Henry Ford used mass production to build the Model T Ford. The process facilitates high production rates per worker. Thus, it created very inexpensive products. The process is, however, capital intensive. It requires expensive machinery in high proportion to the number of workers needed to operate it. From an economic perspective, **mass production** decreases labor costs, increases the rate of production, and thus increases profit. The equipment and start-up costs of implementing mass production techniques are very high. Mass production reduces the amount of non-productive effort. It also reduces the chance of human error and variation. The downside of mass production is its inflexibility. Once a process is established, it is difficult to modify a design or a production process. From the viewpoint of labor, however, mass production can create job shortages.

During the era before and after 1900, a large number of people migrated to the cities of America. Throughout the nineteenth century city populations grew faster than rural populations. The new immigrants were not farmers. For example, Polish immigrants became steelworkers in Pittsburgh; Serbian immigrants became meatpackers in Chicago; Russian Jewish immigrants became tailors in New York City; Slovaks assembled cars in Detroit; Italians worked the factories of Baltimore.

Several factors promoted urbanization during the decade of the 1920s.

1. The decline of agriculture, the drop in prices for grain and produce, and the end of financial support for farming after WWI caused many farmers to go under during the 1920s. Many sold or lost their farms and migrated to cities to find work.
2. Continuing industrialization drew increasing numbers of workers to the areas near or surrounding industrial or manufacturing centers.
3. Cities were becoming the locus of political, cultural, financial and economic life.
4. Transportation to the place of work or shopping for necessities facilitates the growth of cities.

As the cities grew, the demographic composition of those areas began to change. Workers flocked to the cities to be closer to the factories that employed them. As the populations of poorer workers increased, the wealthy moved from the city into the suburbs. The availability of automobiles and the extension of public transportation beyond the city limits enabled the middle and upper classes to leave city centers. **Urbanization** brings certain needs, including: adequate water supply, management of sewage and garbage, the need for public services (such as fire and police), road construction and maintenance, building of bridges to connect parts of cities, and taller buildings were needed. The inventions of steel-framed buildings and the elevator greatly facilitated city growth.

In addition, electricity and telephone lines were needed; department store and supermarket chains grew. The need for additional schools also increased. The increase/growth in all of these areas was directly related to urbanization. With the large migration and low wages came overcrowding, often in old buildings. **Slums** began to appear and soon public health issues began to arise.

COMPETENCY 5.0 UNDERSTAND THE EXPERIENCE OF THE GREAT DEPRESSION AND U.S. INVOLVEMENT IN WORLD WAR II.

Skill 5.1 Analyze the causes and consequences of the Great Depression

The 1929 Stock Market Crash was the powerful event that is generally interpreted as the beginning of the Great Depression in America. Although the crash of the Stock Market was unexpected, it was not without identifiable causes. The 1920s had been a decade of social and economic growth and hope. But the attitudes and actions of the 1920s regarding wealth, production, and investment created several trends that quietly set the stage for the 1929 disaster.

Uneven distribution of wealth: In the 1920s, the distribution of wealth between the rich and the middle-class was grossly disproportionate. In 1929, the combined income of the top 0.1% of the population was equal to the combined income of the bottom 42%. The top 0.1% of the population controlled 34% of all savings, while 80% of American had no savings. Capitalism was enriching the wealthy at the expense of the workers. Between 1920 and 1929, the amount of disposable income per person rose 9%. The top 0.1% of the population, however, enjoyed an increase in disposable income of 75%. One reason for this disparity was increased manufacturing productivity during the 1920s. Average worker productivity in manufacturing increased 32% during this period. Yet wages in manufacturing increased only 8%. The wages of the workers rose very slowly, failing to keep pace with increasing productivity. As production costs fell and prices remained constant, profits soared. But profits were retained by the companies and the owners.

The Legislative and Executive branches of the Coolidge administration tended to favor businesses and the wealthy. The Revenue Act of 1926 significantly reduced income taxes for the wealthy. This bill lowered taxes so that a person with a million-dollar income saw his/her taxes reduced from $600,000 to $200,000. Despite the rise of labor unions, even the Supreme Court ruled in ways that further widened the gap between the rich and the middle/lower classes. In the case of Adkins v. Children's Hospital (1923), the Court ruled that minimum wage legislation was unconstitutional.

This kind of disparity in the distribution of wealth weakens the economy. Demand was unable to equal supply. The surplus of manufactured goods was beyond the reach of the poor and the middle class. The wealthy, however, could purchase all they wanted with a smaller and smaller portion of their income. This meant that in order for the economy to remain stable, the wealthy must invest their money and spend money on luxury items and others must buy on credit.

The majority of the population did not have enough money to buy what was necessary to meet their needs. The concept of buying on credit caught on very quickly. Buying on credit, however, creates artificial demand for products people cannot ordinarily afford. This has two effects: first, at some point there is less need to purchase products (because they have already been bought), and second, at some point paying for previous purchases makes it impossible to purchase new products. This exacerbated the problem of a surplus of goods.

The economy also relied on investment and luxury spending by the rich in the 1920s. Luxury spending, however, only occurs when people are confident with the economy and the future. Should these people lose confidence, that luxury spending would come to an abrupt halt. This is precisely what happened when the stock market crashed in 1929. Business investments produces returns for the investor. During the 1920s, while investing was very healthy, investors began to expect greater returns on their investments. This led many to make speculative investments in risky opportunities.

The disproportionate distribution of wealth between the upper class and the rest of society mirrors the uneven distribution of wealth between industries. In 1929, half of all corporate wealth was controlled by just 200 companies. The automotive industry was growing exceptionally quickly, but agriculture was steadily declining. In fact, in 1921 food prices dropped about 70% due to surplus. The average income in agriculture was only about one-third of the national average across all industries.

Two industries, automotive and radio, drove the economy in the 1920s. During this decade, the government tended to support new industries rather than agriculture. During WWI, the government had subsidized farms and paid ridiculously high prices for grains. Farmers had been encouraged to buy and farm more land and to use new technology to increase production. The nation was feeding much of Europe during and in the aftermath of the war. But when the war ended, these farm policies were cut off. Prices plummeted, farmers fell into debt, and farm prices declined. The agriculture industry was on the brink of ruin before the stock market crash.

The concentration of production and economic stability in the automotive industry and the production and sale of radios was expected to last forever. But there comes a point when the growth of an industry slows due to market saturation. When these two industries declined, due to decreased demand, they caused the collapse of other industries upon which they were dependent (e.g., rubber tires, glass, fuel, construction, etc.).

The other factor contributing to the Great Depression was the economic condition of Europe. The U.S. was lending money to European nations to rebuild after World War I. Many of these countries used this money to purchase U.S. food and manufactured goods, but they were not able to pay off their debts. While the U.S. was providing money, food, and goods to Europe, Americans were not willing to buy European goods. Trade barriers were enacted to maintain a favorable trade balance.

Risky speculative investments in the stock market was the second major factor contributing to the stock market crash of 1929 and the ensuing depression. Stock market speculation was spectacular throughout the 1920s. In 1929, shares traded on the New York Stock Exchange reached 1,124,800,410. In 1928 and 1929 stock prices doubled and tripled (RCA stock prices rose from 85 to 420 within one year). The opportunity to achieve such profits was irresistible. In much the same way that buying goods on credit became popular, buying stock on margin allowed people to invest a very small amount of money in the hope of receiving an exceptional profit. This created an investing craze that drove the market higher and higher. But brokers were also charging higher interest rates on their margin loans (nearly 20%). If, however, the price of the stock dropped, the investor owed the broker the amount borrowed plus interest.

Several other factors are cited by some scholars as contributing to the Great Depression. First, in 1929, the Federal Reserve increased interest rates. Second, some believe that as interest rates rose and the stock market began to decline, people began to hoard money. This was certainly the case after the crash. There is a question whether or not it was a cause of the crash.

In September 1929, stock prices began to slip somewhat, yet people remained optimistic. On Monday, October 21, prices began to fall quickly. The volume traded was so high that the tickers were unable to keep up. Investors were frightened, and they started selling very quickly. This caused further collapse. For the next two days prices stabilized somewhat. On **Black Thursday**, October 24, prices plummeted again. By this time investors had lost confidence. On Friday and Saturday an attempt to stop the crash was made by some leading bankers. But on Monday the 28th, prices began to fall again, declining by 13% in one day. The next day, **Black Tuesday, October 29**, saw 16.4 million shares traded. Stock prices fell so far, that at many times no one was willing to buy at any price.

In the immediate aftermath of the stock market crash, many urged President Herbert Hoover to provide government relief. Hoover responded by urging the nation to be patient. By the time he signed relief bills in 1932, it was too late.

Skill 5.2 **Demonstrate knowledge of the New Deal response to the Great Depression and recognize important environmental and social developments of the 1930s**

Hoover's bid for re-election in 1932 failed. The new president, Franklin D. Roosevelt won the White House on his promise to the American people of a "new deal." Upon assuming the office, Roosevelt and his advisers immediately launched a massive program of innovation and experimentation to try to bring the Depression to an end and get the nation back on track. Congress gave the President unprecedented power to act to save the nation. During the next eight years, the most extensive and broadly-based legislation in the nation's history was enacted. The legislation was intended to accomplish three goals: relief, recovery, and reform.

The first step in Roosevelt's "**New Deal**" was to relieve suffering. This was accomplished through a number of job-creation projects. The second step, the recovery aspect, was to stimulate the economy. The third step was to create social and economic change through innovative legislation.

The National Recovery Administration attempted to accomplish several goals:

- Restore employment,
- Increase general purchasing power,
- Provide character-building activity for unemployed youth,
- Encourage decentralization of industry and thus divert population from crowded cities to rural or semi-rural communities,
- To develop river resources in the interest of navigation and cheap power and light,
- To complete flood control on a permanent basis,
- To enlarge the national program of forest protection and to develop forest resources,
- To control farm production and improve farm prices,
- To assist home builders and home owners,
- To restore public faith in banking and trust operations, and
- To recapture the value of physical assets, whether in real property, securities, or other investments.

These objectives and their accomplishment implied a restoration of public confidence and courage.

Among the "alphabet organizations" set up to work out the details of the recovery plan, the most prominent were:

- **Agricultural Adjustment Administration** (AAA), designed to readjust agricultural production and prices thereby boosting farm income.
- **Civilian Conservation Corps** (CCC), designed to give wholesome, useful activity in the forestry service to unemployed young men.
- **Civil Works Administration** (CWA) and the **Public Works Administ**ration (PWA) were designed to provide employment in the construction and repair of public buildings, parks, and highways.
- **Works Progress Administration** (WPA), sought to move individuals from relief rolls to work projects or private employment.

The **Tennessee Valley Authority** (TVA) was of a more permanent nature, designed to improve the navigability of the Tennessee River and increase productivity of the timber and farm lands in its valley, this program built 16 dams that provided water control and hydroelectric generation.

The **Public Works Administration** employed Americans on over 34,000 public works projects at a cost of more than $4 billion. Among these projects was the construction of a highway that linked the Florida Keys and Miami, the Boulder Dam (now the Hoover Dam) and numerous highway projects.

To provide economic stability and prevent another crash, Congress passed the **Glass-Steagall Act**, which separated banking and investing. The Securities and Exchange Commission was created to regulate dangerous speculative practices on Wall Street. The **Wagner Act** guaranteed a number of rights to workers and unions, including the right to collectively bargain, in an effort to improve worker-employer relations. The **Social Security Act of 1935** established pensions for the aged and infirm as well as a system of unemployment insurance.

While much of the New Deal aimed to immediately resolve the depression, certain permanent national policies emerged. The intention of the public through its government was to supervise and, to an extent, regulate business operations, from corporation activities to labor problems. This included protecting bank depositors and the credit system of the country, employing gold resources and currency adjustments to aid permanent restoration of normal living, and, if possible, establishing a line of subsistence below which no useful citizen would be permitted to sink.

Many of the steps taken by the Roosevelt administration have had far-reaching effects. They alleviated the economic disaster of the Great Depression, they enacted controls that would mitigate the risk of another stock market crash, and they provided greater security for workers. The nation's economy, however, did not fully recover until America entered World War II.

Unemployment quickly reached 25% nation-wide. People thrown out of their homes created makeshift domiciles of cardboard, scraps of wood and tents. With unmasked reference to President Hoover, who was quite obviously overwhelmed by the situation and incompetent to deal with it, these communities were called "**Hoovervilles**." Families stood in bread lines, rural workers left the dust bowl of the plains to search for work in California, and banks failed. More than 100,000 businesses failed between 1929 and 1932. The despair that swept the nation left an indelible scar on all who endured the Depression.

When the stock market crashed, demand for products collapsed along with businesses and industries. This set in motion a domino effect, bringing down the businesses and industries that provided raw materials or components to these industries. Hundreds of thousands became jobless. The unemployed often became homeless. Desperation prevailed. Little has been done to assess the toll hunger, inadequate nutrition, or starvation took on the health of those who were children during this time. Indeed, food was cheap, relatively speaking, but there was little money to buy it.

Everyone who lived through the Great Depression was permanently affected in some way. Many never trusted banks again. Many people of this generation later hoarded cash so they would not risk losing everything again. Some permanently rejected the use of credit.

Skill 5.3   Recognize the origins of U.S. involvement in World War II

World War I had seriously damaged the economies of the European countries, both the victors and the defeated, leaving them deeply in debt. There was difficulty on both sides paying off war debts and loans. It was difficult to find jobs and some countries like Japan and Italy found themselves without enough resources for its populations. Solving these problems by expanding their territory merely set up conditions for war later. Germany suffered horribly with runaway inflation ruining the value of its money and wiping out the savings of millions.

Even though the U.S. made loans to Germany, which helped the government to restore some order and provided a short existence of some economic stability in Europe, the Great Depression only served to undo any good that had been done. Mass unemployment, poverty, and despair greatly weakened the democratic governments that had been formed and greatly strengthened the increasing power and influence of extreme political movements, such as communism, fascism, and national-socialism. These movements promised to put an end to the economic problems.

Nationalism, which was a major cause of World War I, grew even stronger and seemed to feed the feelings of discontent, which became increasingly rampant. Because of unstable economic conditions and political unrest, harsh dictatorships arose in several of the countries, especially where there was no history of experience in democratic government.

In the Soviet Union, **Joseph Stalin** succeeded in gaining political control and establishing a strong harsh dictatorship. **Benito Mussolini** and the Fascist Party, promised prosperity and order in Italy, gained national support and set up a strong government. In Japan, although the ruler was considered **Emperor Hirohito,** actual control and administration of government came under military officers and the leadership of Hideki Tojo. In Germany, the results of war, harsh treaty terms, loss of territory, great economic chaos and collapse all enabled **Adolf Hitler** and his Nazi party to gain complete power and control.

Germany, Italy, and Japan initiated a policy of aggressive territorial expansion with **Japan** being the first act. In 1931, the Japanese forces seized control of Manchuria, a part of China containing rich natural resources. In 1937 Japen began an attack on China, occupying most of its eastern part by 1938. Italy invaded Ethiopia in Africa in 1935, having it totally under its control by 1936. The Soviet Union did not invade or take over any territory but along with Italy and Germany, actively participated in the Spanish Civil War, using it as a proving ground to test tactics and weapons setting the stage for World War II.

In Germany, almost immediately after taking power, in direct violation of the World War I peace treaty, Hitler began the buildup of the armed forces. He sent troops into the Rhineland in 1936, invaded Austria in 1938 and united it with Germany. Then seized control of the Sudetenland in 1938 (part of western Czechoslovakia and containing mostly Germans), the rest of Czechoslovakia in March 1939. On September 1, 1939, Hitler and the Nazis invaded Poland, beginning World War II in Europe. In 1940, Germany invaded and controlled Norway, Denmark, Belgium, Luxembourg, the Netherlands, and France.

France and Britain, who had followed a policy of appeasing Hitler in the hopes that he would be content with Austria, were now concerned as Germany looked next to **Poland**. They pledged to fight Germany if Hitler invaded Poland, which he did in September 1939, after signing a pact with the Soviet Union. Days later, France and Britain declared war on Germany, and the fighting began.

Again, the United States stayed out of the fighting at first. Only when Japan, an ally of Germany, attacked the US naval base in Pearl Harbor, Hawaii on December 7, 1941 did the US enter the war.

Skill 5.4   Recognize major wartime events and developments and identifying prominent wartime figures

After the war began in Europe, U.S. President **Franklin D. Roosevelt** announced that the United States would remain neutral. Most Americans wanted the U.S. to stay out of the war, but hoped for an Ally victory. President Roosevelt and his supporters were called "interventionists." They favored all forms of aid (except sending troops) to the Allied nations fighting Axis aggression. They were fearful that an Axis victory would seriously threaten and endanger all democracies. On the other hand, the "isolationists" were against any U.S. involvement and aid given to the warring nations. They accused President Roosevelt of leading the U.S. into a war that the U.S. was very unprepared to fight. Roosevelt's plan was to defeat the Axis nations by sending to the Allied nations equipment needed to fight: ships, aircraft, tanks, and other war materials.

In Asia, the U.S. had opposed Japan's invasion of Southeast Asia, an effort by the Japanese to gain control of that region's rich resources. Consequently, the U.S. stopped all important exports to Japan, whose industries depended heavily on petroleum, scrap metal, and other raw materials. Later Roosevelt refused the Japanese withdrawal of its funds from American banks. General Tojo became the Japanese premier in October 1941 and quickly realized that the U.S. Navy was powerful enough to block Japanese expansion into Asia. Without warning, the Japanese air force attacked the American Pacific Fleet at **Pearl Harbor,** Hawaii on December 7, 1941. At the moment, it was a success. It destroyed many aircraft and disabled much of the U.S. Pacific Fleet. In the end, it was a costly mistake as it quickly motivated the Americans to prepare for and wage war.

Military strategy in the European theater of war as developed by **Roosevelt, Churchill, and Stalin** was to concentrate on Germany's defeat first, then Japan's. The start was made in the summer of 1942 by, pushing Germans and Italians out of North Africa, and it endedsuccessfully in May 1943. Before the war, Hitler and Stalin had signed a non-aggression pact in 1939, which Hitler violated in 1941 by invading the Soviet Union. The German defeat at Stalingrad, marked a turning point in the war, was brought about by a combination of entrapment by Soviet troops and death of German troops by starvation and freezing due to the horrendous winter conditions. This occurred at the same time that the Allies were driving them out of North Africa.

The liberation of Italy began in July 1943 and ended May 2, 1945. The third part of the strategy was **D-Day, June 6, 1944,** with the Allied invasion of France at Normandy. At the same time, starting in January 1943, the Soviets began pushing the German troops back into Europe and they were greatly assisted by supplies from Britain and the United States. By April 1945, Allies occupied positions beyond the Rhine and the Soviets moved on to Berlin, surrounding it by April 25. Germany surrendered May 7 and the war in Europe was finally over. Meanwhile, in the Pacific, in the six months after the attack on Pearl Harbor, Japanese forces moved across Southeast Asia and the western Pacific Ocean. By August 1942, the Japanese Empire was at its largest size and stretched northeast to Alaska's Aleutian Islands, west to Burma, south to what is now Indonesia. Invaded and controlled areas included Hong Kong, Guam, Wake Island, Thailand, part of Malaysia, Singapore, the Philippines, and bombed Darwin on the north coast of Australia.

The raid of General Doolittle's bombers on Japanese cities and the American naval victory at Midway along with the fighting in the Battle of the Coral Sea helped turn the tide against Japan. Island-hopping by U.S. Seabees and Marines and the grueling bloody battles fought resulted in gradually pushing the Japanese back towards Japan.

After victory was attained in Europe, concentrated efforts were made to secure Japan's surrender, but it took dropping two atomic bombs on the cities of Hiroshima and Nagasaki to finally end the war in the Pacific. Japan formally surrendered on September 2, 1945, aboard the U.S. battleship Missouri, anchored in Tokyo Bay. The war was finally over.

Before the war in Europe ended, the Allies had agreed on a military occupation of Germany. It was divided into four zones – each one occupied by Great Britain, France, the Soviet Union, and the United States and – and the four powers jointly administered Berlin. After the war, the Allies agreed that Germany's armed forces would be abolished, the Nazi Party outlawed, and the territory east of the Oder and Neisse Rivers taken away. Nazi leaders were accused of war crimes and brought to trial.

International organizations received sharp criticism during WWII for their failure to act to save European Jews. The Allied Powers, in particular, were accused of gross negligence. Many organizations and individuals did not believe reports of the abuse and mass genocide that was occurring in Europe. Many nations did not want to accept Jewish refugees. The International Red Cross was one of the organizations that discounted reports of atrocities. One particular point of criticism was the failure of the Allied Powers to bomb the death camp at Auschwitz-Birkenau or the railroad tracks leading there. Military leaders argued that their planes did not have the range to reach the camp; they argued that they could not provide sufficiently precise targeting to safeguard the inmates. Critics have claimed that even if Allied bombs killed all inmates at Auschwitz at the time, the destruction of the camp would have saved thousands of other Jews. The usual response was that, had the Allies destroyed the camp, the Nazis would have turned to other methods of extermination.

It was not until after the war that genocide was accepted by the United Nations as a crime against humanity. Also after the war, there was recognition that the United Nations charter was insufficiently precise as to the rights it protected. The UN then unanimously passed the Universal Declaration of Human Rights. The Nuremberg Trials redefined morality on a global scale. The phrase "crimes against humanity" attained popular currency, and individuals, rather than governments, were held accountable for war crimes.

After Japan's defeat, the Allies began a military occupation directed by American General Douglas MacArthur, who introduced a number of reforms eventually ridding Japan of its military institutions transforming it into a democracy. A constitution was drawn up in 1947 transferring all political rights from the emperor to the people, granting women the right to vote, and denying Japan the right to declare war. War crimes trials of 25 war leaders and government officials were also conducted. The U.S. did not sign a peace treaty until 1951. The treaty permitted Japan to rearm but took away its overseas empire.

Skill 5.5   **Demonstrate knowledge of the contributions of diverse groups to the military effort and the domestic effects of World War II and examine Truman's decision to drop the atomic bomb on Japan**

Internment of people of Japanese ancestry. From the turn of the twentieth century, there was tension between white Americans and the Japanese in California. A series of laws had been passed discouraging Japanese immigration and prohibiting land ownership by Japanese. The Alien Registration Act of 1940 (the Smith Act) required the fingerprinting and registration of all aliens over the age of 14. Aliens were also required to report any change of address within 5 days. Almost 5 million aliens registered under the provisions of this act. The Japanese attack on Pearl Harbor (December 7, 1941) raised suspicion that Japan was planning a full-scale attack on the West Coast. Many believed that American citizenship did not necessarily imply loyalty. Some authorities feared sabotage of both civilian and military facilities within the country. By February 1942, Presidential Executive Orders had authorized the arrest of all aliens suspected of subversive activities and the creation of exclusion zones where people could be isolated from the remainder of the population and kept where they could not damage national infrastructure. These War Relocation Camps were used to isolate about 120,000 Japanese and Japanese Americans (62% were citizens) during World War II.

The Tuskegee Airmen were a group of African American aviators who made a major contribution to the war effort. Although they were not considered eligible for the gold wings of a Navy Pilot until 1948, these men completed standard Army flight classroom instruction and the required flying time. This group of fliers was the first blacks permitted to fly for the military. They flew more than 15,000 missions, destroyed over 1,000 German aircraft earned more than 150 Distinguished Flying Crosses and hundreds of Air Medals.

The 442nd Regimental Combat Team was a unit composed of Japanese Americans who fought in Europe. This unit was the most highly decorated unit of its size and length of service in the history of the U.S. Army. This self-sufficient force served with great distinction in North Africa, Italy, southern France, and Germany. The medals earned by the group include 21 Congressional Medals of Honor (the highest award given). The unit was awarded 9,486 purple hearts (for being wounded in battle). The casualty rate, combining those killed in action, missing in action, and wounded and removed from action, was 93%.

The Navajo Code Talkers have been credited with saving countless lives and accelerating the end of the war. There were over 400 Navajo Indians who served in all six Marine divisions from 1942 to 1945. At the time of WWII, less than 30 non-Navajo people understood the Navajo language. Because it was a very complex language and because it was not a code, it was unbreakable by the Germans or the Japanese. The job of these men was to talk and transmit information on tactics, troop movements, orders and other vital military information. Not only was the enemy unable to understand the language, but it was far faster than translating messages into Morse Code. It is generally accepted that without the Navajo Code Talkers, Iwo Jima could not have been taken.

The statistics on minority representation in the military during WWII are interesting:

African Americans	1,056,841
Chinese	13,311
Japanese	20,080
Hawaiians	1,320
American Indians	19,567
Filipinos	11,506
Puerto Ricans	51,438

The role of women and minority groups at home overturned many expectations and assumptions. Most able-bodied men of appropriate age were called up for military service. Minorities were generally not drafted. Yet many critical functions remained to be fulfilled by those who remained at home.

To a greater extent than any previous war, WWII required industrial production. Those who remained at home were needed to build the planes, tanks, ships, bombs, torpedoes, etc. The men who remained at home were working. But more labor was desperately needed. In particular, a call went out to women to join the effort and enter the industrial work force. A vast campaign was launched to recruit women to these tasks that combined emotional appeals and patriotism. One of the most famous recruiting campaigns featured "Rosie the Riveter."

Yet all of the recruitment efforts emphasized that the need for women in industry was temporary. By the middle of 1944 more than 19 million women had entered the work force. Women worked building planes and tanks, but they also did more. Some operated large cranes to move heavy equipment; some loaded and fired machine guns and other weapons to ensure that they were in working order; some operated hydraulic presses; some were volunteer fire fighters; some were welders, riveters, drill press operators, and cab drivers. Women worked all manufacturing shifts making everything from clothing to fighter jets. Most women and their families tended "Victory Gardens" to produce food items that were in short supply.

The significance and ramifications of the decision to drop the Atomic Bomb.

The development of the atomic bomb was probably the most profound military development of the war years. This invention made it possible for a single plane to carry a single bomb that was sufficiently powerful to destroy an entire city. It was believed that possession of the bomb would serve as a deterrent to any nation because it would make aggression against a nation with a bomb a decision for mass suicide. Two nuclear bombs were dropped in 1945 on the cities of Nagasaki and Hiroshima. They caused the immediate deaths of 100,000 to 200,000 people, and far more deaths over time. This was (and still is) a controversial decision. Those who oppose the use of the atom bomb argued that was an unnecessary act of mass killing, particularly of non-combatants. Proponents argued that it ended the war sooner, thus resulting in fewer casualties on both sides. The development and use of nuclear weapons marked the beginning of a new age in warfare that created greater distance from the act of killing and eliminated the ability to minimize the effect of war on non-combatants. The introduction and possession of nuclear weapons by the United States quickly led to the development of similar weapons by other nations, proliferation of the most destructive weapons ever created, massive fear of the effects of the use of these weapons, including radiation poisoning and acid rain, and led to the Cold War.

Major developments in aviation, weaponry, communications, and medicine were achieved during the war. The years between WWI and WWII produced significant advancement in aircraft technology. But the pace of aircraft development and production was dramatically increased during WWII. Major developments included (1) flight-based weapon delivery systems, (2) the long-range bomber, (3) the first jet fighter, (4) the first cruise missile, (5) the first ballistic missile. Although they were invented, the cruise and ballistic missiles were not widely used during the war. Glider planes were heavily used in WWII because they were silent upon approach. Another significant development was the broad use of paratrooper units. Finally, hospital planes came into use to extract the seriously wounded from the front and transport them to hospitals for treatment.

Weapons and technology in other areas also improved rapidly during the war. These advances were critical in determining the outcome of the war. Used for the first time were: radar, electronic computers, nuclear weapons, and new tank designs. More new inventions were registered for patents than ever before. Most of these new ideas were aimed to either kill or prevent being killed.

The war began with essentially the same weaponry that had been used in WWI. The aircraft carrier joined the battleship; the Higgins boat, the primary landing craft, was invented; light tanks were developed to meet the needs of a changing battlefield; other armored vehicles were developed. Submarines were also perfected during this period. Numerous other weapons were invented and developed in order to meet the needs of battle during WWII: the bazooka, the rocket propelled grenade, anti-tank weapons, assault rifles, the tank destroyer, mine-clearing Flail tanks, Flame tanks, submersible tanks; cruise missiles, rocket artillery and air launched rockets, guided weapons, torpedoes, self-guiding weapons and Napalm. The Atomic Bomb was also developed and used for the first time during WWII.

Skill 5.6 Recognize U.S. postwar aims and the role of the United States in the formation of the United Nations

The American isolationist mood was given a shocking and lasting blow in 1941 with the Japanese attack on Pearl Harbor. The nation arose and forcefully entered the international arena as never before. Declaring itself "the arsenal of democracy", it entered the Second World War and emerged not only victorious, but also as the *strongest power* on the Earth. It would now, like it or not, have a permanent and leading place in world affairs.

In the aftermath of the Second World War, with the Soviet Union having emerged as the *second* strongest power on Earth. The Soviet Union felt that the U.S. took all the credit in winning the war, and growing anxieties about the spread of communism fueled tensions between the US and Soviet Union. The United States embarked on a policy known as "Containment" of communism. The "**Marshall Plan**" and the "**Truman Doctrine**" dictated US foreign policy. The Marshall Plan involved the economic aid that was sent to Europe in the aftermath of the Second World War aimed at preventing the spread of communism. To that end, the US has devoted a larger and larger share of its foreign policy, diplomacy, and both economic and military might to combating it.

The Truman Doctrine offered military aid to those countries that were in danger of communist upheaval. This led to the era known as the Cold War in which the United States took the lead along with the Western European nations against the Soviet Union and the Eastern Bloc countries. It was also at this time that the United States finally gave up on George Washington's' advice against getting involved in "European entanglements" and joined the **North Atlantic Treaty Organization** or NATO. NATO was formed in 1949 and was comprised of the United States and several Western European nations for the purposes of opposing communist aggression.

The United Nations was also formed at this time (1945) to replace the defunct League of Nations for the purposes of ensuring world peace. Even with American involvement, would prove largely ineffective in maintaining world peace.

COMPETENCY 6.0   UNDERSTAND THE EMERGENCE OF THE COLD WAR AND THE POLITICAL, ECONOMIC, AND CULTURAL DEVELOPMENTS IN THE UNITED STATES FROM 1945 TO THE PRESENT.

Skill 6.1   Analyze the causes of the Cold War, demonstrate knowledge of major Cold War developments and recognize the domestic effects of the Cold War on U.S. politics and society

The Cold War was, more than anything else was an ideological struggle between proponents of democracy and those of communism. The two major players were the United States and the Soviet Union, but other countries were involved as well. It was a "cold" war because no large-scale fighting took place directly between the two big protagonists.

It wasn't just form of government that was driving this war, either. Economics were a main concern as well. A concern in both countries was that the precious resources (such as oil and food) from other like-minded countries would not be allowed to flow to "the other side." Resources did not flow between the U.S. and Soviet Union, either.

The Soviet Union kept much more of a tight leash on its supporting countries, including all of Eastern Europe, which made up a military organization called the **Warsaw Pact**. The Western nations responded with a military organization of their own, NATO. Another prime battleground was Asia, where the Soviet Union had allies in China, North Korea, and North Vietnam and the U.S. had allies in Japan, South Korea, Taiwan, and South Vietnam. The Korean War and Vietnam War were major conflicts in which both big protagonists played big roles but didn't directly fight each other. The main symbol of the Cold War was the arms race, a continual buildup of missiles, tanks, and other weapons that became ever more technologically advanced and increasingly more deadly. The ultimate weapon, which both sides had in abundance, was the nuclear bomb. Spending on weapons and defensive systems eventually occupied great percentages of the budgets of the U.S. and the USSR, and some historians argue that this high level of spending played a large part in the downfall of the Soviet Union.

The war was a cultural struggle as well. Adults brought up their children to hate "the Americans" or "the Communists." Cold War tensions spilled over into many parts of life in countries around the world. The ways of life in countries on either side of the divide were so different that they served entirely foreign to outside observers.

The Cold War continued in varying degrees from 1947 to 1991, when the Soviet Union collapsed. Other Eastern European countries had seen their communist governments overthrown by this time as well, marking the shredding of the "Iron Curtain."

The major thrust of U.S. foreign policy from the end of World War II to 1990 was the post-war struggle between non-Communist nations, led by the United States, and the Soviet Union and the Communist nations who were its allies. It was referred to as a "Cold War" because its conflicts did not lead to a major war of fighting, or a "hot war." Both the Soviet Union and the United States embarked on an arsenal buildup of atomic and hydrogen bombs as well as other nuclear weapons. Both nations had the capability of destroying each other but because of the continuous threat of nuclear war and accidents, extreme caution was practiced on both sides. The efforts of both sides to serve and protect their political philosophies and to support and assist their allies resulted in a number of events during this 46-year period.

Skill 6.2   Identify important figures in the Civil Rights Movement, demonstrate knowledge of major events and accomplishments and analyze the consequences of the movement for the United States

The phrase **"the Civil Rights Movement"** generally refers to the nation-wide effort made by African Americans, and those who supported them, to gain equal rights as whites and to eliminate segregation. Discussion of this movement is generally understood in terms of the period of the 1950s and 1960s, but the roots of the movement extend as far back as Abolition. Although in 1868 the 14th Amendment had guaranteed due process of law to all citizens, and despite the 15th Amendment in 1870 granting African Americans the right to vote, by the start of the twentieth entury many blacks still faced great inequality.

The **Great Migration** began in the early 20th Century as millions of blacks left southern farms for northern cities, where they hoped to find better jobs. Instead they found crowded conditions in urban slums. Many also found resentment from whites, fearful of this new population and worried that African Americans would take jobs from whites. Blacks who stayed in the South enjoyed few, if any, civil and political rights.

African Americans became increasingly restive in the postwar years. During both World Wars they had fought discrimination in the military services and in the work force, with limited success. Having fought to defend their country, black servicemen returned home intent on rejecting second-class citizenship. More than one million black soldiers fought in World War II, but those from the South still could not vote. Those who tried faced beatings, loss of job, loss of credit, or eviction from their land. Lynchings still occurred, and **Jim Crow** laws enforced segregation everywhere.

Harry Truman believed in political, though not social, equality, and recognized the growing importance of the black urban vote. Largely as a political move, in 1946 he appointed a committee on civil rights. The committee's report, issued the next year, documented blacks' second-class status in American life.

The **National Association for the Advancement of Colored People (NAACP)**, was founded in 1909 as a a private, not-for-profit organization to protect and expand the civil rights of African Americans. In 1939 the NAACP formed its Legal Defense Fund (**LDF**) to pursue legal cases and strategies on behalf of civil rights for African Americans. **Thurgood Marshall** was the LDF's director during pivotal cases from 1940 to 1961. In 1954, Marshall and the LDF helped the NAACP to win perhaps its greatest legal victory, *Brown v. Board of Education*.

The 1896 court case **Plessy v. Ferguson** had stated that segregation among school students was constitutional if facilities were **"separate but equal."** That decree had been used for decades to sanction rigid segregation in the South, where things were seldom, if ever, equal. Through the actions of the LDF, African Americans achieved their goal of overturning *Plessy* in 1954 when the Supreme Court handed down its **Brown v. Board of Education** ruling. The Court declared unanimously that "separate facilities are inherently unequal." This ruling was applied to public schools. It is important to note, however, that Brown applied only to schools. Segregation in other aspects of daily life remained legal.

In the summer of 1955, **Emmett Till** a teenage boy visiting from Chicago, was murdered by a white mob in Mississippi. The crime of which he was accused was "whistling at a white woman in a store." He was beaten, murdered, and his body was dumped in a river. His two white abductors were apprehended and tried. They were acquitted by an all-white jury. After the acquittal, they admitted their guilt, but remained free because of double jeopardy laws. Though Till was unfortunately one of many, his death gained prominent attention and helped motivate a reexamination of race in the United States.

Then, in December of 1955, **Rosa Parks**, a 42-year-old black seamstress from Montgomery Alabama and activist in the local NAACP, sat down in the front of a bus in a section reserved by law and custom for whites. Tired from a day at work, she'd taken the first seat available. Ordered to move to the back, she refused. Parks was then arrested, tried, and convicted of disorderly conduct and violating a local ordinance – the segregation statutes. When word reached the black community a bus boycott was organized to protest the segregation of blacks and whites on public buses. This event is generally understood as the spark that lit the fire of the Civil Rights Movement. Rosa Parks herself was generally regarded as the "mother of the Civil Rights Movement."

During the boycott, a young Baptist minister named **Martin Luther King Jr.**, became a spokesman for the boycott. He was arrested, as he would be again and again, but a year later, bus segregation was ruled unconstitutional. Dr King would go on to become the most prominent member of the Civil Rights movement, promoting nonviolent methods of opposition to segregation. The **Letter from Birmingham Jail** explained the purpose of nonviolent action as a way to make people notice injustice. "There comes a time when people get tired...of being kicked about by the brutal feet of oppression."

Following up on the decision of the Supreme Court in *Brown vs. Board of Education*, the Arkansas school board voted to integrate the school system. The **NAACP** chose Arkansas as the place to push integration because it was considered a relatively progressive Southern state. In **Little Rock, Arkansas**, in 1957, with the admission of nine black students to a previously all-white high school. Arkansas, Governor Faubus claimed a threat of violence and posted troops to turn the black students away. When a federal court ordered the troops to leave, the students came to school, only to encounter belligerent taunts. President Eisenhower responded by placing the National Guard troops under federal command and calling them back to Little Rock. It was the first time troops had been used to protect Black rights since the late nineteenth century.

Relying on the efforts of black Americans themselves, the Civil Rights Movement gained momentum in the postwar years. Working through courts and legislation, civil rights supporters created the groundwork for an even more extensive movement in the 1960s. After these progressive victories in the 1950s, blacks became even more committed to nonviolent direct action. Groups like the **Southern Christian Leadership Conference (SCLC)**, formed in 1957 by King and other activists, and the **Student Nonviolent Coordinating Committee (SNCC)**, sought reform through peaceful confrontation. One such method was the sit-in.

In 1960 black college students sat down at a segregated Woolworth's lunch counter in Greensboro, North Carolina refusing to leave. Their **sit-in** captured media attention and led to similar demonstrations throughout the South. This led to a rash of similar campaigns throughout the South. Demonstrators began to protest parks, beaches, theaters, museums, and libraries. When arrested, the protesters made **jail-no-bail** pledges, refusing to be bailed out of prison and insisting on staying in jail. This called attention to their cause and put the financial burden of providing jail space and food on the cities.

The next year, civil rights workers organized "**freedom rides**," where activists of all colors, blacks and whites, boarded buses heading South toward segregated terminals. The Supreme Court ordered the cessation of segregated interstate bus terminals, and the freedom rides put the ruling of the Court to the test. Anticipating violence and resitance, civil rights workers hoped that confrontations with local officials attempting to enforce segregation statutes might capture media attention and lead to change. This undertaking was a far more dangerous protest than it might sound. Many buses were firebombed, attacked by the KKK, and the riders beaten. When arrested, they were crammed into small, airless jail cells and mistreated in many ways

James Meredith, an African American, applied for admission to the University of Mississippi in January, 1961. Officials at the school returned his application because he was black. The LDF took the case and the Supreme Court ruled he had the right to attend. Violence erupted as a mob of 2000 clashed with federal troops. When it was over, 2 people were dead, 28 had been shot, 160 were injured. Despite the violence Meredith was admitted and became the first black student at the University of Mississippi.

The **Birmingham Campaign** began in 1963. A campaign was planned to use sit-in, kneel-ins in churches, and a march to the county building to launch a voter registration campaign. The city of Birmingham, Alabama obtained an injunction forbidding all such protests. The protesters, including Martin Luther King, Jr., believed the injunction was unconstitutional, and defied it. They were arrested. While in jail, King wrote his famous **Letter from Birmingham Jail**, one of the clearest statements of the purpose and tactics of the entire movement.

When the campaign began to falter, the Children's Crusade, called students to leave school and join the protests. The events became news when more than 600 students were jailed. The next day more students joined the protest. The media was present and broadcast to the nation vivid pictures of fire hoses being used to knock down children and dogs attacking African Americans. The result was public outrage that led the Kennedy administration to intervene. About a month later, a committee was formed to end hiring discrimination, arrange for the release of jailed protesters, and establish normative communication between blacks and whites.

The penultimate event of the Civil Rights Movement was the **March on Washington** in the late summer of 1963. More than 250,000 people gathered in the nation's capital to demonstrate their commitment to equality for all. This was a march for jobs and freedom, a combined effort of all major civil rights organizations. The goals of the march were: meaningful civil rights laws, a massive federal works program, full and fair employment, decent housing, the right to vote, and adequate integrated education. Amid a day of songs and speeches, the high point came with an address by Martin Luther King, Jr., a man who had emerged as the preeminent spokesman for civil rights. King's speech, referred to as the **I Have a Dream Speech** because of its constant refrain, summed up the hopes of everyone there. "I have a dream," he said, "that one day this nation will rise up and live out the true meaning of its creed, 'We hold these truths to be self-evident, that all men are created equal'."

Then, a little over two weeks after King's speech in Washington, tragedy struck. On Sunday, 15th September, 1963, a white man was seen placing a box under the steps of the **16th Street Baptist Church**, where leaders of the Civil Rights Movement often met.

At 10.22 a.m., the bomb exploded killing four girls who had been attending Sunday school classes. Then more violence occurred a year later, during the **Mississippi Freedom Summer** in 1964. Students were brought from other states to Mississippi to assist local activists in registering voters, teaching in Freedom Schools and in forming the Mississippi Freedom Democratic Party. Three of the workers disappeared – presumed murdered by the KKK. It took six weeks to find their bodies. In both cases, though many sought justice, it would take decades for those who were responsible to be brought to trial.

The national uproar forced President Johnson to send in the FBI. Johnson, a liberal Southerner from Texas was able to use public sentiment to effect passage in Congress of the **Civil Rights Act of 1964**. It outlawed discrimination in all public accommodations, and was a watershed moment in the Civil Rights Movement. The act, however, did not address voting rights.

Another series of marches occurred in 1965. Attempts to obtain voter registration in **Selma, Alabama** had been largely unsuccessful due to opposition from the city's sheriff. Dr King came to the city to lead a series of marches. He and over 200 demonstrators were arrested and jailed. Each successive march was met with violent resistance by police. In March, a group of over 600 intended to walk from Selma to Montgomery (a distance of 54 miles). News media were on hand when, six blocks into the march, state and local law enforcement officials attacked the marchers with billy clubs, tear gas, rubber tubes wrapped in barbed wire and bull whips. The marchers were driven back to Selma. As before in Birmingham, national broadcast of the footage provoked a nation-wide response. President Johnson again used public sentiment to achieve passage of the **Voting Rights Act of 1965**. This law irrevocably changed the political landscape of the South. This law made all barriers on voter registration illegal. Now, literacy tests, poll taxes, and exams on American politics and history can no longer be used as a means of determining voter eligibility.

However, the push for civil rights had more than just one voice. **Malcolm X**, an eloquent activist, argued for black separation from the white race. A prominent member of the Nation of Islam, he rejected the notion of non-violence embraced by the SCLC. He remained a staunch supporter of black power until his assassination in 1965.

Stokely Carmichael was one of the leaders of the Black Power movement that called for independent development of political and social institutions for blacks. Carmichael called for black pride and maintenance of black culture. He was head of the Student Nonviolent Coordinating Committee.

Ralph Abernathy was a major figure in the Civil Rights Movement who succeeded Martin Luther King, Jr. as head of the Southern Christian Leadership Conference.

The **Black Panthers** were founded by Huey Newton and Bobby Seale in 1966 in Oakland, Calif. Originally formed in defense of police brutality, it eventually developed into a revolutionary group that called for the arming of African Americans, their exemption from the draft, the release of all African American prisoners, and payment of compensation to African Americans for centuries of exploitation by white Americans. By the late 1960s it had more than 2,000 members, with chapters in several major cities.

Violence accompanied more militant calls for reform. Riots broke out in several big cities, the biggest in the **Watts** neighborhood of L.A. in 1965. A normally routine traffic stop erupted into five days of violence marked by arson, looting, and armed clashed between police and citizens. It took the National Guard to finally restore order, but the match had been lit and the era of non-violent protest had literally ended in flames.

The final tragedies fell in the spring of 1968 when Martin Luther King was assassinated. Several months later, Senator **Robert Kennedy**, a spokesman for the disadvantaged, brother of the slain president, and presidential candidtate was also killed. To many people, these two assassinations marked the end of an era of innocence and idealism in the movement. Though much had been accomplished, there was also still much to do. However, with the death of the Civil Rights Movement's most prominent members, and growing troubles elsewhere, the nation's attention would shift elsewhere.

The legacy of the movement lived on, however, finding resonance with women's movements, gay rights movements, and similar efforts by the Hispanic and American Indian communities. As a result, a number of anti-discrimination laws have been passed by Congress protecting the civil rights of several groups of Americans. These laws include:

- Civil Rights Act of 1964
- Voting Rights Act of 1965
- Civil Rights Act of 1968
- Age Discrimination in Employment Act of 1967
- Age Discrimination Act of 1975
- Pregnancy Discrimination Act of 1978
- Americans with Disabilities Act of 1990
- Civil Rights Act of 1991

Skill 6.3   Recognize the effects on U.S. society of major political developments from 1960 to the present

John F. Kennedy is widely remembered for his Inaugural Address in which the statement was made, "Ask not what your country can do for you – ask what you can do for your country." His campaign pledge was to get America moving again. During his brief presidency, his economic programs created the longest period of continuous expansion in the country since WWII. He wanted the U.S. to again take up the mission as the first country committed to the revolution of human rights. Through the Alliance for Progress and the Peace Corps, the hopes and idealism of the nation reached out to assist developing nations. He was deeply and passionately involved in the cause of equal rights for all Americans and he drafted new civil rights legislation. He also drafted plans for a broad attack on the systemic problems of privation and poverty. He believed the arts were critical to a society and instituted programs to support the arts.

In 1962, during the Kennedy Administration, Soviet Premier Khrushchev decided to install nuclear missiles in Cuba, as a protective measure against an American invasion,. In October, American U-2 spy planes photographed over Cuba what were identified as missile bases under construction. The decision in the White House was how to handle the situation without starting a war. The only recourse was removal of the missile sites and preventing more being set up. Kennedy announced that the U.S. had set up a "quarantine" of Soviet ships heading to Cuba. It was in reality a blockade but the word itself could not be used publicly as a blockade was actually considered an act of war. The tension that arose from the 13 days of the Cuban Missile Crisis was the closest America and the Soviet Union came to turning the Cold War "hot." The Soviets removed their missiles from Cuba, and the U.S. removed its missiles from Turkey.

Lyndon B. Johnson assumed the presidency after the assassination of Kennedy. His vision for America was called "A Great Society." He won support in Congress for the largest group of legislative programs in the history of the nation. These included programs Kennedy had been working on at the time of his death, including a new civil rights bill and a tax cut. He defined the "great society" as "a place where the meaning of man's life matches the marvels of man's labor." The legislation enacted during his administration included: an attack on disease, urban renewal, Medicare, aid to education, conservation and beautification, development of economically depressed areas, a war on poverty, voting rights for all, and control of crime and delinquency. Johnson managed an unpopular military action in Vietnam and encouraged the exploration of space. During his administration the Department of Transportation was formed and the first black, Thurgood Marshall, was nominated and confirmed as a Supreme Court Justice.

Richard Nixon inherited racial unrest and the Vietnam War, from which he extracted the American military. His administration is probably best known for improved relations with both China and the USSR. However, the Watergate scandal divided the country and led to his resignation during his second term. His major domestic achievements were: the appointment of conservative justices to the Supreme Court, passed new anti-crime legislation, introduced a broad environmental program, sponsored revenue sharing legislation and ended the draft.

Gerald Ford was the first Vice President selected under the 25th Amendment. After Nixon resigned from office, Ford took office as President. The challenges that faced his administration were a depressed economy, inflation, energy shortages, and the need to champion world peace. Once inflation slowed and recession was the major economic problem, he instituted measures that would stimulate the economy. He tried to reduce the role of the federal government. He reduced business taxes and lessened the controls on business. His international focus was on preventing a major war in the Middle East. He negotiated with Russia limitations on nuclear weapons.

During the administration of **President Jimmy Carter**, Egyptian President Anwar el-Sadat and Israeli Prime Minister Menachem Begin met at presidential retreat **Camp David** and agreed, after a series of meetings, to sign a formal treaty of peace between the two countries. In 1979, the Soviet invasion of Afghanistan was perceived by Carter and his advisers as a threat to the rich oil fields in the Persian Gulf. At this time, U.S. military capability was weak to prevent further Soviet aggression in the Middle East. The last year of Carter's presidential term was taken up with the 53 American hostages held in Iran. The Shah had been overthrown and control of the government and the country was in the hands of Muslim leader, Ayatollah Ruhollah Khomeini.

Khomeini's extreme hatred for the U.S. was the result of the 1953 overthrow of Iran's Mossadegh government, sponsored by the CIA. To make matters worse, the CIA proceeded to train the shah's ruthless secret police force. So when the terminally ill exiled shah was allowed into the U.S. for medical treatment, a fanatical mob stormed into the American embassy taking the 53 Americans as prisoners, supported and encouraged by Khomeini.

President Carter froze all Iranian assets in the U.S., set up trade restrictions, and approved a risky rescue attempt, which failed. He had appealed to the UN for aid in gaining release for the hostages and to European allies to join the trade embargo on Iran. Khomeini ignored UN requests for releasing the Americans and Europeans refused to support the embargo so as not to risk losing access to Iran's oil. American prestige was damaged and Carter's chances for reelection were doomed. The hostages were released on the day of Ronald Reagan's inauguration as President when Carter released Iranian assets as ransom.

The foreign policy of **President Ronald Reagan** was, in his first term, focused primarily on the Western Hemisphere, particularly in Central America and the West Indies. U.S. involvement in the domestic revolutions of El Salvador and Nicaragua continued into Reagan's second term when Congress held televised hearings on what came to be known as the Iran-Contra Affair. A cover-up was exposed showing that profits from secretly selling military hardware to Iran had been used to give support to rebels, called Contras, who were fighting in Nicaragua.

In 1983 in Lebanon, 241 American Marines were killed when an Islamic suicide bomber drove an explosive-laden truck into U.S. Marines headquarters located at the airport in Beirut. This tragic event came as part of the unrest and violence between the Israelis and Palestine Liberation Organization (PLO) forces in southern Lebanon.

In the same month, 1,900 U.S. Marines landed on the island of Grenada to rescue a small group of American medical students at the medical school and depose of the leftist government. Perhaps the most intriguing and far-reaching event towards the end of Reagan's second term was the arms-reduction agreement Reagan reached with Soviet General Secretary Mikhail Gorbachev. Gorbachev began easing East-West tensions by stressing the importance of cooperation with the West and easing the harsh and restrictive life of the people in the Soviet Union. In retrospect, it was clearly a prelude to the events occurring during the administration of **President George Bush.**

After Bush took office, it appeared for a brief period that democracy would gain a hold and influence in China, but the brief movement was quickly and decisively crushed. The biggest surprise was the fall of the Berlin Wall, resulting in the unification of all of Germany, the loss of power of the Communists in other Eastern European countries, and the fall of Communism in the Soviet Union and the breakup of its republics into independent nations. The countries of Poland, Hungary, Romania, Czechoslovakia, Albania, and Bulgaria replaced Communist rule with democratic governments.

The former Yugoslavia broke apart into individual ethnic enclaves with the republics of Serbia, Croatia, and Bosnia-Herzegovina embarking on wars of ethnic cleansing between Catholics, Orthodox, and Muslims. In Russia, as in the other former republics and satellites, democratic governments were put into operation and the difficult task of changing communist economies into ones of capitalistic free enterprise began. For all practical purposes, it appeared that the tensions and dangers of the post-World War II "Cold War" between the U.S. and Soviet-led Communism were over.

President Bush, in December of 1989, sent U.S. troops to invade Panama and arrest the Panamanian dictator Manuel Noriega. Although he had periodically assisted CIA operations with intelligence information, at the same time, Noriega laundered money from drug smuggling and gunrunning through Panama's banks.

Though ignored for a short time, it became too embarrassing for the American intelligence community. When a political associate tried unsuccessfully to depose him and an off-duty U.S. Marine was shot and killed at a roadblock, Bush acted. Noriega was brought to the U.S. where he stood trial on charges of drug distribution and racketeering.

During the time of the American hostage crisis, Iraq and Iran fought a war in which the U.S. and most of Iraq's neighbors supported Iraq. In a five-year period, **Saddam Hussein** received from the U.S. $500 million worth of American technology, including lasers, advanced computers, and special machine tools used in missile development. The Iraq-Iran war was a bloody one resulting in a stalemate with a UN truce ending it. Neighboring Kuwait, in direct opposition to OPEC agreements, increased oil production.

This caused oil prices to drop, which upset Hussein, who was deeply in debt from the war and totally dependent on oil revenues. After a short period of time, Saddam invaded and occupied Kuwait. The U.S. made extensive plans to put into operation strategy to successfully carry out **Operation Desert Storm**, the liberation of Kuwait. In four days, February 24-28, 1991, the war was over and Iraq had been defeated, its troops driven back into their country. Saddam remained in power although Iraq's economy was seriously damaged.

President Bill Clinton sent U.S. troops to Haiti to protect the efforts of Jean-Bertrand Aristide to gain democratic power and to **Bosnia** to assist UN peacekeeping forces. He inherited from the Bush administration the problem with Somalia in East Africa, where U.S. troops had been sent in December 1992 to support UN efforts to end the starvation of the Somalis and restore peace. The efforts were successful at first, but eventually failed due to the severity of the intricate political problems within the country. After U.S. soldiers were killed in an ambush along with 300 Somalis, American troops were withdrawn and returned home.

Skill 6.4   **Recognize important changes in U.S. immigration policy and analyze the changing nature of immigration to the United States and its effects**

Immigration has played a crucial role in the growth and settlement of the United States from the start. With a large interior territory to fill and ample opportunity, the US encouraged immigration throughout most of the nineteenth century, maintaining an almost completely open policy. Famine in Ireland and Germany in the 1840s resulted in over 3.5 million immigrants from these two countries alone between the years of 1830 and 1860.

Following the Civil War, rapid expansion in rail transportation brought the interior states within easy reach of new immigrants who still came primarily from Western Europe and entered the US on the east coast. As immigration increased, several states adopted individual immigration laws. In 1875 the US Supreme Court declared immigration a federal matter. Following a huge surge in European immigration in 1880, the United States began to regulate immigration, first by passing a tax to new immigrants, then by instituting literacy requirements and barring those with mental or physical illness. A large influx of Chinese immigration to the western states had resulted in the complete exclusion of immigrants from that country in 1882. In 1891, the Federal Bureau of Immigration was established. Even with these new limits in place, immigration remained relatively open in the US to those from European countries, and increased steadily until World War I.

With much of Europe left in ruins after WWI, immigration to the US exploded in the years following the war. In 1920 and 1921, some 800,000 new immigrants arrived. Unlike previous immigrants who came mainly from western European countries, the new wave of immigrants was from southern and eastern Europe. The US responded to this sudden shift in the makeup of new immigrants with a quota system, first enacted by Congress in 1921. This system limited immigration in proportion to the ethnic groups that were already settled in the US according to previous census records. This **National-Origins Policy** was extended and further defined by Congress in 1924.

This policy remained the official policy of the US for the next 40 years. Occasional challenges to the law from non-white immigrants re-affirmed that the intention of the policy was to limit immigration primarily to white, western Europeans, who the government felt were most likely to assimilate into American culture. Strict limitations on Chinese immigration was extended throughout the period, and only relaxed in 1940. In 1965, Congress overhauled immigration policy, removing the quotas and replacing them with a preference based system. Now, immigrants reuniting with family members and those with special skills or education were given preference. As a result, immigration from Asian and African countries began to increase.

The 40-year legacy of the 1920s immigration restrictions had a direct and dramatic impact on the makeup of modern American society. Had Congress not imposed what amounted to racial limits on new arrivals to the country, the US would perhaps be a larger more diverse nation than it already is today.

Until the middle of the twentieth century, voluntary migrations to America were primarily Europeans. After WWII, a large number of Europeans were admitted to the U.S. and Canada. These were considered the most desirable immigrants. Indeed, immigration policies based upon ethnicity or country of origin were not eliminated until the 1960s. The impact of the Cold War on migration patterns was very significant. American policies toward immigration became more open to political escapees from communist countries, partly out of a desire to embarrass these nations. The number of immigrants from third-world nations was also increasing dramatically. The end of the Cold War marked a shift in migration patterns so that migrations from south to north came to predominate global migration. A significant change in immigration policy occurred after WWII. Both the U.S. and Canada began to distinguish between economically motivated voluntary immigrants and political refugees.

The conditions that existed after the war made it clear that some immigrants must be treated differently on the basis of humanitarian concerns. Fear of persecution caused massive migrations. The United Nations created the International Refugee Organization in 1946. In the next three years this organization relocated over a million European refugees.

Immigration policy in the U.S. was carefully aligned with foreign policy. President Truman introduced the **Displaced Persons Act in 1948** which facilitated the admission of more than 400,000 persons from Europe. During the 1950s, however, the immigration policy became very restrictive. **The McCarran-Walter Immigration Nationality Act of 1952** established a quota system and was clearly anti-Asian.

The number of refugees from Eastern Europe far exceeded these quotas. Both Presidents Truman and Eisenhower urged extension of the quotas, and in time they were abandoned. Refugees from communist Europe were admitted under the President's Escapee Program of 1952 and the Refugee Relief Act of 1953.

Immigration by Asians had been restricted for some time and this policy did not change after WWII. The changes in immigration policies and the great influx of Europeans brought a wide variety of people into the U.S. To be sure, some were farmers and laborers, but many were highly trained and skilled scientists, teachers, inventors, and executives. This migration added to the American "melting pot" experience. The immigrants provided new sources of labor for a booming economy and the introduction of new cultural ideas and contributions to science and technology.

The acceptance and assimilation of European immigrants was, for the most part, easier than the prejudiced assimilation of persons of Asian descent, particularly after the recent hostilities with Japan.

Immigration and Nationality Services Act of 1965

The United States has always been a destination for people from other countries looking to improve their lot. Through most of its history, the majority of newcomers to the US were whites from Europe, particularly in the period between 1890 and 1930, when there was a comparatively liberal immigration policy. Before the Civil War, African slaves who had been brought to the US were primarily in the southern states. Following emancipation, many blacks moved to urban areas where employment was more easily found.

Beginning around 1980, a shift in the nationality of new immigrants began, with an increase in the number of immigrants from Asian and Latin American countries. Political unrest and economic downturns led to surges in immigrants from troubled countries such as the Dominican Republic and Cambodia. The disparity between the US and Mexican economies created a situation where laborers from Mexico could find ample work in America.

Initially, the increase in Latin American and Asian immigration affected the few traditional "gateway" states such as New York, Florida, Texas and California. In the decades since, immigration has moved increasingly into interior areas of the US such as the Midwestern states of Iowa and Nebraska, where agricultural and meatpacking industries provide a source of employment for immigrant labor. This movement of immigrants from the border states has had the effect of spreading ethnic and cultural diversity into small, previously homogenous towns, making a permanent impact on American culture.

Skill 6.5   Analyze the growing influence of technology on U.S. society and demonstrate knowledge of changes to the U.S. economy

The **microscope** first appeared about 1590, and was steadily improved upon. The microscope revealed an entire world of invisible activity by bacteria and fungus, and laid bare the cell structure of complex organisms. Advancements in microscopy led directly to important discoveries concerning germs, viruses and the cause of disease, greatly aiding the field of medicine.

The use of machines in industry enabled workers to produce a large quantity of goods much faster than by hand. With the increase in business, hundreds of workers were hired, assigned to perform a certain job in the production process. This was a method of organization called "**division of labor**" and by its increased rate of production, businesses lowered prices for their products making the products affordable for more people. As a result, sales and businesses were increasingly successful and profitable.

A great variety of new products or inventions became available such as: the typewriter, the telephone, barbed wire, the electric light, the phonograph, and the gasoline automobile. From this list, the one development that had the greatest effect on America's economy was the automobile. The availability of automobiles and the extension of public transportation beyond the city limits enabled the middle and upper classes to leave city centers.

The **microchip** was developed in the 1950s as a way to reduce the size of transistor-based electronic equipment. By replacing individual transistors with a single chip of semiconductor material, more capability could be included in less space. This development led directly to the microprocessor, which is at the heart of every modern computer and most modern electronic products.

Political factors have affected scientific advancement, as well, especially in cultures that partially support scientific research with public money. Warfare has traditionally been a strong driver of technological advancement as cultures strive to outpace their neighbors with better weapons and defenses. Technologies developed for military purposes often find their way into the mainstream. Significant advances in flight technology, for example, were made during the two World Wars.

Socially, many cultures have come to value innovation and welcome new products and improvements to older products. This desire to always be advancing and obtaining the latest, newest technology creates economic incentive for innovation.

New technologies have made production faster, easier, and more efficient. People found their skills and their abilities **replaced by machines** that were faster and more accurate. To some degree, machines and humans have entered an age of competition. Yet these advances have facilitated greater control over nature, lightened the burden of labor, and extended human life span. These advances in science, knowledge and technology have also called into question many of the assumptions and beliefs that have provided meaning for human existence. The myths that provided meaning in the past have been exposed and there are no new structures of belief to replace them. Without the foundational belief structures that have given meaning to life, an emptiness and aimlessness has arisen. Technology and science have extended life and made life easier. They have provided power and knowledge, but not the wisdom to know how to use it effectively. It was not accompanied by self-mastery, the willingness to prevent class conflicts and prejudice, or to stop war, cruelty and violence.

The extraordinary advances in science and technology opened new frontiers and pushed back an ever-growing number of boundaries. These influences have had a profound effect in shaping modern civilization. Each discovery or machine or insight built upon other new discoveries or insights or machines. By the twentieth century the rate of discovery and invention became literally uncontrollable. The results have, in many cases, been beneficial. But others have been horrifying. Advances in biology and medicine have **decreased infant mortality** and **increased life expectancy** dramatically. Antibiotics and new surgical techniques have saved countless lives. Inoculations have essentially erased many dreadful diseases. Yet others have resulted from the careless disposal of by-products and the effects of industrialization upon the environment and the individual.

Tremendous progress in **communication** and **transportation** has tied all parts of the earth and drawn them closer. There are still vast areas of the former Soviet Union that have unproductive land, extreme poverty, food shortages, rampant diseases, violent friction between cultures, the ever-present nuclear threat, environmental pollution, rapid reduction of natural resources, urban over-crowding, acceleration in global terrorism and violent crimes, and a diminishing middle class.

New technologies have changed the way of life for many. We are now living in the computer age and in most places, computers are even in grade schools. Technology makes the world seem a much smaller place. Even children have cell phones today. The existence of television and modern technology has us watching a war while it is in progress. **Outsourcing** is now popular because of technological advances. Call centers for European, American and other large countries are now located in India, Pakistan, etc. Multinational corporations located plants in foreign countries to lower costs.

In many places technology has resulted in a mobile population. After World War II, air travel started to boom making domestic and international travel easier. Popular culture has been shaped by mass production and the **mass media**. Mass production and technology has made electronic goods affordable to most. The Internet and email allow people to communicate with others anywhere in the world and to allow people to learn about world events. In the industrial countries and in many others, the popular culture is oriented towards the electronic era.

The Soviet Union was the first industrialized nation to successfully begin a program of **space flight and exploration,** launching Sputnik and putting the first man in space. The United States also experienced success in its space program successfully landing the first space crew on the moon. In the late 1980s and early 1990s, the Berlin Wall was torn down and communism fell in the Soviet Union and Eastern Europe. The fifteen republics of the former USSR became independent nations with varying degrees of freedom and democracy in government and together formed the Commonwealth of Independent States (CIS). The former communist nations of Eastern Europe also emphasized their independence with democratic forms of government.

Globalization refers to the complex of social, political, technological, and economic changes that result from increasing contact, communication, interaction, integration and interdependence of peoples of disparate parts of the world. The term is generally used to refer to the process of change or as the cause of turbulent change. Globalization may be understood in terms of positive social and economic change, as in the case of a broadening of trade resulting in an increase in the standard of living for developing countries. Globalization may also be understood negatively in terms of the abusive treatment of developing countries in the interest of cultural or economic imperialism. These negative understandings generally point to cultural assimilation, plunder and profiteering, the destruction of the local culture and economy, and ecological indifference.

The global economy had its origins in the early twentieth century, with the advent of the **airplane**, which made travel and trade easier and less time-consuming than ever. With the recent introduction of the Internet, the world might be better termed a global neighborhood.

Globalization also involves exchange of money, commodities, information, ideas, and people. Much of this has been facilitated by the great advances in technology in the last 150 years. The effects of globalization can be seen across all areas of social and cultural interaction. Economically, globalization brings about broader and faster trade and flow of capital, increased outsourcing of labor, the development of global financial systems (such as the introduction of the Euro), the creation of trade agreements and the birth of international organizations to moderate the agreements.

From a social and cultural point of view, globalization results in greater exchange of all segments of the various cultures, including ideas, technology, food, clothing, trends, etc. Travel and migration create multicultural societies. The media facilitates the exchange of cultural and social values. As values interact a new shared set of values begins to emerge.

Skill 6.6 **Recognize major foreign policy issues and developments affecting the United States and analyze the effects of these developments on the United States and its place in the global community**

The **Middle East** is defined by its name and its geographic position. It is the joining point of Europe, Africa, and Asia, a position that enables it to exert tremendous influence on not only the trade that passes through its realm of influence but also the political relations between its countries and those of different parts of the world.

From the beginnings of civilization, the Middle East has been a destination—for attackers, for adventure-seekers, for those starving for food and a progressively more technologically advanced series of other resources, from iron to oil. Now, as then, the countries of the Middle East play an important role in the economics of the world.

First and foremost is the importance of oil. **Saudi Arabia** most notably but also Iran, Iraq, Kuwait, Qatar, Dubai, and the United Arab Emirates are huge exporters of oil: in some cases, the amount of oil that one of these countries exports exceeds 90 percent of its' total economic outflow. These countries are also members of OPEC, the Organization of Petroleum Exporting Countries. Most of the world requires oil in huge numbers, to run its machines and especially its transportation vehicles—cars, trucks, airplanes, and buses. The vast majority of the world's developed nations would be helpless without this oil, and so the governments of these nations will pay nearly any price to keep that oil flowing from the Middle East into their countries. The oil-rich exporters of the Middle East can hold the rest of the world hostage by increasing the price of oil even slightly, since the consumption for even a small developed nation numbers in the billions of gallons every month. (The Middle East is not the only place to get oil by any means; Russia, for example, is another excellent source of oil. The appeal of the Middle East countries as sources of oil is that it is much easier to get at and put on tankers than it is to procure from the wilds of central Russia.)

It can be argued that whoever controls a country in the Middle East controls the oil. With few exceptions, all of these countries have strong central governments, which control the collection and export of oil. If a country were to take over one of these big exporters, the infrastructure would already be in place to control the flow of oil. The recent American occupation of Iraq illustrates this, since the existing oil companies were taken over by American operations.

The countries of the Middle East, despite their economic similarities, have important differences in their government, belief systems, and global outlooks. Iran and Iraq fought a devastating war in the 1980s. Iraq invaded Kuwait in the late 1990s. It is not outside the realm of possibility that other conflicts will arise in the future.

Another large factor of the instability in the Middle East is ethnic strife. It's not just Muslims who occupy these countries. Each country has its own ethnic mix. A good example of this is Iraq, which has a huge minority of Kurdish people. Saddam Hussein, the former dictator of Iraq, made a habit of persecuting Kurds just because of who they were. Iraq is an example of a religious conflict, with the minority Shiites now in power and Hussein's Sunnis out of power. These two people agree on next to nothing except that "There is no God but Allah, and Muhammad is his Prophet." The prospect of a civil war in Iraq looms large, as it does in other neighboring countries, which have their own ethnic problems.

Religious conflict is the name of the game in Israel as well, as Israelis and Palestinians continue a centuries-old fight over religion and geography. This conflict goes back to the beginnings of Islam, in the seventh century. Muslims claimed Jerusalem, capital of the ancient civilization of Israel, as a holy city, in the same way that Jews and Christians did. Muslims seized control of Palestine and Jerusalem and held it for a great many years, prompting Christian armies from Europe to muster for the Crusades, in a series of attempts to "regain the Holy Land." For hundreds of years after Christendom's failure, these lands were ruled by Muslim leaders and armies. The Turkish Ottoman Empire controlled the land of Palestine from the 1500s until 1917. After World War I, the League of Nations divided up many Middle Eastern nations among the British and the French. The British Mandate of Palestine was set to terminate in 1948 (as stipulated in UN Resolution 181). The same day that the British left Palestine, the State of Israel declared independence. Since that last event, in 1948, the conflict has escalated to varying degrees.

The addition of Israel to the Middle East equation presents a religious conflict not only with the Palestinians but also with the Arab peoples of neighboring Egypt and Syria. The armed forces of all of these countries have so many advanced weapons that they would seem to be a deterrent to further bloodshed, yet the attacks continue. In the last 40 years, Israel has won two major wars with its neighbors. Nearly daily conflict continues, much as it has for thousands of years. This conflict is not so much an economic one, but a full-blown war in this region would certainly involve Israel's neighbors and, by extension, other large countries in the world, most notably the United States.

During the administration of **President Jimmy Carter**, Egyptian President Anwar el-Sadat and Israeli Prime Minister Menachem Begin met at presidential retreat **Camp David** and agreed, after a series of meetings, to sign a formal treaty of peace between the two countries. In 1979, the Soviet invasion of Afghanistan was perceived by Carter and his advisers as a threat to the rich oil fields in the Persian Gulf but at the time, U.S. military capability to prevent further Soviet aggression in the Middle East was weak. The last year of Carter's presidential term was taken up with the 53 American hostages held in Iran. The shah had been deposed and control of the government and the country was in the hands of Muslim leader, Ayatollah Ruhollah Khomeini.

Khomeini's extreme hatred for the U.S. was the result of the 1953 overthrow of Iran's Mossadegh government, sponsored by the CIA. To make matters worse, the CIA proceeded to train the shah's ruthless secret police force. So when the terminally ill exiled shah was allowed into the U.S. for medical treatment, a fanatical mob stormed into the American embassy taking the 53 Americans as prisoners, supported and encouraged by Khomeini.

President Carter froze all Iranian assets in the U.S., set up trade restrictions, and approved a risky rescue attempt, which failed. He had appealed to the UN for aid in gaining release for the hostages and to European allies to join the trade embargo on Iran. Khomeini ignored UN requests for releasing the Americans and Europeans refused to support the embargo so as not to risk losing access to Iran's oil. American prestige was damaged and Carter's chances for reelection were doomed. The hostages were released on the day of Ronald Reagan's inauguration as President when Carter released Iranian assets as ransom.

In 1983 in Lebanon, 241 American Marines were killed when an Islamic suicide bomber drove an explosive-laden truck into U.S. Marines headquarters located at the airport in Beirut. This tragic event came as part of the unrest and violence between the Israelis and Palestine Liberation Organization (PLO) forces in southern Lebanon.

The **Persian Gulf War** was fought in 1990-91 in Kuwait and Iraq and along the border of Saudi Arabia. The combatants were Iraq and a coalition of nations led by the United States. The immediate cause of the war was the invasion of Kuwait by Iraq on August 2, 1990. Iraqi leader Saddam Hussein justified the invasion by accusing Kuwait of slant drilling into Iraqi oil fields, and by renewing a former dispute over Kuwait's independence from Iraq. Prior to World War I, Kuwait was considered part of larger Iraq. Following the war, the British gained administrative control of Kuwait and treated it as an independent nation. Iraq did not recognize Kuwait's independence. Iraq also owed Kuwait a large debt for aid it received while fighting a war against Iran. Iraq claimed that because it acted as a buffer between Iran and Kuwait and Saudi Arabia, its war debts to these countries should be forgiven.

Immediately following Iraq's invasion of Kuwait, the United Nations imposed economic sanctions. Within a week, the United States, fearing that Iraq might next invade Saudi Arabia, began to send troops to that country in what was called Operation Desert Shield. Two naval battle groups were sent to the Persian Gulf as part of the operation.

As the U.S. amassed military resources in the region, it began to organize a coalition of other nations to give support in the case of conflict. The United Nations passed a resolution in November, 1990, giving Iraq until January 15, 1991 to leave Kuwait. On January 12, the U.S. Congress authorized military action in Iraq. Iraq did not withdraw by the deadline, and the following day the U.S. began heavy aerial assaults on the country. Iraq responded with missile attacks and ground forces, but was quickly forced back into Iraq. The fighting was largely over in a matter of weeks, with the U.S. beginning to withdraw its forces from the area in early March, 1991.

DOMAIN II.   WORLD REGIONS

COMPETENCY 7.0   UNDERSTAND MAJOR HISTORICAL, SOCIAL, POLITICAL, AND ECONOMIC DEVELOPMENTS IN LATIN AMERICA AND THE GEOGRAPHIC FACTORS INFLUENCING THEM.

Skill 7.1   Demonstrate knowledge of the location and characteristics of the major physical and political features of Latin America

Mexico and Central America

Mexico is a rising industrial power in Latin America that has established industries in the fields of telecommunication, natural gas distribution and electric generation, as well as seaport and railroad construction. Its agricultural output mainly consists of the production of corn, beans, cotton and, potatoes. It is the world's major producer of silver, which produces close to one quarter of the total revenue of the economy. It is one of the world's leading producers of natural gas and petroleum. It has the seventh largest oil reserve in the world.

Its capital, Mexico City, was founded by Hernán Cortes on the ruins of Tenochtitlan, former Aztec capital, in 1521. It has many points of interest. Among them are: "el Paseo de la Reforma" (the most elegant avenue in the capital), "el Zócalo" (the major square), "el Palacio de Bellas Artes" (the largest theater in the country; which also contains a huge Mexican art collection), "el Museo de Antropología," "la Cuidad Universitaria," "la Basílica de Guadalupe" patron saint of Mexico, "la Catedral," "Templo Mayo" (important ruins), the floating gardens on Xochimilco and the pyramids and temples of Teotihuacán. Other important cities include: Guadalajara (principal center of agriculture and cattle raising), Veracruz and Tampico (important ports on the Gulf of Mexico), Acapulco and Puerto Vallarta (famous beaches), Taxco (national monument of architecture and industrial center of silver) and Chichen Itza (ruins of former Mayan city).

Geographically, Mexico is considered to be part of North America. It is the northernmost and westernmost country in Latin America. Its central region, which is the most densely populated in the whole country, is a great plateau that opens up to the north into dry and hot desert areas. The east and west feature two mountain ranges: the Sierra Madre Occidental and the Sierra Madre Oriental, which are outwardly surrounded by oceanfront facing lowlands. To the south, forest and tropical rainforest areas make up the land. The Tropic of Cancer divides the country into tropical zones to the south, and temperate zones to the north. Its northern border with the United States, along the Río Bravo or Río Grande, is the longest border in the world. The Isthmus of Tehuantepec is the southernmost point of North America and the northernmost point of Central America. It is the most populated Spanish speaking country in the world.

Guatemala's hot tropical climate permits for farming of various types of agricultural products. Its principal products are coffee, bananas and sugar. In the north are lowlands and in the south is a costal area where the majority of the population resides, the rest of the country being mountainous. Mayan languages are prominent in rural areas. Its capital is Guatemala City.

Honduras is historically an agriculturally producing country producing sugar, bananas and coffee. It recently has found a burgeoning textile and shrimp industry as a new source of revenue. The ruins of Copan are a point of interest for once being the center of Mayan civilization. Eighty percent of Honduras consists of mountains with plains along its costal area, lowland jungles in the northeast and a valley in the northwest which is its most heavily populated area. The Negro River is its boundary with Nicaragua. Its capital is Tegucigalpa.

El Salvador has the second strongest economy in Central America with a thriving telecommunications, banking and textile industry. Coffee is its main agricultural product, but it also produces cotton, and sugar cane. In El Salvador rest the Mayan ruins of Tazumal, Chalchuapa and San Andrés. It is the only Central American country without a coastline to the Caribbean Sea.

Two mountain ranges cross El Salvador from east to west: the Sierra Madre on the north and the southern range is made up by volcanoes. It has a central plateau that consists of rolling plains resting between both mountain ranges. The plateau serves as the land for the majority of the country's population. There are narrow plains on its coastline with the Pacific. The Lempa River emptying into the Pacific Ocean is its only navigable river. El Salvador is the smallest country in Central America. It is known offhand "el pulgarcito de las Américas," (America's little thumb). Its capital is San Salvador. Nahuatl, an ancient Mayan language is prominent in all parts of El Salvador.

Nicaragua is mainly an agricultural country producing corn, cotton, coffee, bananas and tobacco. It is the largest cattle raising country in Central America. It contains seven percent of the world's bio-diversity. It is the largest country in Central America. It has mountains in the north central region and lowlands adjoining the Atlantic and Pacific. One fourth of the country is protected as a natural park or biological reserve. The Masaya Volcanic national park is a point of interest. Its capital is Managua.

Costa Rica's chief products for exportation are coffee and bananas. It also produces cocoa, sugar cane, potatoes and many types of fruit. Recently the fields of pharmaceuticals, electronics, financial outsourcing and software development have become main economic sources. Costa Rica is one of the oldest democracies in the Western Hemisphere. It is the only one that does not have an army and a civil guard maintains order. Costa Rica is home to five percent of the world's bio-diversity. The Corcovado and Tortuguero national parks, as well as the Monterey cloud forest are points of interest. Its capital is San José.

Costa Rica is the only country in Central America whose population consists mostly of Caucasian people. Spanish is the first and most common language, but English is often spoken.

Panama's principal agricultural product is bananas, but the main source of its economy is banking and commerce. The Colón free trade zone is the largest free trade zone in the Western Hemisphere. Panama is the smallest populated Spanish-speaking country in the Americas. It is considered a land bridge between South and Central America. The Isthmus of Panama is the dividing point where Central America ends and South America begins. Cristóbal is the terminus of the Canal Zone. Balboa is the port on the Pacific side. Its capital is Panama City. Panama is a melting pot; nine percent of its population is Chinese.

The Antilles (group of islands in the Caribbean Sea)

Cuba is the number one producer of sugar cane in the world. Cattle raising and fishing are also important industries and the country is rich in mineral deposits. It also produces tobacco – known worldwide for its quality – nickel, rice and a large variety of fruits. Its organic agriculture initiative is noted for its innovation and the pharmaceutical industry is being heavily invested in.

Cuba's healthcare system, with free universal health care for the entire country, is ranked as being one of the best in the world. Cuba is the largest island in the Caribbean and the last surviving communist state in Latin America. Cuba was the first of the Antilles to be discovered by Columbus on his first trip to the New World. It is known as the Pearl of the Antilles because of its beautiful country sides and fertile land. Its capital is Havana. The Castle of "el Morro" is a place of great historical interest because it was a fort used to protect the island from pirates in the seventeenth century. Guantanamo is an American naval base located on the island.

The **Dominican Republic's** economy is based on agriculture. Its main products are sugar cane, cocoa, coffee, plantains and corn. Citrus, green vegetables, pineapples, and flowers have grown important. Fishing is also becoming a major industry. It also bears the world's largest open-pit gold mine. It has three mountain ranges – the central, septentrional, and eastern – that cut the island from east to west. In the south, where most of the population concentrates, are rolling plains, while the west is arid and is made up of shrubs and cacti. The north side of the island is made up mostly of beaches. The Dominican Republic occupies two-thirds of the island of Hispañola. The other third is occupied by Creole speaking Haiti. Lake Enriquillo is the lowest point in the Caribbean. Its capital is Santo Domingo. There one can find the first chapel, first hospital and first cathedral in the New World, as well as the New World's oldest university – Thomas Aquinas University, known today as the University of Santo Domingo.

Puerto Rico's main staple is sugar cane. The petrochemical, pharmaceutical and technology industries are a rising addition to the current economy. It is mostly a mountainous island with coastlines on its north and south faces. The "Cordillera Central," the central mountain range, runs through the island. To the northwest lie beautiful beaches such as Jobos beach, María's beach, Domes beach and Sandy beach. The island came into possession of the United States, in 1898. Today it is known as a commonwealth. Its inhabitants have United States citizenship (since 1917). The island was discovered by Columbus, in 1493. The largest telescope in the world, the Arrecibo observatory, is situated on the island. Its capital, San Juan, was established in 1508 by Ponce de León. It is an active commercial port and possesses beautiful and ancient forts from the Spanish Colonial era.

South America

Argentina has a traditional, middle class economy that is largely self-sufficient. Livestock and grains are the country's major source of revenue. Its economy's famed products, wines, and meats are recognized to be excellent by the rest of the world. Textiles, leather goods and chemicals are prominent products within the overall economy. It is the second largest country in South America and the seventh largest in the world. The "Tierra del Fuego" (Land of Fire) and Patagonia in the south are made up of grassland and thorny forests.

The Chaco, in the north and northeast, is made up of jungles, swamps, mountains and the Iguazu falls lie within it. The Pampas, the country's central fertile plains, are home to the majority of the country's population and agricultural industry. Buenos Aires, its capital, possesses one of the most active seaports in the world. It is a very sophisticated city with a triage of elegant avenues, stores and theatres. Its second most important city is Rosario, a port city and industrial center. German, Spanish and Italian immigrants make up most of the population with native Indians representing a small percentage of the total race makeup. It has the largest Jewish population in all Latin America.

Uruguay's principal industry is cattle raising. It is also one of the world's leaders in the production of cotton. Tobacco and sugar are agricultural staples. Textiles, soy beans, cement and lime are produced as well. Vegetable oils are a rising industry. It is the smallest Spanish-speaking country in South America. It is made up of rolling plains and hundred of miles of beautiful beaches along the coast. El Negro River bisects the country from east to west. Montevideo is its capital and major port.

Paraguay's economy is agriculturally based. Its most important products are tea leaves and wood. It is landlocked on both sides, east and west, but it has many navigable outlets to the River Plate estuary bordering the Atlantic Ocean. The Paraguay River cuts the country into two east-west sections. In eastern Paraguay, between the Parana and Paraguay rivers, is the country's largest concentration of people. The west is mostly made up of marshes, lagoons, dense forests and jungles. Its capital is Asunción and is also its major port. Guaraní is its other dominant language, besides Spanish.

Chile is the world's largest producer of copper and mineral ore. Its chief products are grapevines and cereals. It is the world's longest country. The southernmost point of South America Cape Horn; Punta Arenas, the southernmost urban area in the world; Easter Island, home to a mysterious ancient civilization; Patagonia, the polar south region adjoining Antarctica, are all points of interest. The central valley's rolling plains are home to the majority of the country's population and agricultural industry. The north region is the Atacama Desert, known as the driest place on earth. Its most important cities: Santiago, the capital; Valparaíso, the principal seaport; Viña del Mar, a famous beach. The Andes Mountains runs along the coast line of Chile.

Bolivia has very rich mineral reserves that produce tin, copper, zinc, lead, sulfur and gold. It has the second largest natural gas industry in South America. It is a landlocked country that only has access to the Atlantic through the Paraguay River. Bolivia's population is concentrated on the western part: a great plateau called the "Altiplano," where half its population lives. East are grasslands and rainforests. Lake Titicaca, located between Bolivia and Peru, is the tallest commercially navigable lake in the world and South America's largest freshwater lake. Within the department of Potosi lies the "Salar de Uyuni," the world's largest salt flats. The country is named after Simón Bolívar.

Its capital is La Paz: the capital with the tallest altitude in the world. Bolivia has the highest indigenous population ratio in all America. Spanish, Quechua and Aymara are all equally recognized in Bolivia.

Peru's mining industry producing copper, gold and other precious minerals for a major source of its revenue. It has widespread agricultural sectors, with a variety of products for both domestic and foreign markets such as corn, cotton and different fruit trees. Fishing has always been a popular industry. Along the north coast, llamas, sheep and goat-like animals are kept. Cebu cattle roam, fit to the Amazonian climate. The Andes mountain ranges divide the country into three regions: the Pacific coast, which is desert-like; the sierra, which is dominated by the Andes and where more than half the country's population lies; the jungles of the Amazon, which cover more than sixty percent of the country. The Sechura desert is located in the northwestern area close to the Pacific coastline. The roots of the Amazon River are located in Peru. Peru is home to eighty-four of the one hundred and four remaining ecosystems on earth. The Manu National Park is the most diverse rainforest in the world.

The mysterious Nazca lines are found within the coastal plains. Near the city of Cuzco one can find the ruins of Machu Picchu, a former Incan city. There one can also find the University of San Marco, the first university on the continent, founded in 1551. Lima is its capital and an agricultural and industrial center – originally a fishing village. The city of Arequipe "la Ciudad Blanca" (The White City) is protected by UNESCO and is Peru's second largest city. Quechua is Peru's second official language.

Ecuador's main agricultural product is bananas, but petroleum is the economy's mainline. It also produces coffee, cacao, fine woods, flowers, shrimp and tuna. It has a complete range of geographical features that include islands, mountains, beaches and jungles. Most of the country's population is concentrated in the Pacific coast and in the central Andean sierra region. Cotopaxi, south of Quito, is the world's tallest active volcano. The Galápagos Islands, the site of Charles Darwin's inspiration for the "Theory of Evolution," are a point of interest. Quito is Ecuador's capital and Guayaquil is its main port city. Cuenca is the center for the most part, of all the artisans who produce pottery, silver plates and gold work within the country.

Colombia's main products for exportation are: coffee –which it is world-famous for, topsoil, bananas and petroleum. It is the United States' largest exporter of flowers. It also produces carbon, gold, silver, platinum and emeralds. The Andes mountain range separates the country from the southeastern Ecuadorian border and the northwestern Venezuelan border. It separates into three mountain ranges, the "Cordillera Oriental," the east mountain range; the "Cordillera Central," the central mountain range; the "Cordillera Occidental," the west mountain range, all at the Colombian Massif. The Magdalena River runs to the coast and starts where the eastern and central mountain ranges separate. It is the country's principal river. East of the eastern mountain range are "llanos," extensive grasslands.

The Cauca River, which separates the central and western mountain ranges into a fertile valley, is the second largest river and one of the Magdalena's main tributaries. The plateau in its central region and its extending basins are the country's most populated areas. There are lowlands west of the western mountain range and in the north, by the Caribbean coastline. The south is made up mostly of jungle and dense forest. Colombia is one of the most bio-diverse countries in the world. "Parque Tayrona" (Tayrona National Park), is a point of interest conjoining beaches, mountains and mountain forests. Bogotá is its capital and Medellín is its second most important city –it is the industrial nexus of coffee production and one of the fastest growing economic regions in South America.

Cartagena is its principal commercial seaport and within it one can find intact colonial artifacts and architecture. It has many points of interest like: "la Ciudad Vieja" (The Old City,) the old colonial city with colonial houses and churches; "La Muralla" (The Old wall), a wall surrounding the city, bridled with cannons, that was utilized to protect it from English pirates; "El Castillo San Felipe" (San Felipe's Castle), a large castle built for the same purposes.

Venezuela produces coffee and cocoa. However, the agricultural industry is minimal –petroleum is the base of its economy. It has the world's seventh largest oil reserve. The northeastern extension of the Andes mountain range lies in the country's northwest region. Its population is concentrated in the mountainous regions of the east and in its coastal regions. The central region is made up of "llano," savannahs, which extend to the banks of the Orinoco, its main river and border with Colombia. The south, called the Guiana Highlands, is featured by mountain forests and jungles. Lake Maracaibo is the largest body of water in northern Venezuela and if considered a lake. It is connected to the Caribbean Sea by a fifty-four mile strait and is the largest body of water in South America. The world's tallest waterfall, "Salto Ángel" (Angel Falls), lies in the south. The "Cuevas de Guacharo" (Guacharo Caves) is Venezuela's largest and most magnificent set of caves. Caracas is both the political and commercial capital of the country. It is a modern city with beautiful streets and buildings.

In 1826, Simón Bolívar made the first attempt to bring world leaders together. He invited representatives from all the nations of the New World to come together in Panamá. Though only four countries sent delegates, the Panama Conference was still a success. The First International Conference was held in the United States (Washington, D.C.) in 1889 – 1890. Its purpose was to maintain peace and better commercial relations between countries. In the Conference of Buenos Aires, in 1920, the Pan-American Union was created. Its purpose was to establish cultural and economic ties between 21 nations.

In 1948, the ninth Panamerican Conference took place in Bogotá. The alliance was recognized and given a new name "Organización de Estados Americanos - OEA" (Organization of American States). It is now part of the United Nations and has many functions. Some of these functions are: to maintain peace among its members, to mutually assist each other in times of need and to work towards cultural, social and economic progress.

The "Área de Libre Comercio de las Américas," (Free trade Area of the Americas), a United States initiative to reduce trade barriers, was initiated by NAFTA (North American Free Trade Agreement) with Mexico, in 1994. It eventually aims to enact multiple TLCs' "Tratados de Libre Comercio," (Free Trade Agreements) with every nation in the American continent, except Cuba.

Skill 7.2   Identify the major ethnic groups of Latin America, including indigenous groups and peoples from other regions of the world, and demonstrate knowledge of their areas of settlement, religions, customs, and traditions

Indian Civilizations

Mayan – the most advanced of the Indian civilizations, the Myans flourished from the third century to the sixteenth. The Mayans occupied what is now the Yucatán Peninsula, Belize, Guatemala and parts of Honduras and El Salvador. They were a very advanced culture in science, astronomy and mathematics. They had made a calendar that managed to calculate with incredible accuracy, the duration of a solar year. They also had invented the numeral zero. They were also the only Indian civilization to create a system of writing to record influential events.

Aztec – moved to the central Mexican valley in the twelfth century, remaining there until the sixteenth. They were an ambitious and religious people who had managed to conquer every tribe in the central Mexican valley and were still increasing their territory when the Spanish invaded them. They built large city-states and were the first civilization to practice mandatory education for all, regardless of gender or social status. All males, ages seventeen to twenty-two were put in the army and even peasants could rise to the rank of officer, if they worked hard enough. Their enormous capital Tenochtitlán, with a population of 500,000, had causeways and canals surrounding it.

Inca – At the height of the Incan empire it was the largest empire on earth and remains the largest state to have ever existed in the Western Hemisphere. Cuzco, its capital "The Navel of the World," was the richest city in the New World. Their empire was located in the Andes and extended from Ecuador to central Chile, including parts of Bolivia and Argentina. The center of their nation was in Peru. They had an extensive political and social system. The Incans were also known for their royal family, well-organized army and system of roads. They spoke Quechua, a language that is still spoken in parts of Peru, Bolivia, Ecuador, and northern Chile.

Lesser Civilizations – In the Caribbean, at the time of Columbus's discovery of the Antilles, there were many Indian tribes living on those Islands that were similarly featured and related: the Arawaks, Taíno and "Caribes" or Carib. Numbering two to three million, they were reduced to mere thousands by the conquistadors. In the mountains of Colombia, the "Chibchas" were the dominant civilization. They were a calm and religious people, famed for their expertise in their workings with gold and rituals, such as "el Dorado" (The Golden One) that revolved around it. Their works can be seen in the "el Museo de Oro" (The Gold Museum), in Bogotá.

The "Guaraniés," in Paraguay spoke Guaraní, which is still spoken in certain parts of Paraguay. The "Araucanos" or "Mapuches" in Chile and Argentina, between the Bío Bío River and the Toltén River, were a warrior-tribe that resisted both the Incan Empires' and the conquistadors' advances.

In 1503, the "Casa de Contratación" (House of Trade), was organized in Seville, Spain. It was the centre for tax recollection and commercial regulation over the crown's property, including the many colonies. In 1524, the Crown of Castille incorporated the new domains into the existing administrating organ of the "Consejo de Castilla" (Council of Castille), with Juan Rodríguez Fonseca as its head, resulting in the creation of the "Consejo de Indias" (Council of the Indies) and the "Real y Supremo Consejo de Indias" (Royal and Supreme Council of the Indies); priests and lawyers administered all colonies in America and the Phillipines. Combining legislative, executive, and judicial functions under one organ of command it reported to the king weekly decisions over issues that would have been handled previously by the "Casa de Contratación" (House of Trade). In 1680, the council's decisions were formally codified. In 1714, Borbon reforms enacted the creation of new posts: the "Ministro de Indias" (Minister of the Indies) and the "Secretario de Guerra, Marina e Indias," (Secretary of War, Navy and Indies), to assume the authority of the old council. The colonies were divided into four administrative territories. They were as follows:

1) New Spain, which included Mexico, Central America, part of the United States and the Antilles;
2) Peru and Chile;

3)   New Granada, which included Ecuador, Colombia, Panama and Venezuela; and

4)   "Río de la Plata," which included Argentina, Bolivia, Paraguay, Uruguay and part of Brazil.

A viceroy appointed by the king of Spain governed each.

The Spanish crown had two main goals: to civilize the Indians (which included converting them to Catholicism), and to exploit the riches of the colonies for the sole benefit of Spain.

Spanish society was divided into four classes:

1)   The Spaniards, who governed and enjoyed all privileges

2)   The "Criollos" (of Spanish origin but born in the colonies), who were well-off financially but could not govern

3)   The Mestizos (the mixture of a Spaniard and a Indian), mulattos (the mixture of a Spaniard and a Black Slave), and Zambo (the mixture of a Indian and a Black slave); who had no social category nor political rights

4)   The Native Indians and Black slaves.

Skill 7.3   Demonstrate knowledge of the Mayan, Aztec, and Incan civilizations; the colonization of Latin America by European nations; the effects of European diseases on the indigenous peoples of Latin America; important features of colonial life; Latin American independence movements; and major issues in Latin America during the twentieth century

Also Refer to Skill 7.2 and 7.5.

Independence

The inhabitants of the colonies grew tired of social and political injustice and of the economic restrictions placed on them by Spain. They were encouraged to seek their independence by three occurrences: the independence of the United States, the French Revolution, and the invasion of Spain by Napoleon's forces. There were four major revolutionary movements. They are:

Mexico – In 1808, Napoleon installed his brother Joseph into the throne as the King of Spain. In the colony that consisted of modern day Mexico, conservative criollos found their beliefs and values at odds with the liberal agenda of the newly installed French government and the local governors who adhered to its rule. Resistance sprang up and allegiance to the former King of Spain, Fernando VII, served as a spark for the "Grito de Dolores" (Cry of Dolores), beginning the Mexican revolution.

Initiated on September 16, 1810, by Miguel Hidalgo, a priest at his own parish in the town of Dolores under the banner of the Virgin of Guadalupe, attracted both followers and victory. Hidalgo, his wife and his partner Ignacio Allende, marched towards Mexico City leading the revolution. Reaching the edge of the city and threatening to invade it, Hidalgo turned back and they were both eventually executed, in 1811. José María Morelos, a priest as well, became the new leader of the revolutionary movement. He occupied Oaxaca in November 24, 1812. He invoked the first Mexican national congress in Chilpancingo, Guerrero, in 1813. It adopted a manifesto that elected him Generalissimo and granted him executive powers. He was about to possess his hometown of Valladolid (now called Morelia in his honor), but was defeated and hindered into retreat, leading to his execution, in 1815. He was apprehended by a royalist patrol led by a former follower.

After losing its principal leader, Vincente Guerrero resurged as the new head of the revolutionary movement and was named protector of the independent Mexican congress. He moved the congress to Tehuacán and in 1818, he defeated General Armiso. This led to the announcement of talks over an armistice between the government and the revolutionaries, in 1819, between himself and viceroy Apocada,. As both sides came to the bargaining table, a coup was staged in Spain, in 1820 that changed the Spanish monarchy into a liberal institution, one that the central government in Mexico disfavored. The general placed in command to quell the revolutionary movements' military force and set the terms for their surrender, Augustín de Iturbide, was pushed into total defeat and opted instead to offer his own version of a truce.

In reconciling both opposing sides on Jan 20, 1821, under the "Iguala" plan –also known as the "Three Guarantees" –had three goals: establishing Mexico as a country with the Roman Catholic faith as its one religion; proclaiming Mexico as an independent nation; and achieving social equality for every social and ethnic group within the country. That popularized it sufficiently with the revolutionary forces to give him enough momentum to form an alliance with them. The "Trigaranté army" (Army of the Three Guarantees) was formed with the revolutionary armies and the government's troops under his own command, concluding the war for independence in Mexico. He signed "The Treaty of Córdoba" on August 24, 1821, with Don Juan O'Donnojú, a Spanish replacement meant to be the new viceroy, assuring Mexico as an independent empire from Spain and its own constitutional monarchy recognized by the Spanish throne. In the treaty, Iturbide was decreed First Chief of the Imperial Mexican Army and on May 18, 1822, following his rousing, a popular movement named him Emperor Augustín I. On March 19, 1823, he abdicated power after his opponents had grown too numerous.

They declared his disrespect of exercising power under the provisions of previous treaties and he was exiled to Italy. In 1824, he was executed after chasing the rumor of a possible Spanish invasion of Mexico. Guadalupe Victoria, an old revolutionary, was named the first president of Mexico, in 1824.

New Granada (northern South America) – In 1808, Venezuela proclaimed its Independence from Spain and sent Andrés Bello, Luis López Mendez, and Simón Bolívar to Great Britain on a diplomatic mission. They were sent with a plan to foment full independence from Spain for all the colonies from the New World. On returning to Venezuela on June 3, 1811, he enlisted under the command of Francisco de Miranda, who acted as dictator of Venezuela, fighting with him until he was defeated and imprisoned by royalist forces. Bolívar traveled to Cartagena and wrote the Cartagena manifesto. It it, he argues for the cooperation of all the different kingdoms of New Granada. He was persuasive and successful, and he continued leading the revolutionary cause, invading Venezuela, taking the city of Merida and the capital, Caracas. There he was proclaimed "el Libertador" (The Liberator). He was defeated by the Royalists, in 1814 and found asylum in Nueva Granada where he intervened and assisted in freeing Bogotá after being appointed commander in chief of the forces of the federal republic. After falling out with province leaders, he sought refuge in Jamaica and there wrote the "Letter from Jamaica": a document on the current struggle and purpose of Latin American independence. He returned to Venezuela in 1817, with assistance from newly independent Haiti and continued fighting.

On August 7, 1819, Bolívar defeated the Spanish at the battle of Boyacá and founded "la Gran Colombia" (The Great Colombia) at the Angostura congress: it represented the now present-day areas of Venezuela, Colombia, Panama and Ecuador. He was named president. His military hand: Antonio José de Sucre, Francisco Antonio Zea and Francisco Paula Santander, all kept fighting for a stronger and more independent state. Northern South America was completely liberated from all Spanish and royalist authority on May 22, 1822, when Antonio José de Sucre defeated the Spanish at Pichincha, in Ecuador. He began talks with the "Knight of the Andes," the liberator of southern South America, José de San Martín, to begin planning a total victory over the Spanish royalists. Eventually, Bolívar was made chief and defeated the Spanish in the battle of Junin on August 6, 1824 and the battle of Ayacucho on December 9, 1824. Spanish rule over South America no longer existed. On August 6, 1825, the Republic of Bolivia was created at the congress of upper Peru, which had been invoked by Antonio José de Sucre.

Peru and "el Río de la Plata" (southern South America) – In 1810 a momentous French invasion of Spain allowed for the wealthy residents of Argentina to seize power, asserting their own authority under King Fernando VII and deposing the viceroy. On July 9, 1816, the Argentine Declaration of Independence was signed. The connecting ties to the Spanish monarchy began their eventual separation. In the north remained the Royalist viceroy of Peru. Revolutionary movements, created to sever any possibility of Spanish rule, were starting to formulate. The splintered factions looking for personal gain which had earlier assumed authority were now in a position to claim complete control.

José de San Martín, a lifelong soldier and veteran of the Napoleonic wars, offered his services, in 1812. In 1814, San Martín was appointed to command the Revolutionary Army, to which he later resigned. While at the edge of the Chilean Andes, and with the help of his longtime friend and Chilean patriot Bernard O'Higgins, he enlisted support from the patriots residing in Chile and the Argentine government, raising an army: "el Ejército de los Andes" (The Army of the Andes). They crossed the Andes with success and defeated the Spanish on February 2, 1817, re-establishing a national government in Santiago, placing O'Higgins at the head as the Republic's first president, Chile was fully independent in April, 1818.

After failing in negotiations with the Royalists, in Peru, upon Martin's suggestion that they themselves form an independent monarchy, Martín's forces began incursions into Peru and backed the remaining Spaniards into defeat, in 1821, as a result of blocking their last remaining seaport. San Martín was proclaimed the protector of Peru. In 1822, he abdicated his powers at the first invocation of the Peruvian congress and he then left them in Bolívar's hand.

Cuba – Cuba remained loyal to Spain until 1868, when Carlos Manuel de Céspedes began the freedom movement in Cuba, with what was known as the "Grito de Yara" (Cry of Yara). This began a ten-year war waged by Cuban guerrillas, known as the Mambises and they fought with victory and acclaim. As Cuba prepared for its independence, José Martí, a famous poet and writer, started the Cuban Revolutionary Party. In 1878, the remaining revolutionaries in Cuba signed the pact of Zajón, providing general amnesty for all combatants and freeing all slaves involved in the act. Yet, independence had not been reached and the United States had begun implementing its interests in expanding its reign over the small and treasured island. A small effort saw its initiation in Major Calixto García's and José Maceo's attempt at independence, called "la Guerra Chiquita" (The Little War). It was time for a renewed strategy. Calixto García, Antonio Maceo, Máximo Gómez and José Martí banded together most of the veterans alive from the ten-year war and set sail from Florida to fight in Cuba. Combat led to a stalemate with the Spanish, which the United States took advantage of, citing the precedent of the destruction of the U.S.S. Maine as a reason to engage Spain and annex Guam, Cuba, the Philippines, and Puerto Rico from them. Martí died in 1895 during an Invasion to Cuba. Cuba finally became a republic in 1901.

Revolution
The development of Latin-American nations after their independence from Spain varied from country to country and was influenced by several factors that all held in common and that resulted in different stages and degrees of statehood.

Arriving at a stable position in government, conflict between bilateral opposing parties (Liberal and Conservative) and reaching a peace with guerrilla movements or the democratically transforming, authoritarian, repressive regime has been the end-in-sight for most Latin-American nations in the 21st century.

The mixture of the lower classes and ethnic Indian groups into the governmental structure and the balance of foreign influence and encroachment were central causes for conflict and stagnation. Of those nations that did not sustain a democratic process, armed conflict between the government and its critical or armed opposition ensued in the form of armed and unarmed revolutionary movements, military coups and state-sponsored military repression.

After independence, Mexico fought in the Mexican-American war (1846-1848), with the United States. During which, Antonio López Santa Anna reigned over the then unsettled state of Texas, eventually became part of the United States. In 1855, Ignacio Comonfort bridged the gap between Liberals and Conservatives by becoming the nation's first moderate president. In 1857, the newly enacted constitution left the exclusivity of the Catholic Church as Mexico's sole religion unremarked and set off a bloody four year civil war that had liberals allying with moderates to stunt the conservatives' inclinations towards the Church's interest. The Liberals were victorious, making Benito Júarez president.

In the 1860s, Mexico was invaded by France, who then created the Second Mexican Empire under Habsburg Archduke Ferdinand Maximilian of Austria. They were then overthrown by him and General Porfirio Díaz – the next president, aided by the United States. Their final victory on May 5, 1862, led by Ignacio Zaragosa, is the origination of the "Cinco de Mayo" celebrations. Porfirio Díaz inaugurated his presidency in 1876, through the Plan of Tuxtepec and remained in office for thirty years. His reign was called the "Porfiriato" because of its length and consistent production of public works aided by heavy foreign capital investment. The lower classes were systematically exploited and unrepresented in their motivations for social change. Francisco Madero intended to run against Díaz for the presidency in 1910 and was jailed by his opponent. He fled to the United States and initiated a revolt, with native Indians supporting him. This put him in power through the support of other opposition leaders such as Zapata, Carranza and the United States. Disagreements over the issue of land reform with Zapata (who had written the "Plan de Ayala"), led to the loss of popular support and instigated a coup d'etat by his military commander, Victoriano Huerta, who executed him and his vice-president one week later. Other leaders disagreed with his station and issued the "Plan de Guadalupe," initiating a front-face conflict with him. Villa, Zapata, Carranza and Obregón fought him and forced him to flee to Puerto Mexico; the United States invaded Vera Cruz and these predicaments led him to flee to Spain. Carranza became the next president and was himself deposed by Villa and Zapata –the former who became president in 1915. Carranza adopted a new constitution, becoming president in 1917 and was again deposed, in 1920, by Obregón. He had assassinated Zapata in 1919. Carranza and Villa were assassinated in 1920 and 1923, respectively. Obregon's successor Plutarco Elías Calles, assumed the presidency in 1928, in all but in name, after Obregon's assassination.

The Cristeros' Rebellion: the Christian resistance to the government oppression of their faith – predicated within the constitution of 1917, ended in 1929. The same year he created the National Revolutionary Party "PNR," that has had a nominee in every election held until 2001. In 1934, the progressive General Lázaro Cárdenas was elected president and in the following four decades coined the term "El Milagro Mexicano" (The Mexican Miracle) because of the nation's industrial rise and social advancement.

The Dominican Republic was occupied by Haiti for twenty-two years after their independence from Spain. They became free again in 1844, after Pedro Santana's military force expelled the invaders. He volunteered the Dominicans back into the Spanish Empire in 1861 and following a rebellion to this measure the Dominicans restored their independence, in 1865. The United States ruled the Dominican Republic from 1916-1924, through a military government. Horacio Vásquez was the first elected president in 1924 . In 1930, Rafael Trujillo, a prominent army commander ousted President Vásquez and established absolute political control as dictator. He modernized the nation through many public works, but his repressive regime fell hard upon any critics of its rule.

He massacred twenty thousand Haitian sugar cane workers in a response to the Dominicans working in Haiti, across the border, to overthrow him. After trying to form a plan to assassinate the Venezuelan President Rómulo Betancourt his government was singled out and acted against by the Organization of American States (OEA) and the United States. He was assassinated by his own troops. His son Ramfis Trujillo was president for a short while, but was then exiled as Joaquín Belaguer came into power. He resigned in 1962, and a council under President Rafael Bonnely held power, until 1963, when Juan Bosch of the "Partido Revolucionario Dominicano" (PRD or Dominican Revolutionary Party) was inaugurated president. He was overthrown by a right-wing military coup in 1963. A civilian triumvirate adopted a joint dictatorship, until 1965, when military elements vying for Bosch's return and the proponents of a new general election came to a head – anti-Bosche forces called in the United States for assistance. In 1966, Balaguers' Reformers Party had him assume the presidency, as well as in 1970 and 1974. In the 1978 election, he was defeated by Antonio Guzmán Fernández, marking the first peaceful transfer of power to an opposing party in the nation's history.

After becoming a possession of the United States, the Republic of Cuba gained formal independence on May 20, 1902. Tomás Estrada Palma was the country's first president. In 1906, a revolt in Cuba led to United States intervention – as was specified in their special amendments to the Cuban constitution. In 1908, José Miguel Gómez was elected president and power was transferred back to Cuban control. In 1925, Gerardo Machado y Morales suspended the constitution and made himself Cuba's first dictator. In 1933, a military coup deposed him and installed Carlos Manuel de Céspedes – not the same from the Cry of Yara, as Cuba's new leader.

Later that year, Sergeant Fulgencío Batista overthrew him and replaced him with Carlos Mendieta y Montefur. Aiming for Cuban sovereignty, Batista himself ran for president in 1940, but was opposed by the leader of the constitutional liberals Ramón Grau San Martín. He turned instead to the Communist Party of Cuba which eventually generated his election. Grau became president, in 1944 and Carlos Prío Socarrás of the same party, in 1948. In 1952, he staged a coup – for he had slim chances of winning and became dictator. In 1956, Fidel Castro and a group of young nationalists sailed to Cuba, on a boat called "Granma" from Mexico and began their insurrection in the Sierra Madre Mountains. Batista fled in 1959 and Castro assumed power that has lasted to this day. In 1959, Osvaldo Dorticós Torrado became President as Castro was the first secretary of the communist party. In 1976, a new constitution was introduced that made him President, while still remaining chairman of the council of ministers.

In 1838, Costa Rica proclaimed itself a sovereign and independent nation from its prior allegiance to "The United Provinces of Central America": consisting of the areas of Guatemala, El Salvador, Honduras and Nicaragua under the rule of Braulio Carrillo. In 1856, William Walker, a United States explorer bent on conquering Central America and claming it to be part of the United States, invaded Costa Rica. He was repelled by the national army. In 1899, the first democratic elections were held under peaceful auspices. In 1917, Federico Torinco Granados ruled as dictator and was ousted, in 1919. In 1948, José Figueres Ferrer led an armed uprising to challenge the recent and questionable elections. In 1949, he abolished the army after two thousand casualties came out from a forty-four day civil war.

Rafael Carrera was the leader who broke Guatemala away from "The United Provinces of Central America." He ruled until 1865. Starting in 1871, as president, Justo Rufino Barrios was the leader of the country's trend in modernization and also fought to reunite the Central American provinces. He was killed on the battlefield, fighting to achieve this, in 1885. Manuel José Estrada came into power, in 1898 and invited the United Fruit Company to do business with the country. A coup d'etat, in 1920, installed General José Orellana into the presidency. In 1931, Jorge Ubico, a member of the Progressive party, was unanimously elected president and he recognized himself as dictator. In 1944, his office was overthrown by the "October Revolutionaries," lead by Jacobo Arbenz and Francisco Javier Arana. A general election chose Juan José Arévalo, as president in 1945. In a failed coup, Arana was killed, but Arbenz managed to succeed Arévalo in 1951, in a general election. The United States orchestrated a coup against his communist aligned government and Colonel Carlos Castillo Armas assumed power. He was assassinated in 1958, and General Ydígoras Fuentes assumed power. In 1960, a group of junior officers began their own rebellion, which was stammered and led to their extending ties with Cuba. In 1966, President Julio César Méndez Montenegro began counter-insurgency operations in the countryside.

The Guerrilla Army of the Poor (EGP), the Revolutionary Organization of Armed People (ORPA), the Rebel Armed Forces (FAR), and the Guatemalan Labor Party (PGT) all battled against the government and joined together as the Guatemalan National Revolutionary Unit (URNG), in 1982. Right-wing groups like The Secret Anti-Communist Army (ESA) and The White Hand battled the civilian population whom they identified as possible perpetrators and enemies. In 1982, junior officers willing to prevent the ascension of General Ángel Aníbal Guevara, as President, staged a coup d'etat. General Efraín Ríos Montt was elected. He promptly annulled the 1965 constitution, dissolved Congress, suspended political parties and cancelled the electoral law. He began forming local civilian defense patrols (PACs) and the resulting imbroglio constituted a mass genocide of the rural and Indian population. He was deposed in 1983 by General Óscar Humberto Mejía Victores, whom allowed a return to democracy and a new constitution to be drafted, in 1985.

Honduran Francisco Morazán became the president of "The United Central American Provinces," in 1830 and upon its dissolution in 1838 intended to reunite them through force. He was ousted by General Francisco Ferrera, who became President, in 1841. Morazán was executed, in 1842, in Costa Rica. United States soldier of fortune William Walker intended to invade, but was captured by the British and executed in Honduras, in 1860. Internal conflict between liberals and conservatives was swayed by the influence of like-minded-parties in neighboring Guatemala, El Salvador and Nicaraua. The United Fruit Company shipped its first shipment of bananas from Honduras and so became its center of exploitation. In 1899, the peaceful transfer of power from Liberal Policarpo Bonilla to General Sierra marked the first constitutional shift of power. After him Manuel Bonilla assumed power and set the foundation for the "Partido Nacional de Honduras" (National Party of Honduras or PNH) which exists to this day. In 1956, a coup d'etat led by the former president's son ousted Lozano Díaz, the then current President. The military dissolved congress, in 1963 and assumed power. Suazo Córdova was the first civilian elected President in ten years, in 1981.

In 1823, El Salvadorian Manuel José Arce formed "The United Central American Provinces." In 1832, Anastasio Aquino led an indigenous revolt against criollos and mestizos. In 1838, El Salvador became independent after "The United Central American Provinces" dissolved. General Maximiliano Hérnandez Martínez came into power during a coup in 1931, and embraced a brutal oppression of all resistance movements. Farabundo Martí's peasant uprising, in 1932, was decimated into "La Matanza" (The Massacre). The National Conciliation Party held power from the early 1960s, until 1979. In 1967, Fidel Sánchez Hernández became President and manned the helm during the brief "Soccer War," against Honduras. In 1972, opposing military rule, José Napoleón Duarte ran for President and lost. An ensuing coup d'etat to impose his own rule led to his exile. Leftist guerrilla groups began to form and total war erupted in both the cities and the countryside.

Right-wing death squads began to kill indiscriminately. The Salvadorian Armed forces perpetrated the "El Mozote" massacre. In 1979, the Revolutionary Government Junta, a group of military officers and civilian leaders, ousted the President's and General Carlos Humberto Romero's right-wing government. In 1980, the murder of Archbishop Óscar Arnulfo Romero, whom had asked for the United States to stop granting aid to El Salvador's armed forces, led to a new constituent assembly. Álvaro Alfredo Magaña Borja was selected its provisional president. In 1980, all left-wing guerrilla groups coalesced into the Farabundi Martí National Front (FMNL). After drafting a new constitution, in 1983, Duarte was elected President, in 1984. In 1989, the Nationalist Republican Alliance's (ARENA) Alfredo Cristiani became president. This marked the first time a switch within political power, between opposing sides, occurred without violence.

After FMNL led an attack on the capitol San Salvador, in 1989, the FMNL and the government were invited to Peace talks with the UN, eventually leading to the Chapultepec Peace accord and a cease-fire in 1992.

Nicaragua separated from "The United Central American Provinces," in 1838. In 1853, Conservative General Fruto Chamorro took over the government and exiled the liberals who previously held it in control. A civil war ensued. William Walker assumed power later, in 1856. In 1857, a constituent assembly convened and named General Martínez, as president. A revolt, in 1893, ousted Roberto Sacasa. General José Santos Zelaya, the man who initiated the revolt, was eventually called to be President. In 1926, General Emiliano Chamorro forced previous president Carlos Sólorzano from power. The "Ejército Defensor de la Soberanía de Nicaragua" (Army for the Defense of Nicaraguan Sovereignty) fought against social inequality under Augusto César Sandino. Anastasio "Tacho" Somoza García established a military dictatorship, in 1937, after assassinating Sandino – whilst in negotiations about the possibility of a peace accord. Leonardo Argüelo was named President, in 1947 and then replaced, through Somoza's handywork, by Benjamín Lacayo Sacasa. Somoza was assassinated, in 1956 and was proceeded by his son. The "Frente Sandinista de Liberación Nacional" (Sandinista National Liberation Front), a student activist group, was created in 1961. In 1972, a three-man junta ruled the government. Following a Sandinista revolution, Dictator Anastasio Somoza Debayle was deposed and they took control of the government, in 1979. The United States granted aid to former National Guard members, organized and called "contrarevolucionarios" (counterrevolutionaries or contras) starting in 1981. Daniel Ortega was sworn in as President, representing the new government, in 1985.

Panama seceded from Colombia, in 1903, with support from the United States, brought on by the upper circles' desire to govern independently. Liberal and Conservative parties were organized and arrayed to govern. A revolutionary junta controlled the government. In a 1969 coup d'etat, General Omar Torrijos assumed power. He died in a plane crash, in 1981. General Manuel Norriega assumed governmental control. He annulled the elections, in 1989, that elected Guillermo Endara to power. Norriega was overthrown by the United States and left Endara in control.

In 1830, "La Gran Colombia" (The Republic of Greater Colombia) broke away into separate states: Venezuela, Quito (now known as Ecuador) and "Nueva Granada" (New Granada – is now Colombia and Panama) in which Bolívar became President. In 1850, "el Partido Liberal" (The Liberal Party or PL) and "el Partido Conservativo" (The Conservative Party or PC) were created and a Federalist-Nationalist friction was set into being. In 1853, the elected liberal president was deposed in a coup d'etat by General José María Melo, who dissolved congress and named himself dictator, in 1854. His term lasted for eight months and was followed by conservative rule.

In 1857, PC candidate Mariano Rodriguez adopted a new constitution and renamed the country the "La Confederación Granadina" (Grenadine Confederation). In 1861, conservative president Bartolomé Calvo was deposed by liberals led by General Mosquera. He drafted the constitution of Ríonegro, in 1863, lasting until 1886. He renamed the country "The United States of Colombia." Mosquera was ousted and exiled in 1867. The federalist trends within the previous constitution were remade into a centrally organized political system in the new constitution of 1886, put into place by nationalist opposition candidate Rafael Nuñez. Disenchanted liberals began "La Guerra de los Mil Días" (The Thousand Day War) with the Conservative government. They eventually signed a peace agreement, in 1902. Panama seceded from the country, in 1903. General Rafael Reyes became President, in 1904. He replaced Congress with a National Assembly. In 1930, Liberals took charge of the government through their first elected President in many years, Enrique Olaya Herrera. The current reformist policy encountered resistance and in 1946, the PL's candidate, who differed with previous policy, spurred Gaitán – a popular reformist – into running independently.

In 1948, he Gaitán murdered, causing riots ensued throughout the capital destroying much of its downtown area in an incident called "El Bogotazo." "La Violencia" (The Violence), a period of undeclared war between liberals and conservatives, claiming two hundred thousand lives over the next ten years, followed. Congress was closed, in 1949, by Mariano Ospina and General Rojas Pinilla assumed power through a coup d'etat, in 1954. An alternating system of government was set in place called "El Frente Nacional" (The National Front). One term would be assumed by a Conservative candidate and the next one by a Liberal candidate. Alberto Lleras Camargo, a liberal, was the first president elected on the basis of the previous accord. During this period any opposition to the current agreement had no outlet in government and various guerrilla groups formed: "Ejército de Liberación Nacional" (National Liberation Army or ELN), "Fuerzas Armadas Revolucionarias Colombianas" (Armed Colombian Revolutionary Forces or FARC), "Ejército Popular de Liberación" (Popular Liberation Army or EPL) which were all based in communist ideology. In 1974, the National Front ended and Alfonso López Michelsen became President, in a peaceful change of power.

Venezuela separated from "La Gran Colombia" (Republic of Great Colombia), in 1830. General Páez was elected under the new 1830 constitution. In 1846, Páez selected Liberal General José Tadeo Monangas as his successor and was exiled alongside every other conservative in the country. In 1858, almost all local caudillos (local leaders) were involved in "La Guerra Federal" (Federal War). General Juan C. Falcón was elected president after the war's termination. Antonio Guzmán Blanco established a dictatorship in 1870, centralizing the government. Later, in 1945, a coup d'etat placed Rómulo Betancourt in power which led to constituent assembly elections, in 1946. The elected President in 1948, Rómulo Gallegos, was overthrown by the military and along with prior coup leaders and sent into exile.

A three-man military junta was put in control of government and the 1936 traditionalist constitution replaced the recent 1947 draft. Dictator Pérez Jiménez was forced to abdicate in 1958. A five-man provisionary military junta formed and invoked a general election in 1959. Rómulo Betancourt was elected president. The "Fuerzas Armadas de Liberación Nacional" (Armed Forces of National Liberation or FALN) surfaced in the 1960s as a left-wing opposition group. Raúl Leoni proved in 1964 to be the first Venezuelan democratically elected leader to receive previous office while remaining at peace.

Independent Peru's first President was Simón Bolívar. General Andrés Santa Cruz y Calahumana marched into Peru and imposed a Peru-Bolivia confederation in 1839. General Marshal Ramón Castilla assumed power in 1845. Meanwhile, in 1872 the first elected civilian President came to power, Manuel Pardo, leader of the "Partido Civilista" (Civilian Party or PC). General Andrés Avelina Cáceres assumed power, being elected President in 1886. José Nicólas de Piérola overthrew him through the "Revolución de 1895" (1895 Revolution) and assumed power. Colonel Oscar Raimundo Benavides seized governmental power in 1914. In 1919, Augusto B. Leguía y Salcedo assumed the presidency through a preemptive coup d'etat. He was overthrown in 1932 by the military and later died in prison. The "Alianza Popular Revolucionaria Americana" (American Popular Revolutionary Alliance or APRA) founded in Mexico, in 1924, was brought by Haya de la Torre, into Peru. In 1931, Sánchez Cerro was elected President, beating APRAs' Haya de la Torre. He was assassinated in 1993. The military overthrew the government in 1948. They installed General Manuel A. Odría as President; the "Partido Demócrata Cristiano" (Christian Democratic Party or PDC) and "Acción Popular" (Popular Action or AP) were then newly created democratic organs. Haya de la Torre returned from exile in 1962 and upon winning the elections was ousted by the military, led by General Ricardo Pérez Gódoy, who held a provisional junta for one year. Fernando Belaúnde, a member of the PDC, was President after the junta re-convened elections in 1963. General Vásquez Alvarado overthrew the government, in 1968. Elections were held in 1978 for a constituent assembly and the drafting of a new constitution. Former President Belaúnde was re-elected in 1980.

The Guerrilla group "Sendero Luminoso" (Luminous Path or SL) was spawned in 1980, by a philosophy professor Abimáel Guzmán Reynoso. In 1984, the "Movimiento Revolucionario Túpac Amaru" (Túpac Amaru Revolutionary Movement or MRTA) was created in Lima.

Bernardo O'Higgins was Chile's first President after independence from Spain. The "Partido Liberal" (Liberal Party or PL), "Partido Conservador" (Conservative Party or PC) and "Partido Nacional" (National Party or PN) were created in 1857. Congress led a revolt against President José Manuel Balmaceda Fernández, in 1891 and assumed power. He later committed suicide in Argentina.

President Alessandri Dipalma was deposed by the military, in 1924 and then reinstated by supporters led by Carlos Ibáñez del Campo and Marmaduke Grove Vallejo, in 1925. The "Frente de Acción Popular" (Popular Action Front or FRAP) socialist party was created in 1958. In 1973, leftist UP (Popular Union or Union Popular) president Salvadore Allende was either murdered or committed suicide after his government was ousted in a military coup d'etat, led by General Augusto Pinochet Ugarte, who established a dictatorship. Chileans elected Christian Democrat Patricio Ailwyn as interim President, in 1989.

Bernardino Rivadavia was the first president of the Republic of Argentina, within the "Provincias Unidas de el Río de la Plata" (The United Provinces of the River Plate) in 1826. General Juan Manuel de Rosas established a Dictatorship in 1835. Rosas was overthrown by General Justo José de Urquiza, who called a constituent assembly and promulgated a constitution in 1853. In 1930, General José F. Uriburu ousted President Hipolito Irigoyen. President Ramon S. Castillo was overthrown in 1944 by army colonels, led by General Juan Peron. He was victorious in the 1946 election and established a dictatorship. The "Revolución Libertadora" (Liberating Revolution) ousted him in 1955 and placed an interim government in power under General Eduardo Lonardi. He was deposed and General Pedro Aramburu assumed power in 1955. General Juan Carlos Onganía was deposed in 1970 and General Roberto M. Levingston was made President. Peron, returning from exile, in 1973, was elected President and died one year later. His wife María Isabel Peron, the vice president, assumed power. In 1976, she was deposed by the "Proceso de Reorganización Nacional," a military junta, under the leadership of Jorge Rafael Videla. In 1983, Raúl Alfonsín was elected President.

Ecuador separated from "La Gran Colombia" (Republic of Great Colombia) in 1830. Gabriel García Moreno unified the country under the Roman Catholic Church in 1865. He was assassinated in 1875. In 1895, the "Partido Liberal Radical" (Radical Liberal Party) came to power, and reduced the power of the clergy ushering in a liberal plutocracy. In 1941, an Amazonian border dispute with Peru led to a war which Peru won, annexing two hundred thousand kilometers of its territory. In 1972, a nationalist military regime seized power. In 1979, Ecuador returned to constitutional democratic rule under President Róldos.

Skill 7.4   **Recognize the effects of location, climate, physical characteristics, the distribution of natural resources, and population size on the development of Latin America**

The climate of **Latin America** varies across the full spectrum, from desert areas of Mexico to tropical regions with dense plant growth through South America. Areas of extreme climate such as these were barriers to the European settlers who began to arrive in Latin America in the seventeenth century, although indigenous peoples were able to survive and establish communities.

The oldest European settlements are along the Atlantic Coast of Latin America, where Spanish and Portuguese explorers began to visit in the seventeenth century. Today, much of the population of the region is concentrated along the Atlantic Coast. Large cities developed at key river access points to the Atlantic, where the raw materials from the interior were brought for export. Rio de Janeiro in Brazil and Buenos Aires in Argentina are located at such key points.

Former indigenous settlements also became sites for growth and development, such as Cuzco, Peru, which was once the center of the ancient Inca Empire. The Aztec Empire in Mexico was based in Tenochtitlan, which later became Mexico City. Spanish conquistadors, upon seizing control of the region, continued to develop these population centers.

The relatively small size of the Central American countries limits the amount of natural resources available for economic development. As a result, much of the area remains rural, with nearly half of the people reliant on subsistence agriculture for food and clothing.

Panama's location on the isthmus between North and South America led to its selection for the location of a canal connecting the Atlantic and Pacific oceans. The **Panama Canal** is a vital link in international trade, allowing ships to avoid the longer and more treacherous route around the southern tip of South America.

Skill 7.5   **Recognize the effects of human-environment interaction on the development of Latin America and the approaches Latin American countries have taken to address these and other environmental problems**

Mexico City is one of the largest and most polluted cities in the world and has a particular problem with air pollution. Situated in a high basin, Mexico City is shielded from the surrounding weather patterns that would otherwise move air through the area. As a result, air becomes trapped over the city, and fills with smoke and emissions. Because of the size and physical nature of Mexico city, the estimated 4 million automobiles that are used by its residents are mainly old and emit high levels of pollutants that loom over the city.

Mexico has been slow to address the air pollution problem in Mexico City. As part of the **North American Free Trade Agreement** (NAFTA,) Mexico is now required to bring its emission standards up to those of the United States. Air pollution in industrial areas near the U.S. border has a direct impact on air quality in the U.S.

The tropical rain forest of Brazil has been impacted by human industry and population expansion. Farmers burn portions along the edge of the forest to clear land for grazing and growing crops. The logging industry cuts sections of the forest to obtain exotic woods for export. This destruction sometimes takes place at an alarming rate. The **rain forest** is an important ecosystem, housing many rare species of plants and animals that are not found elsewhere. It is also important to the world environment, providing an important link in the cycle of carbon dioxide and oxygen. As a result, Brazil has been joined by international groups to reduce the rate of destruction of the rainforest. Brazil has set aside large areas of national forest that is protected by the government. Because of the large size of these areas and the rapid recent growth of the Brazilian economy and population, enforcing protective measures is often difficult. Some groups are trying to encourage economic activities in and around the rainforests that do not impact it negatively.

Oil has been an important part of the Venezuelan economy for nearly 100 years and is also one of its primary sources of pollution. The Venezuelan oil fields are primarily off shore, increasing the risk that spills from production and drilling operations will contaminate the water. Pipelines that run below and along the ocean have been the target of attacks in neighboring Colombia, creating spills that have affected Venezuela's sources of drinking water. In Ecuador, which borders Colombia on the west, inland oil drilling is a key source of water pollution, contaminating agricultural land and seeping into the groundwater. Oil shipping along the northern coast of South America has produced tanker accidents that have released oil into the environment. While these oil-producing countries have nominal regulations in place to prevent excessive pollution and spillage, they are hesitant to be too restrictive on oil development for fear of discouraging international investment.

Skill 7.6   Demonstrate knowledge of the basic structure of national governments in Latin America

The type of governments overwhelmingly present in the countries of Latin America is the democratic republic or federal republic. These are based on a constitution and provide for the separation of executive, legislative, and judicial powers. All adults have the right to vote throughout Latin America. In some countries voting is obligatory.

In practice, the balance of power in many countries is heavily tilted toward the executive, as is the case in **Bolivia**, for example. Bolivia has a **bicameral congress** that must approve all legislation, but traditionally the congress simply serves to approve the proposals of the president. Bolivia has a tiered judicial system headed by a supreme court. However, this system is widely corrupted. In 2006, Bolivia held a Constituent Assembly to review and possibly amend its constitution. Bolivia requires all adults to vote. Uruguay also has a traditionally strong presidency with a system of legislative and judiciary checks.

Venezuela has a similarly strong executive presence in its government. The Venezuelan president is elected to a six-year term. The unicameral congress elects the 32 members of the Supreme Court.

Until 1992, **Paraguay's** government was highly centralized. A new constitution passed in 1992 provided for a division of powers. Paraguay has a bicameral legislature and a Supreme Court. An elected president is head of the executive powers. Voting in Paraguay is obligatory for all citizens between 18 and 75 years old.

Ecuador's constitution was ratified in 1998. It calls for 4-year terms for the offices of president, vice president and members of the unicameral congress. Presidents cannot serve two consecutive terms, but can be re-elected after an intervening term. The judicial system is headed by a Supreme Court whose members are appointed by the congress for life. Voting is compulsory for literate citizens between 16 and 65 years of age. Ecuador is unique in that it does not allow active military personnel and police to vote.

Colombia's government is a republic with an elected president and bicameral congress. It has a tiered judicial system with a supreme court at the top. Voting rights are extended to all citizens over 18.

Argentina is a republic with a bicameral legislature, an elected president and a tiered judicial system. All adults over 18 are eligible to vote.

The **Brazilian** system of government is a federal republic made up of 26 states overseen by federal government of an elected president, a bicameral legislative body and supreme federal tribunal made up of 11 justices appointed by the president.

Mexico is also a federal republic, with 31 states. Mexico has a president, bicameral congress and a Supreme Court. The executive branch of the Mexican government is traditionally the strongest of the three.

Shortly after gaining independence in 1822, the Central American countries were for a time united in one federal republic. This federation collapsed in 1840, however, as rifts between member states erupted into civil war. In recent years, the concept of a unified government has re-emerged in the form of the Parliamento Centroamericano, or **Parlacen**. The Parlacen is an international parliament made up of representatives from El Salvador, Guatemala, Honduras, Nicaragua and Panama. Each country elects 20 deputies. Costa Rica has not joined the association.

Skill 7.7   Identify major features of the different types of economic systems found in Latin America, recognize the involvement of Latin America in international trade, and analyze factors that have encouraged and discouraged economic growth in the region

The countries of Mexico, Central America and South America all have open market economies heavily based on international trade. The important exports of agricultural, mineral and petroleum products have made the region a crucial part of the world economy. Free trade agreements among Latin American countries have encouraged the movement of goods within the region, expanding nearby markets. At the same time, international agreements with countries such as the United States have facilitated trade outside the region.

Mexico's primary trade partner is the United States, which it borders on the north. The North American Free Trade Agreement between Mexico, the U.S. and Canada has made trade among these three nations less restrictive in recent years with the intention of expanding this trade. Because of their strong trade relationship the economy of Mexico is closely tied to that of the U.S.

The economies of the Central American countries of El Salvador, Guatemala, Honduras, Nicaragua, Panama and Costa Rica are mainly agricultural. Sugar, coffee and bananas are chief exports from this area of Latin America. Guatemala is also a producer of oil. Approximately half of the people in Central America live in rural areas where there is only a basic subsistence economy. **Tourism** is an increasingly important part of the economies of Central America.

The economies of the countries of South America have historically been characterized by instability often related to turbulent political situations. In recent years, most South American governments have taken steps to reform economic policy to promote stability and growth.

The countries of Bolivia, Peru and Colombia have had highly regulated economies in the past, with many industries controlled or operated by the government. In recent years, reforms have been made to promote more open markets and return industries to the private sector. In Venezuela, the current government is taking more control over the oil industry which was formerly mainly private. All petroleum-based industry in Venezuela must now be jointly owned by the government.

The economy of Argentina went through a serious crisis in 2002, when the value of its currency collapsed. Argentina has recovered, partly through currency reforms and by addressing its high international debt.

Brazil's economy is growing steadily, owing to a boom in exports and good international debt relations. Brazil is the largest member of the MERCOSUR trade association, along with Argentina, Paraguay, Uruguay and Venezuela. This important economic agreement allows for free flow of goods between the member countries and has been an important part of Argentina's recovery and Brazil's growth.

Chile has seen a long period of economic growth, fueled by conservative banking policies and the government's encouragement of foreign investment.

Foreign investments have played a central role in the recent growth of many Latin American countries as governments have stabilized. Uncertain political conditions have scared off foreign investors historically. This uncertainty can limit economic growth in countries where economic reforms are not yet complete, or where internationally controversial governments are in charge, as in Venezuela.

The proliferation of free trade agreements has helped Latin American countries in particular, owing to their heavy reliance on international trade. By lowering customs duties and import/export barriers, Latin American partners to these agreements have been able to strengthen a central part of their economies.

Skill 7.8   Demonstrate familiarity with major literary, artistic, and musical forms of the peoples of Latin America

Gabriel García Márquez is the foremost proponent of the literary style dubbed "Magic Realism," the casual meshing of supernatural and everyday events. He is a pioneer of the Latin-American "Boom" and was given the Nobel Prize for Literature in 1982 for the novel "Cien Años de Soledad" (One Hundred Years of Solitude). He is Colombia's most accomplished author and writes extensively in novels, short stories, and articles on the history and the mosaic picture of its daily life.

Jorge Luis Borges is Argentina's most prolific writer. His intellectually based themes are written in the form of short stories that compound philosophy and the entire universe of its ideas.

Gabriela Mistral is a Chilean educator, poet, and diplomat whose wonderful works of poetry are conformed by contemplations of death, faith, and motherhood. She was Latin-America's first Nobel Prize winner, receiving it in 1945 for literature.

Octavio Paz was a Mexican poet and writer, whose focus in his writings tended to the union of civil liberty and nature and its corresponding love. He is Mexico's most prestigious poet of the twentieth century. He won the Nobel Prize for Literature, in 1990.

Pablo Neruda was a Chilean Poet who wrote poetry that's main theme is the historical power of Latin America and its reflection within its vitality and living soul. He was the Nobel Prize Laureate in 1971.

Sor Juana Inés de la Cruz was a nun from Mexico. She was famous for being one of the most prodigious scholars of all times. She wrote poetry and prose that affirmed women's strength and their individual rights.

Latin-American Art
When the conquistadors arrived in the early fifteenth century, they found a very advanced art form left behind by the Indians. They had made pyramids, palaces and temples. They had made statues of their gods out of gold and silver and had made jewelry out of precious stones. They had also made elaborate pottery.

The Spaniards brought a religious form of art to the New World, which served to convert the Indians to Catholicism.

One of the most famous Mexican painters is Diego Rivera. He began his early career influenced by cubism and post-impressionism. In his twenties, he decided to dedicate himself to painting murals that represented political and social themes. His murals can be seen today decorating many public buildings in Mexico.

José Clemente Orozco was also a Mexican muralist who depicted the Mexican Revolution in his paintings. He also painted the frescos of the Palace of the Arts in Mexico City and can also be found in the United States in Dartmouth College.

David Alfaro Siqueiros was a Mexican painter famous for his expression of idealism. He was arrested several times for his political expressions.

Rufino Tamayo was a famous Mexican painter who depicted the happiness and tragedy of his country's history. He won many international art prizes and his paintings adorn famous public buildings like the National Palace of Beautiful Art and the Museum of Anthropology, both in Mexico City and the UNESCO building in Paris.

Miguel Covarrubias, also Mexican, was famous both in his country and in the United States as a painter of caricatures. His drawings have been printed in several magazines.

Cesáreo Bernaldo de Quirós was an Argentinean impressionist whose paintings represented the life of a "gaucho." His paintings depict the history of the "Pampas."

Wilfredo Lam was a Cuban surrealist painter. His paintings contained Afro-Cuban elements. Some of his works are on display in the Museum of Modern Art in New York City.

Some other artists: Emilio Pettoruti, an Argentinean cubist painter; Roberto Matta, a Chilean surrealist; Oswaldo Guayasamin, an Ecuadorian cubist; Alejandro Obregón, a Colombian abstract painter; Rómulo Macció, a vanguard Argentinean painter; Fernando Botero, a Colombian figurative painter; Gerardo Chávez, a Peruvian surrealist.

Most Hispanic music is a conjunction of rhythms brought by African slaves to the Caribbean or native rhythms and melodies preexisting in various indigenous cultures transplanted to the Western instruments brought by the Spanish. Salsa, Merengue, Calypso, Mambo, Cumbia and Vallenato are mixed African and western musical genres that originate in Puerto Rico, Cuba, the Dominican Republic, Honduras, Guatemala, El Salvador, Panamá and the coasts of Venezuela and Colombia. Inland in Mexico, Mariachi and Ranchera music are original and popular musical genres.

Within Peru, Colombia, Ecuador, Bolivia, Uruguay, Paraguay, Chile and Argentina, Andean music is frequently played and listened to. "Música Andina," a genre representing native indigenous musical rhythms and melodies. In Argentina, the music of choice and the genre most listened to is tango – song and dance form both classics and folklore. It is a profound dance technique for couples to participate in, and developed from the expression of Argentinean and Uruguayan folklore.

COMPETENCY 8.0   UNDERSTAND MAJOR HISTORICAL, SOCIAL, POLITICAL, AND ECONOMIC DEVELOPMENTS IN CANADA AND THE GEOGRAPHIC FACTORS INFLUENCING THEM.

Skill 8.1   Demonstrate knowledge of the location and characteristics of the major physical and political features of Canada

Canada has the longest coastline of any country in the world, bordering on three oceans, the Atlantic, Pacific and Arctic. Canada is the second largest country in the world in terms of area. The main part of Canada stretches across the northern half of North America and includes several large islands such as Vancouver Island off the Pacific Coast, Newfoundland off the Atlantic Coast, and Victoria, Baffin and Ellesmere Islands in the seas bordering the Arctic Ocean. In the eastern part of Canada, Hudson Bay juts deep into the country from the north. On the east coast, the Gulf of St. Lawrence is fed by the St. Lawrence River, which connects to the Great Lakes System, which forms part of the border between Canada and the United States. The northernmost settlement in the world is in Canada, at Alert on Ellesmere Island. Canada also claims a portion of the Arctic Ocean extending to the North Pole that includes the magnetic North Pole.

The **Continental Divide** extends across the western part of Canada running north and south. This mountainous region includes the Rocky Mountains and several related mountain chains. Mt. Logan, Canada's highest point and the second highest peak in North America, is part of the Divide and is located in the St. Elias Mountains in the Yukon Territory. In the eastern part of Canada, the Appalachian Range extends into parts of Quebec and New Brunswick.

The St. Lawrence River is a major feature in the southeastern part of Canada, forming part of the border with the United States. The St. Lawrence River flows from Lake Ontario to the Atlantic Ocean. It is a major transportation route. The St. Lawrence Seaway, a series of connected locks and passages, follows the river between Montreal and Lake Erie.

Canada is divided into ten provinces and three territories. The provinces of Canada are: Alberta, British Columbia, Manitoba, New Brunswick, Newfoundland and Labrador, Nova Scotia, Ontario, Prince Edward Island, Quebec, and Saskatchewan. The three territories are Northwest Territories, Nunavut, and Yukon. Toronto, Ontario, is the largest city in Canada, with a population of over 4 million. It is located on the northwestern shore of Lake Ontario. Montreal, Quebec is Canada's second largest city with a population over 3 million. Montreal is situated on an island at the confluence of the St. Lawrence and Ottawa Rivers. At nearly 2 million in population, Vancouver is Canada's third largest city. Vancouver is on the Pacific Coast of Canada, along the Strait of Georgia at the foot of the Coast Mountains. The capital of Canada is Ottawa, found in the province of Ontario.

Skill 8.2   **Identify the major ethnic groups of Canada, including Inuit and other indigenous groups and peoples from other regions of the world, and demonstrate knowledge of their areas of settlement, religions, customs, and traditions**

There are three officially recognized indigenous peoples in Canada, the First Nations, the Métis, and the Inuit.

First Nations are the Native peoples who are entitled to official recognition as part of an Indian tribe or nation. Many members of the First Nations live on reserves throughout Canada and concentrated in the provinces of British Columbia and Ontario. There are currently over 600 recognized First Nations bands or nations.

The First Nations are a diverse group of people with different histories and traditions. Along the Pacific Coast, tribes such as the Haida and Tlingit lived in small settlements near the ocean and rivers and subsisted on salmon fishing and gathering wild foods. Natives on the Atlantic Coast also relied on fishing. In the Canadian Plains, native tribes like the Blackfoot were nomadic, living in teepees and hunting wild bison. In the woodlands across the northern part of Western Canada and extending into the East, bands such as the Cree hunted caribou and moose and later became involved in the fur trade. Along the St. Lawrence River Valley and the shores of Lake Ontario, groups such as the Iroquois came in early contact with European explorers, engaging in trade and sometimes warfare with them.

The **Métis** are the recognized descendents of Native peoples and early French Canadian and British explorers and settlers. The Métis at one time spoke a common language called Michif, which has declined in use in favor of English and French. They have settled throughout Canada.

The **Inuit** people of Canada live along the northern Arctic Coast, where they traditionally derived nearly all their needs from fish and sea mammals, including food, tools from bone, oil for heat and light, and skins and fur for clothing.

Most residents of Canada describe their ethnicity as "Canadian" with many recognizing the British and French ties to their heritage. Canada is also home to large populations of immigrants from Asia, especially on the Pacific Coast in cities like Vancouver, which has a large Chinese community.

Skill 8.3   **Demonstrate knowledge of the development of Canada from its colonization by France and Great Britain, important features of colonial life, and key events in Canada's becoming an independent nation**

The French were the first Europeans to settle permanently in Canada. Samuel de Champlain established a fortification in 1608 at what would become the modern city of Quebec City. de Champlain's settlement became the capital of New France, which grew slowly over the next 150 years to a population of about 60,000. French settlers relied on the cod fishery and fur trapping, and had small subsistence farming.

To the south of New France were the thirteen British colonies. Britain also controlled the Hudson Bay region to the north. Britain and France had a long history of conflict, and their hostilities were carried to the New World as well. Conflict broke out between the colonies several times in the seventeenth and eighteenth centuries. The British eventually took control of much of the French regions of Canada and in 1763 France ceded its lands to Britain. Portions of former New France retained their language and customs, however. There were occasional rebellions against British rule, but the British maintained control. They did later make concessions to the French-speaking regions, however, as Canada gained more autonomy from Britain.

The economy of colonial Canada was largely dominated by the fur trade, which was in turn completely controlled by the **Hudson Bay Company,** one of the oldest companies in the world. Beginning in the seventeenth century, the Hudson Bay Company supported explorers and trappers and established a network of trading posts through the regions that laid claim to large portions of what would become the Dominion of Canada. As the fur trade declined, the Hudson Bay Company turned to supplying Canadian settlers with merchant goods. The company still maintains a chain of department stores throughout Canada.

During the early nineteenth century, the British also established settlements along the Pacific Coast of Canada, creating the colonies of Vancouver and British Columbia. These settlements became part of the dispute between Britain and the United States over the border between their two territories. The border was eventually placed at the 49th parallel. In 1864, the provinces of Canada adopted a resolution calling for autonomy from Britain, and in 1867 Britain proclaimed Canada a dominion, a self-governing colony of the British Empire. The three initial provinces were the Province of Canada, New Brunswick and Nova Scotia, which formed a federation under the British monarchy. Manitoba joined the Dominion in 1870. British Columbia, including the united colony of Vancouver, joined in 1871. As the Canada Pacific Railroad expanded and opened new lands to settlement, the people of Canada moved eastward. Saskatchewan and Alberta were admitted as provinces in 1905.

Skill 8.4 Analyze major issues in Canada during the twentieth century

Canada's sense of nationhood was solidified when it entered the First World War, sending troops to Europe. Between the World Wars, Canada saw both prosperity and depression. The Great Depression that had brought hard times to American farmers was also devastating to Canadian farmers. As commodity prices fell and American trade declined, many had to give up farming altogether. In the industrial regions, production declined and unemployment became widespread.

Britain assisted Canada by increasing its imports, but recovery was slow. Not until the beginning of World War II, which Canada entered in 1939, would the Canadian economy begin to fully recover. Following the Second World War, Canada once again saw prosperous growth.

In the 1960s a movement arose in the province of Quebec calling for sovereignty as an independent state. French-speaking Quebec had retained its language and traditions from the time it was part of New France before British domination. In deference to its national heritage, Quebec provincial law was based on French common law, not the English common law that presided in the rest of Canada. Beginning in the early 1960s, Liberal politicians in the Provincial government began adopting plans that would place more authority over education and the economy in the hands of the French-speaking residents of Quebec. The Quebec Assembly created several state companies to control the province's natural resources. A series of civil laws were passed that reformed labor and marriage laws.

This growth in nationalism among the French-Canadians of Quebec is sometimes called the *Quiet Revolution*. It is during this time that supporters of the increased autonomy of Quebec began referring to themselves as "Quebecois" instead of French-Canadians, accentuating the growing sentiment toward complete independence. Political parties were formed to advocate for the independence of Quebec. Eventually two referendums were held on whether the Quebec should secede and become a separate state. In 1980, the question failed by a vote of 60% against and 40% for independence. Another popular vote was taken in 1995 and independence was defeated by a slim margin.

Since the earliest days of Canadian autonomy, the relationship with the indigenous people of Canada has been one toward acculturation and assimilation. Natives were banned from practicing many of their traditions, and were required to attend schools run by Christian missionaries. Prime Minister Jean Chrétien expressed officially support this policy in 1969. He proposed the abolition of the Indian Act of Canada that gave indigenous people official recognition. The proposal was opposed by Native leaders and members of the Liberal party, and was not adopted.

In 1996, a commission under Prime Minister Brian Mulroney produced a report that proposed the establishment of the First Nations peoples as a political unit within Canada and the payment of federal monies to help improve economic conditions for First Nations peoples. Since that time, First Nations groups have entered into several agreements with the federal and provincial governments to provide economic opportunities and political involvement among First Nations peoples.

Skill 8.5   Recognize the effects of location, climate, physical characteristics, the distribution of natural resources, and population size on the development of Canada

The earliest residents of Canada lived in close association with the natural resources available to them. Some First Nations people settled along the coastal regions and many rivers where fish were an important source of food. Others moved over the plains or through forested regions following game animals. The Inuit have managed to subsist in the forbidding Arctic regions by hunting seals and whales and relying on them for many of their needs. The earliest European settlements were also along the waterways, which provided access to the sea and to trade. Canada's vast wilderness contained expansion during the early years of settlement, and population growth took place mainly in the southeastern part of the country, along the Great Lakes and St. Lawrence River. The Hudson Bay provided sea access to the interior of Canada, and settlements supplying the fur trade were established on its shores.

The distribution of fur animals had an impact on the patterns of Canadian settlement in the form of trading posts set up by the Hudson Bay Company to transport pelts from the forested interior to the sea where they could be shipped back to England. Most of these trading posts were small operations that disappeared when the fur trade declined. Some grew into permanent settlements, however. Outlets on the Pacific Coast were established to serve the fur trade, as well, which later became towns and cities.

As industrial technology advanced in the nineteenth century, waterpower and shipping transportation became crucial. Southeastern Canada, with prime access to water, became an important industrial area. This is the location of Canada's largest urban areas, which still take advantage of their proximity to the water as major shipping ports. The availability of hydroelectric power from the region's large river system has fueled this growth. Canada's extensive international trade has also helped expand its cities with port access, including Vancouver on the Pacific Coast. Agriculture in Canada was mainly for subsistence in the earliest days. When the railroad began to facilitate expansion into the more fertile plains of central Canada, wheat and other crops became profitable. The railroad provided transportation for these crops to market, and allowed for the settlement of the Canadian interior as communities started up along the railroad to provide support to the surrounding agricultural areas.

Skill 8.6   Recognize the effects of human-environment interaction on the development of Canada and the approaches Canada has taken to address these and other environmental problems

Canada contains large areas of undisturbed natural land as well as some heavily settled urban and industrial areas. As humans have interacted with their environment to carve out settlements and develop industry, pollution and other environmental problems can arise.

Acid rain occurs when sulfur dioxide, which is emitted from the burning of fossil fuels, enters and absorbed in the atmosphere and then falls to earth with rain. This rain can change the acidity of soil, lakes and streams, changing the kinds of organisms that can survive there. Canada has made an official effort to reduce acid rain by regulating the companies that produce it, particularly power companies that burn fossil fuels to make power. Most of these industries are located in the eastern provinces of Canada, where the United States also has large industrial areas near the Canadian border. Because pollution is not limited to political borders, Canada has made international agreements with the U.S. to cooperate on reducing air pollution.

Water quality is another international issue that Canada and the United States address together. Water forms much of the eastern part of the boundary between the two countries, including the Great Lakes and the St. Lawrence River. The Great Lakes are ringed with urban and industrial areas that produce polluting substances that can end up in water. These pollutants affect the wildlife in and around the lakes. Several species of fish that were once caught for trade have now disappeared. To reduce pollution, Canada and the U.S. have cooperated to clean up problem areas and to monitor specific chemicals known to be the cause of pollution problems. The countries also must report on their efforts to the international community.

Forestry and related industries such as pulp and paper manufacturing are important industries in Canada, which has nearly half of its land covered in forest. Old growth forests are areas where the trees have reached a great age and are characterized by a layered vegetation of plants of varying ages. Many species of plants and animals are only found in old growth forests. These forests are also attractive to the lumber industry because of the massive trees that can be found there. Logging of old growth forest disturbs the species that rely on it, and can have other environmental effects such as increasing soil erosion. To protect old growth and other forested areas, Canada has increased the amount of forestland that is strictly protected from logging. Canada also hosted an international conference on the subject of forest resource management, which resulted in a set of guidelines called the Montreal Process.

Skill 8.7   Demonstrate knowledge of the basic structure of national government in Canada and Canada's relationship to the United Kingdom

The **Dominion of Canada** was established in 1867 by the British Parliament with the passing of the British North America Act, now called the Constitution Act of 1867. In this act, Britain set up the form of provincial and federal government that is still largely in place today.

While Canada is effectively considered an independent country, its Head of State is still the reigning monarch of England, presently Queen Elizabeth II. The Queen holds executive power in Canada, which she enforces through an appointed Governor General. The Queen makes the appointment of Governor General based on the recommendation of the **Prime Minister**, who is the actual head of the Canadian government.

The legislative branch of the Canadian government is a parliamentary system with two houses, the House of Commons and the Senate. Members of the House of Commons are elected from 308 constituencies distributed through the country. The Governor General, with the recommendation of the Prime Minister, appoints senators.

The Governor General appoints the Prime Minister, who is usually the leader of the political party that controls the House of Commons. The Prime Minister then forms a cabinet, appointing fellow members of parliament to head various government departments. It is the practice that the Prime Minister and his cabinet ministers are members of the parliament, but legally speaking, any Canadian adult is eligible for appointment to these positions.

Provincial governments mirror the federal government in form, with a legislature, a premier, and a lieutenant governor. However, provincial governments have only one legislative assembly.

The federal government enforces civil law in Canada. All powers not granted to the provinces by the Canadian Constitution are the jurisdiction of the federal government. In practice, many of these powers have been assigned to the provinces by the federal government, resulting in a highly de-centralized federal system.

Canada has a federal judicial system to determine matters of law. At the head of the judiciary sits a Supreme Court with nine justices appointed by the Governor General. The Canadian Supreme Court is the final appeals court of Canada, and lower courts are required to follow its rulings.

Canada has an open, democratic system for electing public officials. All Canadian citizens age 18 and above are eligible to vote.

Skill 8.8   Identify major features of the Canadian economic system, recognize the involvement of Canada in international trade, and analyze factors that have encouraged and discouraged economic growth in the region.

Canadian raw materials and products have been shipped around the world from its earliest days as a major supplier of fur and timber. Canada has continued in this vein of economic development to the present day, while also developing related industries of its own such as pulp and paper manufacturing and oil and mineral refining.

As energy producing technology has advanced, Canada has positioned itself as one of the world's few energy exporters, providing electricity to the United States from its productive hydroelectric power systems.

Canada's economy is closely linked to that of the United States, which is its largest trade partner. Its economic growth has largely mirrored that of the U.S., with its industrial regions in the southeast developing across the border from American industrial areas.

Canada's economic links to the U.S. are sometimes closer than those within the country itself, owing largely to the wide expanse of the country and the expense of transporting materials across the Canadian interior. Oil, for instance, is abundant in western Canada, but can be transported more cheaply to the western U.S. than to the industrial areas in the east. As a result, Canadian industry cannot make use of all of Canada's resources, reducing its growth potential. In recent years, Canada has followed the trend of most Western countries toward a service-based economy.

Agriculture is an important sector of the Canadian economy and another area where Canada is a significant exporter. The United States is the primary purchaser of Canadian food products.

In recent years, Canada's population growth has not kept up with economic demands, prompting the government to promote immigration as a way to boost Canada's population. Canada now has the highest per capita immigration rate in the world.

COMPETENCY 9.0 UNDERSTAND MAJOR HISTORICAL, SOCIAL, POLITICAL, AND ECONOMIC DEVELOPMENTS IN EUROPE SINCE THE RENAISSANCE AND THE GEOGRAPHIC FACTORS INFLUENCING THEM.

Skill 9.1   Demonstrate knowledge of the location and characteristics of the major physical and political features of Europe and analyze the geographic and cultural boundaries of Europe

Europe is traditionally considered one of the seven continents of the world. It is bordered on the south by the Mediterranean and Black Seas, on the west by the Atlantic Ocean, on the north by the North Sea and Arctic Ocean, and on the east by the continent of Asia. Europe also includes several islands such as Iceland, Ireland and Great Britain, as well as several smaller islands that are part of mainland countries.

The Alps mountain range extends along the northern edge of the Italian Peninsula in the southern part of the region. The Alps contain numerous high, rocky peaks, the highest of which is Mont Blanc, at over 15,000 feet elevation. Several large lakes are fed by Alpine glaciers. Such lakes include, Lake Como in Italy, Lake Constance which borders Germany, Switzerland and Austria, and Lake Geneva between Switzerland and France. To the east of the Alps, the Carpathian Mountains arch northward, forming the boundary of a large plain. In Western Europe, the Pyrenees Mountains form a natural border between France and Spain.

The Danube River is the longest river system in Europe. It flows eastward from the Black Forest of Germany through Austria, Slovakia, Hungary, Serbia and Romania into the Black Sea. The Rhine River is another important European river, originating in the Swiss Alps and flowing northward into the North Sea.

Europe is densely populated, with several large urban centers. The cities of London, England, Paris, France, Madrid, Spain, Rome, Italy and Berlin, Germany are some of the Europe's larger cities.

Skill 9.2 **Recognize the diversity of cultures in Europe, including differences and similarities in religion, customs, and traditions, and compare the political, social, and economic structures of eastern and western Europe**

Europe contains a wide variety of different cultures in a relatively small area. Cultural links can be seen along linguistic lines, such as between the French-speaking countries of France, Belgium, Monaco and parts of Switzerland, the English-speaking countries of England and Ireland, and the German-speaking countries of Germany and Austria, as well as those countries with Germanic languages such as The Netherlands and Denmark. Cultural differences still exist between groups that share a language, however. Also, language borders do not always coincide with political boundaries, with some cultural groups spanning the regions between two countries. The country of Switzerland, for instance, contains regions of Italian, French and German speakers.

Christianity is the primary religion of Europe. At one time in history, the Roman Catholic Church dominated European religion. Spain contained significant settlements of Muslims and Jews for a time, but these peoples were forcibly driven from the region in the fifteenth century. Europe is home to the Protestant Revolution of Martin Luther, and Protestant faiths still predominate in some parts of the continent. The Catholic Church remains strong in the countries of Ireland, Spain, France, Portugal and Italy, where the Vatican City, the home of the Catholic Pope, is located. The Eastern Orthodox Church, which split from the Roman Catholic Church in the eleventh century, remains strong portions of in southeastern Europe, particularly in Greece.

Following World War II, the Communist government of the Soviet Union held tight control over the countries of Eastern Europe, creating a buffer between Russia and Western Europe, where the United States had established a permanent military presence. These countries were politically and economically linked to the Soviet Union through the Communist Party, which controlled their governments. Foreign policy was also dictated by Russia, which clamped down on emigration from Eastern Europe through strict border control, the most famous example being the Berlin Wall that separated the German city of Berlin.

After the reunification of Germany and the collapse of the Soviet Union, many former Soviet Bloc countries found themselves in difficult circumstances after having relied upon the Soviet Union to support their economies. Many regions were far behind Western Europe in the condition of their infrastructure and technology. Outdated methods of agriculture and manufacturing created challenges to entering the western economy.

These challenges still face many regions of Eastern Europe. The European Union is working to bring these areas into the western economy, and has admitted some of the former Soviet Bloc countries into the Union.

Skill 9.3 **Recognize the causes, major figures, and consequences of the Renaissance, Reformation, Scientific Revolution, and Age of Discovery; examine the significance of the Enlightenment in European history and the influence of Enlightenment ideas on Europe and the world; demonstrate knowledge of the Industrial Revolution and examine its effects on European life and society; and analyze major political and economic developments in Europe during the twentieth century**

The Reformation period consisted of two phases: the **Protestant Reformation** and the **Catholic Reformation** also known as the Inquisition. The Protestant Reformation came about because of religious, political, and economic reasons.

The religious reasons stemmed from abuses in the Catholic Church including fraudulent clergy with their scandalous immoral lifestyles; the sale of religious offices, indulgences, and dispensations; different theologies within the Church; and frauds involving sacred relics. But the underlying reasoning was that the Catholic Church did not follow the Bible it touted. Several religious rites now existed that were not in the Bible. The Bible was also forbidden to be read by anyone during this period who was not clergy.

The political reasons for the Protestant Reformation involved the creation of an increase in the power of rulers who were considered "absolute monarchs." They desired all power and control, especially over the Church. The growth of "nationalism" or patriotic pride in one's own country was another contributing factor.

Economic reasons included the concerns of ruling monarchs to regarding the size and wealth of the Church, the deep animosity against the burdensome papal taxation, the rise of the affluent middle class and its clash with medieval Church ideals, and the increase of an active system of "intense" capitalism.

The Protestant Reformation began in Germany with the revolt of Martin Luther, a monk, against Church abuses. Luther was incensed with the sale of indulgences. It is said that John Tetzel went about selling Indulgences (a paper from the Pope that feed people an Purgatory), which people would buy for those they knew who had died. Tetzel is said to have advertised his Papal Indulgences while crying out, "When a penny in the coffer rings, a soul from Purgatory springs." The spark of the Reformation was started when Luther nailed his 95 Theses to the door of the church at Wittenberg in 1517. These articles questioned Papal tenets of faith when compared to the Bible, where he could find no justification for their existence. The Reformation would have died in Germany if it were not for Gutenberg's invention of the printing press. The printing press allowed Luther's questions, sermons, and books to be published and shared with people throughout Europe.

Luther's works and preaching brought about a church council known as the Diet of Worms. In this meeting Luther was asked if he would reject his books and the "errors" they contained. Tradition holds that Luther stated "Unless I am convicted by Scripture and plain reason — I do not accept the authority of popes and councils, for they have contradicted each other — my conscience is captive to the Word of God. I cannot and will not recant anything, for to go against conscience is neither right nor safe." It is also said that he ended his reply with *"Here I stand. I can do no other. God help me. Amen."*

The Protestant Reformation spread to Switzerland where it was led by John Calvin. It began in England with the efforts of King Henry VIII to have his marriage to Catherine of Aragon annulled so he could wed another and have a male heir. The results were the increasing support given not only by the people but also by nobles and some rulers, and of course, the attempts of the Church to stop it.

The Catholic Reformation was undertaken by the Church to "clean up its act" and to slow or stop the Protestant Revolution.

The major efforts to this end were supplied by the Council of Trent and the Jesuits. Six major results of the Reformation included:

- Religious freedom,
- Religious tolerance,
- More opportunities for education,
- Power and control of rulers limited,
- Increase in religious wars, and
- An increase in fanaticism and persecution.
- The creation of the Index of Forbidden Books which forbid the Bible in the common tongue.

A number of individuals and events led this time of exploration and discoveries. The Vivaldo Brothers and Marco Polo wrote of their travels and experiences, which signaled the early beginnings. Survivors from the Crusades made their way home to different places in Europe bringing with them fascinating, new information about exotic lands, people, customs, and desired foods and goods such as spices and silks.

The **Renaissance** ushered in a time of curiosity, learning, and incredible energy sparking the desire for trade to procure these new, exotic products and to find better, faster, cheaper trade routes to get to them. The work of geographers, astronomers and cartographers made important contributions and many studied and applied the work of such men as Hipparchus of Greece, Ptolemy of Egypt, Tycho Brahe of Denmark, and Fra Mauro of Italy.

The word "Renaissance" literally means "rebirth." It signaled the rekindling of interest in the glory of ancient classical Greek and Roman civilizations. It was the period in human history marking the start of many ideas and innovations leading to our modern age.

The Renaissance began in Italy with many of its ideas starting in Florence, controlled by the infamous Medici family. Education, especially for some of the merchants, required reading, writing, the study of law, math, and the writings of classical Greek and Roman writers.

A combination of a renewed fascination with the classical world and new infusion of money into the hands of those so fascinated brought on the Renaissance. In the areas of art, literature, music, and science, the world changed for the better.

Most famous are the Renaissance artists, first and foremost Leonardo da Vinci, Michelangelo, and Raphael, but also Titian, Donatello, and Rembrandt. All of these men pioneered a new method of painting and sculpture — the portrayal of real events and real people as they really looked, not as the artists imagined them to be. Michelangelo's *David* illustrates this concept.

Literature was also focus during the Renaissance. Humanists Petrarch, Boccaccio, Erasmus, and Sir Thomas More advanced the idea of being interested in life here on earth and the opportunities it can bring, rather than constantly focusing on heaven and its rewards. The monumental works of Shakespeare, Dante, and Cervantes found their origins in these ideas as well as the ones that drove the painters and sculptors. All of these works, of course, owe much of their existence to the invention of the printing press, which occurred during the Renaissance.

The Renaissance changed music as well. Music could be fun and composed for its own sake, to be enjoyed in fuller and more humanistic ways than in the Middle Ages, where it was used for religious experiences. Musicians worked for themselves rather than for the churches, and so could command good money for their work, increasing their prestige.

Science advanced considerably during the Renaissance, especially in the area of physics and astronomy. Copernicus, Kepler, and Galileo led a Scientific Revolution in proving that the earth was round and certainly not perfect, an earth-shattering revelation to those who clung to medieval ideals of a geocentric, church-centered existence.

All of these things encouraged people to see the world in a new way, more real, more realized, and more realistic than ever before. Contributions of the Italian Renaissance period were in:

Art - the most important artists were **Giotto** and his development of perspective in paintings; **Leonardo da Vinci** was not only an artist but also a scientist and inventor; **Michelangelo** was a sculptor, painter, and architect; and others including **Raphael**, **Donatello**, **Titian**, and **Tintoretto.**

Political philosophy - the writings of **Machiavelli (*The Prince).***

Literature - the writings of **Petrarch** and **Boccaccio.**

Science - Galileo

Medicine - the work of Brussels-born **Andrea Vesalius** earned him the title of "father of anatomy" and had a profound influence on the Spaniard **Michael Servetus** and the Englishman **William Harvey**

In Germany, Gutenberg's invention of the **printing press** with movable type facilitated the rapid spread of Renaissance ideas, writings and innovations, thus ensuring the enlightenment of most of Western Europe. Contributions were also made by Durer and Holbein in art and by Paracelsus in science and medicine.

The effects of the Renaissance in the Low Countries can be seen in the literature and philosophy of **Erasmus** and the art of **van Eyck** and **Breughel the Elder**. In France, **Rabelais** and **de Montaigne** also contributed to literature and philosophy. In Spain, the art of **El Greco** and **de Morales** flourished, as did the writings of **Cervantes** and **de Vega**. In England, **Sir Thomas More** and **Sir Francis Bacon** wrote and taught philosophy and inspired by **Vesalius**. **William Harvey** made important contributions in medicine. The greatest talent was found in literature and drama and given to mankind by **Chaucer, Spenser, Marlowe, Jonson**, and the incomparable **Shakespeare.**

Skill 9.4   **Recognize the of location, climate, physical characteristics, the distribution of natural resources, and population size on the development of Europe**

The climate of Europe ranges from the mild, warm regions along the Mediterranean Sea to the frigid, Arctic north of Scandinavia. The earliest human migrations to Europe probably took place along the eastern edge of the Mediterranean, where the climate and fertile interior plains made attractive new lands for settlement. It was in this region that the early European populations thrived in Greece and Rome. The Roman Empire radiated outward from this region, eventually colliding and succumbing to the Germanic tribes in the northern areas.

The rivers of Europe have provided transportation and resources for Europeans since ancient times, and have provided advantageous sites for the development of some of Europe's major cities. **The Rhine River** cuts deep into the interior of Europe, providing a crucial link to the sea and to outside trade. The Rhine was also the northern border of the Roman Empire, forming a natural defensive barrier. Castles and fortifications line the banks of the river where trade traffic could be stopped to extract tolls. The Rhine retains its ancient role as a natural border, and forms part of the border between France and Germany. Its long association with trade and industry is evident from the string of major industrial cities that are situated along its length such as Mannheim, Düsseldorf, Bonn, Cologne and Rotterdam.

The Danube Rover formed a similar natural border to the former Roman Empire and provided a crucial link to the Black Sea and the East. This eastern link has extended the influence of eastern peoples into southeastern Europe. It is one of the longest rivers in Europe.

Geography has played a central role to the development of Europe's dense, diverse population. The mountain ranges, rivers and numerous valley regions of Europe have provided natural borders that have allowed distinct cultures to survive over long periods of time. This diversity has often been the source of regional conflict, particularly following the rise of nationalism in the nineteenth century. **Prussia** sought to unite smaller regions by appealing to similarities in language and culture. Both the First and Second World Wars were centered in Europe and arose out of regional conflicts that expanded as other nations joined in.

Being almost completely surrounded by water, Europe has a traditionally strong link to the sea and seafaring. The natural water borders have also confined the people of Europe, prompting them to develop **exploration** and **colonization** beginning in the fifteenth century. By forging links to other parts of the world, Europeans were able to obtain **raw materials** that were in short supply in Europe, or that could not be found or grown there, such as gold, cotton, tobacco, coffee and chocolate. Through colonization and trade, Europe built and maintained a strong influence throughout the world that was disproportionate to its relatively small size.

Skill 9.5   **Recognize the effects of human-environment interaction on the development of Europe and the approaches European countries have taken to address these and other environmental problems**

Air pollution in Europe has been an environmental problem since the Industrial Revolution, when more and more people began to settle in urban areas. As personal automobile use and burning of fossil fuels expanded, air pollution continued to increase in the urban and industrial areas of Europe.

In the 1960s, the countries of Europe began to address the problem of air pollution seriously. Environmental scientists discovered evidence that air pollutants could travel great distances and affect areas thousands of miles from where they originated. One of the first studies of this kind demonstrated that pollution created in continental Europe was contaminating lakes in Scandinavia.

Water pollution is a similar problem for Europe, which has several rivers that form and flow across country borders. Pollution produced in one area can be transported to other areas, or affect downstream water quality.

These factors make air and water pollution a major international concerns in Europe. Starting in the 1970s, European nations began to hold discussions on ways to cooperate to reduce pollution. In 1979, 34 countries agreed to an international convention to conduct research and set pollution standards and policies. This was the first regional convention of its kind to address pollution and has been used as an example for similar international agreements in other parts of the world.

One such agreement is the the **Kyoto Protocol**. It addresses the formation of greenhouse gas emissions that are linked to global warming. Named after the city in Japan where it was negotiated, Kyoto is a United Nations treaty that sets goals for reducing the kinds of air pollution that cause climate change. The nations of Europe, as part of the European Union, were strong proponents of the Kyoto Protocol, which went into effect in 2005.

When the rising price of oil drove up energy costs in the 1970s, many European countries sought to gain energy independence by building nuclear power plants. While nuclear plants do create radioactive waste, they do not produce the airborne chemicals that contribute to air pollution. This was another factor in the development of nuclear power in Europe.

Nuclear power can produce major environmental problems in the event of leaks or accidents, however. In 1982, an explosion at a nuclear power plant in Chernobyl, Ukraine sent a huge cloud of radioactive particles into the air that floated over much of Europe. Concern over potential radioactive pollution has led some European countries such as Germany and Spain to make plans to eliminate nuclear power. At the same time, countries such as France, which currently gets almost 80% of its power from nuclear plants, have plans to construct more facilities.

Skill 9.6   Demonstrate knowledge of the basic structure of European governments and examine the transition of central European countries from authoritarian systems to democratic systems

The most common form of government among the countries of Europe is the parliamentary republic. This form of government has an elected representative body from which an executive leader is chosen. The executive and legislative powers of government are usually combined in a parliamentary government, unlike other forms that separate these powers. Some countries such as France have a parliamentary system combined with an elected president who shares executive authority with a prime minister. This is called a semi-presidential system.

The Scandinavian countries, Spain, The Netherlands, Belgium, Luxembourg, Denmark and the United Kingdom have **constitutional monarchy** governments. These systems recognize a hereditary monarch as the leader of the government, but the monarch actually has little involvement in the government. Two exceptions are the principalities of Monaco and Liechtenstein, where monarchs hold real executive power as heads of the government. The constitutional monarchies of Europe use a parliamentary system of government.

The **Vatican City** is a tiny independent city-state. It is under the administration of the Catholic Church headed by the Pope. As such, it is sometimes considered an absolute monarchy.

Following the devastation of the Second World War, European countries began to forge political and trade alliances to assist one another and to prevent future hostilities. As these agreements developed, the idea of an economic union of European countries began to gain momentum. In 1958, the European Economic Community was formed to standardize tariffs and allow for free trade within the member states. This community eventually grew into the European Union, which was formed in 1992.

The **European Union** is made up of 27 European countries and is an international government with a parliamentary system. Members of the European Parliament are directly elected every five years. The parliament is based in Brussels, Belgium. There is also a European Union judicial system, and several other commissions that oversee the administration of the European Union, which are established in cities throughout Europe.

The constitution and laws of the European Union have precedence over those of the individual member states, however individuals maintain rights granted to them by their home countries. Member states also agree to form a common economy, with uniform regulations and economic policies. Thirteen European countries have adopted the European Union currency, the euro.

Membership in the European Union is open ended. Countries wishing to join the union must apply and meet certain political and economic requirements before being considered and admitted. The European Union is an example of supranationalism.

Skill 9.7   Identify major features of the different types of economic systems found in Europe, recognize the involvement of Europe in international trade, and analyze factors that have influenced economic growth in various regions of Europe

All the countries of Europe have free-market economies. Because of the relatively small size of the countries of Europe, most do not contain a full range of natural resources to support self-sufficient economies, making trade an important part of all European economies.

Following World War II, much of Eastern Europe came under the control of the Communist Soviet Union and was enrolled in the Council for Mutual Economic Assistance, a communist market controlled by the USSR. After the war, many Western Europe's ndustrial infrastructure had been demolished in the fighting, and countries such as Germany were faced with rebuilding an economy nearly from scratch. With the extensive involvement of the United States, the Western European countries adopted free-market systems, and with help from the U.S. began to recover from the devastation.

Germany, which had been the center of the final battles of the war, was split into two regions, with the city of Berlin divided between western and eastern control. West Germany received particular attention from the United States, and with American support, eventually surpassed the United Kingdom to become the largest economy in Europe.

In the 1980s and 1990s, division between Eastern and Western Europe began to crumble, and the reunification of East and West Germany began, culminating in the collapse of the Soviet Union. The former communist market states of Eastern Europe rapidly made efforts to convert to free market systems, with varying degrees of success. Countries such as Poland, which already had strong, modern industrial bases, made the transition fairly quickly and easily. Other states that had relied on the economic assistance of Russia and the Soviet Union had a more difficult time. Yugoslavia, which was an independent communist country that was not directly controlled by the USSR, dissolved into civil war in the years after the collapse of Soviet Communism.

In recent years, the countries of Europe have consolidated many of the regional trade agreements and treaties into a common, central economy under the European Union. The European Union seeks to reduce the barriers to trade within European countries and to pool the various resources and industries of the European region into a large world economic force to compete with the United States and Asia. This economy has a common currency and a central bank, and has grown rapidly since its inception, both in economic strength and in the number of member states.

To counter the influence of the European Union, Russia has formed a trade group called the **Commonwealth of Independent States**, which is open to former states of the Soviet Union.

Skill 9.8   Demonstrate familiarity with major literary, artistic, and musical forms of the peoples of Europe

Europe has been the cultural center of Western culture for centuries, and is where many present forms of literary, artistic, and musical expression were first developed.

Classical music is dominated by European figures like Brahms, Bach, Mozart and Beethoven. The classical symphony grew out of the eighteenth century Italian overture, which usually had three separate movements and was played as a prelude to an operatic or vocal concert. Early symphonies were short and were included on musical programs with other works, mainly vocal. In the early years of the nineteenth century, Ludwig von Beethoven began to experiment with the form of the symphony, expanding it into an extended orchestral work that is usually the main piece in a program. Modern symphony orchestras are assembled to perform these classical works, and are found in all major European and cities. Europe was home to the development of most modern classical instruments, as well.

Closely related to European classical music are the forms of **opera** and **ballet**. Opera is a form of staged performance combining orchestral music and dramatic action with the dialogue in song. Operas are often elaborately produced affairs, with large sets and many performers in costume. The Italians and French have traditionally embraced opera, and many operas are performed in these languages.

Ballet is a formal style of dance that emphasizes smooth, graceful movements and perfect balance. Like opera, classical ballets often depict dramatic events set to music, but rely on the movement of the dancers to convey expression and emotion.

Popular music is an important part of European culture. Europe's recording industry produces albums by popular singers and groups that are widely purchased and played on television and radio stations. European and American popular music scenes are closely linked, with many American singers and groups gaining acclaim in Europe. European pop groups such as The Beatles, Abba and U2 have had major influences on American popular music, as well.

The **novel**, in its modern sense, emerged in Europe during the eighteenth century. Lengthy pieces of fiction had appeared before 1700, but they were extensions of romantic tales, or were written in verse. *Pamela, or Virtue Rewarded* by Samuel Richardson was published in 1740, and was a full length, realistic prose story in a contemporary setting. It is widely considered the first novel. The form grew popular, and by the 1840s was the prominent form of important fiction. It remains a popular and important literary form in Europe and throughout the world.

The literary form of staged drama presented in multiple acts reached its pinnacle in sixteenth century England with the **plays** of Christopher Marlowe, Francis Bacon and William Shakespeare. These plays are still performed and enjoyed, especially those of Shakespeare, which have come to represent a highpoint in English literature.

Europe has a tradition of respect for the literature of other world cultures. One of the most prestigious awards in the field, the Nobel Prize for Literature, is given every year by a committee based in Sweden.

During the Renaissance, European artists perfected the method of introducing perspective into painting, beginning an age of realism in **painting** and **sculpture** that reached its height with the European masters such as Rembrandt and Vermeer in the seventeenth century. The Impressionist style of Monet and Van Gogh moved away from this strictly realistic style of painting and led to the development of the abstract ideals of Braque and Picasso. These European forms of expression have been influential throughout the world of art, and examples hang in all major museums today.

COMPETENCY 10.0   UNDERSTAND MAJOR HISTORICAL, SOCIAL, POLITICAL, AND ECONOMIC DEVELOPMENTS IN SUB-SAHARAN AFRICA AND THE GEOGRAPHIC FACTORS INFLUENCING THEM.

Skill 10.1   Demonstrate knowledge of the location and characteristics of the major physical and political features of Sub-Saharan Africa

The region south of the Sahara desert is known as Sub-Saharan Africa and is made up all the regions of West Africa, East and Equatorial Africa and Southern Africa, as well as the island of Madagascar, off the east coast of Africa. There are a variety of landforms in Sub-Saharan Africa. The world's longest river, the **Nile**, originates in Sub-Saharan Africa, and some other major rivers are the Zaire, Zambezi and Niger Rivers. Some of the rivers flow from higher elevations to huge basins, such as the Zaire Basin. Great plateaus span much of the Sub-Saharan region, as well as some mountains, including Mount Kilimanjaro and Mount Kenya. Several large rift valleys are found in this region. A rift valley is a deep narrow valley formed by cracks in the earth's surface millions of years ago. The Great Rift Valley is the largest rift valley and it is made up of several smaller rift valleys. A significant area of the Sub-Saharan land consists of wide expanses of grasslands called savannas. Savannas have an extremely hot dry season, followed by a season of heavy rain which waters the land. Savannas are good for farming millet and sorghum, and they are the major habitat of African wildlife. Just south of the Sahara Desert is an area of dry grassland that extends across Africa. This is called the **Sahel**. Bordering the coast of South Africa is the tropical rainforest, where it rains throughout the year. The equator runs across the middle of Africa, and the climate is tropical. Most areas have hot, dry climates and other areas have seasonal rain.

Sub-Saharan Africa is a region of great political instability. Traditionally, this area had been inhabited by thousands of ethnic groups that each had its own language, culture, customs, and its own system of governments. Ethnic groups were often made up of tribes of extended families and were ruled by their own kings, chiefs or by a system similar to basic democracy, where a council of elders takes political decisions. These systems were deeply rooted in the history of Africa. During the 1500s, European colonists took over most of this region. Before the end of the age of colonialism, starting in about the 1960s, the Europeans created state borders for the modern states of this region. These borders had little to do with what the people living there had in common. Africans often found themselves united in a state with ethnic tribes who had been former enemies, or who spoke different languages and had different values. As a result, people had little loyalty for their state and were more passionate about their ties to their clan and ethnic group. The Europeans tried to set up governments that were modeled on European government, but these had limited success. Nations were often ruled by dictators or single party governments. When political parties were created, they were often based on ethnic ties rather than political ideology.

The nations of this region have had numerous coups, uprisings, rebellions, civil wars and wars with neighboring states. An additional challenge to South Africa has been the European laws of **apartheid,** or racial segregation, created many political conflicts until apartheid laws were abolished in the 1990s. Today the nations of Africa are attempting to move away from single party governments and are trying to introduce forms of government that are more democratic. This is having varied success in different states in the region.

Skill 10.2   Identify the major ethnic groups of Sub-Saharan Africa, including indigenous groups and peoples from other regions of the world, and demonstrate knowledge of their areas of settlement, religions, customs, and traditions

Sub-Saharan Africa is made up of many ethnic groups native to the region, each possessing a unique culture, language, way of life and religion. As many as 1,000 languages are spoken in Africa.

Some of the major groups in West Africa are the Ibo, who lived in areas with more rain, and made a living as farmers. They used a council system to govern their tribe. The Fulani and the Tuaregs lived in areas of the savanna and lived by keeping livestock and cattle. These groups were affiliated with the Muslim countries and were politically influenced by Muslim leaders. In Eastern and Equatorial Africa, the Bantu are the largest group. There are several ethnic groups (Kikuyu of Kenya and the Baganda of Uganda) who migrated from the Cameroon area about 2,500 years ago into what is now central Africa. This migration took many centuries and the original Bantu languages and customs underwent many changes. The Kushites are another ethnic group in East Africa, and they made their living by farming. The major ethnic group that traditionally inhabited southern Africa and many other parts of Africa are the Bushmen. When the Bantu migration reached southern Africa, the Bushmen were forced into the Kalahari Desert. Today, the majority of the people living in the southern region of Africa are of Bantu descent.

Groups of people foreign to Africa also settled there. In 650 AD, Muslim merchants began trade with areas on the Eastern coast of Africa. Muslims brought the religion of Islam to Africa, as well as the Arabic language. They also started new crops such as coconuts and bananas. The religion of Islam, Arabic and the new crops spread through much of East Africa. Today, several African nations are mainly Muslim, including Mauritania, Gambia and Senegal.

Starting from the 1400s, European traders began arriving in Africa. They brought the religion of Christianity, various European languages. Eventually the Europeans brought a long era of colonialism to Africa. A major Dutch colony named Cape Colony was set up in South Africa in 1652. European traders from France and Germany joined the colony. A new language developed in the south of Africa, consisting of the words and rules from Dutch, French, German and Bantu.

This language was named Afrikaans. The white people who spoke Afrikaans were called **Boers** and they are the largest European group in Africa today. When the Boers were forced out of their colony by the British in the 1700s, they migrated to other areas of Africa and settled there. The Boers and the British spread their influence in Africa and were important in forming the unique culture of Sub-Saharan Africa.

Skill 10.3   **Identify major characteristics of early Sub-Saharan African empires and demonstrate knowledge of the effects of the colonial period on the development of Sub-Saharan Africa, important features of colonial life in Sub-Saharan Africa, Sub-Saharan African independence movements, major challenges faced by Sub-Saharan African nations since independence, and efforts by Sub-Saharan African nations and individuals to address these challenges**

During the fourteenth and fifteenth centuries, the Muslim Empire experienced great expansion. The conquest of Ghana by Muslim Berbers in 1076 permitted rule to devolve to a series of lesser successor states. By the thirteenth century, the successor state of Kangaba established the Kingdom of Mali. This vast trading state extended from the African Atlantic Coast to beyond Gao on the Niger River in the east.

Much of the history of **Mali** was preserved by Islamic scholars because the Mali rulers converted to Islam and were responsible for the spread of Islam throughout Africa. The expansion of the Mali kingdom began from the city of Timbuktu and gradually moved downstream along the Niger River. This provided increasing control of the river and the cities along its banks, which were critical for both travel and trade. The Niger River was a central link in trade for both west and North African trade routes. The government of the Mali Kingdom was held together by military power and trade. The kingdom was organized into a series of feudal states that were ruled by a king. Most of the kings used the surname "Mansa" (meaning, "sultan"). The most powerful and effective of the kings was Mansa Musa.

The religion and culture of the Kingdom of Mali was a blend of Islamic faith and traditional African belief. The influence of the Islamic empire provided the basis of a large and very structured government which allowed the king to expand both territory and influence. The people, however, did not follow strict Islamic law. In traditional African fashion, the king was thought as a divine ruler removed from the people. A strong military and control of the Niger River and the trade that flourished along the river enabled Mali to build a strong feudal empire.

Farther to the east, the king of the Songhai people had earlier converted to Islam in the eleventh century. **Songhai** was at one time a province of Mali. By the fifteenth century, Songhai was stronger than Mali and it emerged as the next great power in western Africa. Songhai was situated on the great bend of the Niger River. From the early fifteenth to the late sixteenth centuries, the Songhai Empire stood, one of the largest empires in the history of Africa. The first king Sonni Ali conquered many neighboring states, including the Mali Empire. This gave him control of the trade routes and cities like Timbuktu. His successor, Askia Mohammad, initiated political reform and revitalization. He also created religious schools, built mosques, and opened his court to scholars and poets from all parts of the Muslim world.

During the same period, the Zimbabwe Kingdom was built. "Great Zimbabwe" was the largest of about 300 stone structures in the area. This capital city and trading center of the Kingdom of Makaranga was built between the twelfth and fifteenth centuries. It was believed to have housed as many as 20,000 people. The structures were built entirely of stone, without mortar. The scanty evidence that is available suggests that the kingdom was a trading center, believed to be part of a trading network that reached as far as China.

The area known today as the Republic of Benin was the site of an early African kingdom known as **Dahomey**. By the seventeenth century, Dahomeny included a large part of West Africa. The kingdom was economically prosperous because of slave trading relations with Europeans, primarily the Dutch and Portuguese, who arrived in the fifteenth century. The coastal part of the kingdom was known as **"the Slave Coast."** This kingdom was known for a very distinct culture and some very unusual traditions. In 1729, the kingdom started a female army system. A law was passed stating that females would be inspected at the age of 15. Those thought beautiful were sent to the Palace to become wives of the king. Those who were sick or were considered unattractive were executed. The rest were trained as soldiers for two years. Human sacrifice was practiced on holidays and special occasions. Slaves and prisoners of war were sacrificed to Dahomenian gods and ancestors.

The slave trade provided economic stability for the kingdom for almost three hundred years. The continuing need for human sacrifices caused a decrease in the number of slaves available for export. As many colonial countries declared the slave trade illegal, demand for slaves subsided steadily until 1885 when the last Portuguese slave ship left the coast. With the decline of the slave trade, the kingdom began a slow disintegration. The French took over in 1892.

Skill 10.4   Recognize the effects of location, climate, physical characteristics, the distribution of natural resources, and population size on the development of Sub-Saharan Africa

As with all regions, the environment of Sub-Saharan Africa has greatly influenced all areas of its development and livelihood.

Africa is the second largest continent and it has tropical climate, where it is mostly hot and dry. Large deserts span the continent, as well as huge expanses of grassy savannah, long rivers, high mountains and a few areas of tropical rainforests. This variation in climate and landforms combined with other factors has given rise to certain patterns of development in the region.
Africa is ideally located between Europe and Asia and the Americas. This centralized location had made it a suitable trading base with countries all over the world.

Tropical climate in Sub-Saharan Africa has made it suitable for certain kinds of agriculture. **Cacao** is one of Africa's major exports and the plant thrives in tropical conditions. Coffee, rubber and palm oil are other crops that are well suited to the climate. African **rainforests** are a major source for wood throughout the world. The savanna's pattern of seasonal rain makes it good ground for farming corn and millet.

However, the harsh climate in the Sub-Sahara also brings problems. As a result of strong desert winds, extended dry seasons cause **drought** and **famine** – two consistent problems in this area. Drought destroys crops and results in widespread famine. Millions of African lives have been lost to famine. Another persistent problem with the tropical climate is that it is a suitable breeding climate for certain disease-carrying insects such as mosquitoes and the tsetse fly. These diseases threaten both people and livestock and they are a great influence on how the population is distributed, since people try to avoid insect infested regions.

Sub-Saharan Africa has a wealth of minerals such as **diamonds, gold, copper, uranium and iron**, as well as **petroleum**. This has no doubt attracted traders and settlers alike and the industry of mining is a thriving one.

The rivers and lakes of Africa provide valuable, if insufficient water supply to a region in dire need. Not surprisingly, many clusters of settlements are around the water resources of Sub-Saharan Africa. Some parts of Africa are experimenting with hydroelectric power generated from waterfalls. In coastal areas, a fishing industry has developed.

Another natural resource of the Sub-Saharan continent is the variety of wildlife in the savanna. This has supported a large tourism industry which continues to grow.

Skill 10.5   Recognize the effects of human-environment interaction on the development of Sub-Saharan Africa and the approaches Sub-Saharan African countries have taken to address these and other environmental problems

Environmental resources in Sub-Saharan Africa are rapidly depleting, due to increased population and industry practices that are not conservative of the environment. In addition, extreme poverty in this region has made it challenging to efficiently manage environmental resources and establish ways to remedy problems.

Air and water **pollution** are difficult issues faced by Sub-Sarahan Africa. Oil production has made significant increases, but has released natural gas and carbon dioxide into the environment and poisoned the atmosphere. Oil trade has also led to the use of the rivers of Africa for transporting oil. Problems with oil spills and leakages have led to polluting the waters, causing shortages of drinking water and affecting fishing and other industries. Governments have been trying to reduce these effects by fining companies that contribute to such pollution.

Deforestation and **desertification** are two other persistent problems. The tropical rain forests of the Sub-Sahara have been some of earth's largest natural air detoxifiers, by absorbing carbon dioxide from the atmosphere. The growing population and the increased use of wood for fuel has led to wide deforestation. Almost 70% of this region's forests have been depleted. Other than creating a shortage of fuel wood, this has altered the biodiversity of the area and created disruptions in the natural ecosystem. International attention has focused on these issues and some natural conservation programs have been put in place to preserve these natural resources.

Deforestation leads to desertification, or loss of soil that is good for farming. The reduced number of trees allows soil to be washed away by rain into the rivers and water sources. This has contributed to reduced water quality, dust storms and respiratory illnesses. The remaining soil there is poorly served by the traditional farming methods used. All the countries of Sub-Saharan Africa have entered into The Convention to Combat Desertification, in attempts to reduce the effects of this problem.

There has been new interest in other sources of power such as **hydropower** from the waterfalls of Africa. However installation of hydropower plants has been expensive and has affected the biodiversity of rivers and interfered with fishing and tourism industries.

Overall, there is growing awareness of the environmental issues of the sub-Sahara and national and international activists are trying to reverse and prevent further damaging effects.

Reference: Sub-Saharan Environmental Issues. www.eia.doe.gov

Skill 10.6   Demonstrate knowledge of the basic structure of Sub-Saharan African governments and analyze the effects of ethnic conflicts and civil wars on Sub-Saharan African governments

Historically, the region of Sub-Saharan Africa has been inhabited by thousands of ethnic tribes and groups, each having independent forms of government. Some groups had a single-leader government, while others were led by councils of elders who took decisions as a group.

The age of colonialism brought changes to these forms of governments. Sub-Saharan regions were divided into states and official governments were established. Some of these governments are monarchies and authoritarian regimes, others are military governments and others are attempts at representative governments. Representative governments have had limited success at democracy, and few of them have real democracy as a basis. Few countries allowed multiple political parties with the goal of unifying peoples who already had different cultures and ethnic loyalties. These deep-rooted differences have caused numerous civil wars, uprisings and military coups in the region. Governments had little credibility and were very unstable. Political instability and natural disasters increased poverty and dissatisfaction with the performance of the governments.

Towards the end of the last century there have been movements toward advancing democracy. Laws were passed to end the ban on multiple party systems. Some nations are holding elections and developing modern forms of legislature. Younger generations of Africans are contributing to political ideologies that are more tolerant of differences and less inspired by ethnic identity. Governments in the Sub-Saharan region continue to remain unstable, but there are continuous efforts by the governments to improve living standards and quality of life for the people, which will contribute toward political stability.

Skill 10.7   Identify major features of the different types of economic systems found in Sub-Saharan Africa, recognize the involvement of Sub-Saharan Africa in international trade, and analyze factors that have influenced economic growth in various parts of the region

Sub-Saharan economy depends on several different kinds of economic activity. **Farming** was traditionally one of the major economic activities. In many parts of the savanna, land was jointly owned by tribes of ethnic groups. They would all work in the fields and share in the expenses, the yield and the wealth. No one was allowed to sell the land since it was joint property. Some farmers practice subsistence farming, producing only what they need for the consumption of their own families. Other farmers produce cash crops, or crops for selling, including cacao, coffee and peanuts. Farming has been faced with tremendous challenges as the region underwent severe drought. Much of the farmland dried up. The area of the Sahel, south of the Sahara Desert, used to have land that was good for limited farming but is be,ginning to show increasing features of desertification and can sustain very few crops. In areas of the savanna, which receives slightly more rain, farmers have traditionally used a system of shifting cultivation, where fields are planted for one season, then left fallow to enable soil restoration over a few seasons. This practice requires plenty of arable land to allow farmers to maintain a constant supply of fields. Land shortages have required farmers to shorten the resting periods for land, which produces a smaller yield per field, and poorer quality of harvest. Most regions of the Sub-Sahara cannot afford the high cost of artificial irrigation. Climate conditions are thus forcing more and more people out of farming.

Another common economic activity is cattle rearing. Cattle shepherds follow a nomadic lifestyle, moving their herds to places with more water and vegetation as lands dry up. This activity has also suffered under the conditions of harsh climate.

As farming becomes less able to sustain the economy, Sub-Saharan Africa is slowly becoming more industrialized. Instead of selling raw products and resources, factories and manufacturing plants are being built to process these materials and sell them both locally and internationally for profit. **Industrialization** has created thousands of jobs, but remains challenged by limited spending power to modernize industry, and poor methods of transportation for goods.

Africa's wealth of natural resources is an important pillar in the economy. Oil and mining industry are expanding and are supporting many jobs for people that were formerly employed in farming.

The biggest challenges the economy have been the climate and inability to invest sufficient money in industrial growth. In addition, political instability and frequent civil wars have taken their toll on the economy of Sub-Saharan Africa.

The exception to these conditions has been the region of southern Africa, particularly in the country, South Africa. South Africa enjoys a diversified economy which depends on advanced industry and mining. It has a great wealth of mineral resources including gold, diamonds, coal, iron, chrome, uranium and platinum. These minerals are processed and exported all over the world. South Africa is able to afford methods of artificial irrigation, and their farming industry produces enough to support international trade. However, even in these positive conditions, problems of racial segregation have been a factor in holding back the economy. Black workers were always subject to lower wages and sub-standard working conditions. With the laws of racial equality, some economic stability has been attained. South Africa is undergoing rapid economic expansion and growth.

Skill 10.8 Demonstrate familiarity with major literary, artistic, and musical forms of the peoples of Sub-Saharan Africa

Sub-Saharan Africa is a region rich in culture and tradition. Traditional arts and literature have been kept alive from generation to generation and are ever present in many aspects of life.

Storytelling is a favorite art form practiced in all parts of the sub-Sahara. Storytelling is a well developed ancient art that has the goal of preserving history and wisdom and maintain ethnic values and beliefs. Storytellers called **griots** are versed in the art of storytelling and they often tell stories accompanied by traditional songs and dances. Story themes relate to all. Even the younger generation needs to learn about their traditions, including values, beliefs, historical events, and personal stories of significance and wisdom. Becoming familiar with history inspires feelings of belonging and unity among ethnic group members.

Other popular art forms are dance and music, which are not just for entertainment, but often represent beliefs and values. Many rites of passage ceremonies are accompanied by song and dance (marriage, death, birth, puberty, etc.) The most common musical instrument is the drum. Drummers are able to produce infinite rhythms and beats for every occasion. Dancers and singers often wear costumes and beautifully decorated masks to symbolize beliefs and ethnicity.

Poetry is another important art form, and African poems relate to many themes, including the environment, feelings, beliefs, events and identity. Sub-Saharan Africa has been the birth place of many proverbs that educate humanity in African wisdom. Some famous African proverbs show the importance of family and children, e.g., blood is thicker than water, it takes a village to raise a child.

Reference for all above skills:

World Regions: Adventures in Time and Place. McGraw-Hill, 1998.

COMPETENCY 11.0   UNDERSTAND MAJOR HISTORICAL, SOCIAL, POLITICAL, AND ECONOMIC DEVELOPMENTS IN NORTH AFRICA/SOUTHWEST ASIA (THE MIDDLE EAST) AND THE GEOGRAPHIC FACTORS INFLUENCING THEM.

Skill 11.1   Demonstrate knowledge of the location and characteristics of the major physical and political features of North Africa/Southwest Asia

The countries of North Africa and southwest Asia are usually grouped together in social and geographical study because they share many features. This region is referred to as the Middle East, since it is to the east of Europe, but it is closer than the region referred to as the Far East.

The Middle East consists of land extending across two continents, connected by a narrow land bridge known as the Sinai Peninsula. This area is surrounded by seas and gulfs. The countries of North Africa are along the coast of the Mediterranean Sea, across from Europe. The Arabian Peninsula is separated from mainland Africa by the Red Sea, and is surrounded by two other seas, The Arabian Sea and the Persian Gulf. The country of Turkey, which connects Europe to Asia, forms the Anatolia Peninsula, and it is surrounded by the Black Sea and the Aegean Sea.

There is great variety in the physical features of the region. The world's largest desert, the Sahara, is located in North Africa. Other deserts are commonly found in the area, including the Libyan Desert, the Syrian Desert and the Rub' Al-Khali Desert in Saudi Arabia. Some farmland is also found in the Middle East surrounding the rivers. The area of the Rivers Tigris and the Euphrates is known as the Fertile Crescent and it has plentiful farmland. The Nile River, the longest river in the world, passes through Egypt and provides it with valuable farmland. Turkey, Syria and Iran receive enough rain to support farming along their coasts.

Historically, the Middle East region has been home to several ancient civilizations and through the ages has seen periods of great civilization, stability, wars and unrest. Today, the region is going through many tensions because of the Israeli-Palestinian conflict, a transitional government in Iraq and different governments in other countries who are struggling with political instability.

Skill 11.2 **Identify the major ethnic groups of North Africa/Southwest Asia, including indigenous groups and peoples from other regions of the world, and demonstrate knowledge of their areas of settlement, religions, customs, and traditions**

The region of North Africa and Southwest Asia (the Middle East) has historically been a center of trade and cultural exchange, and it has had many influences from all over the world.

The main group of people inhabiting the region is the **Arabs**. The Arabs originally lived in the Arabian Peninsula and spoke Arabic. They made their living by trading along several different trade routes. Many of them were Bedouins, living in the desert and following a nomadic lifestyle, moving around to settle in different areas, depending on availability of sources of food and trade. Today, Arabs live in large cities and towns. Many live in groups of extended families, and elders are held in high respect as wise and experienced community members. Arabs follow the religion of Islam, and many of their customs and traditions are derived from Islam. Some of the most widespread traditions accompany the month of **Ramadan**, the Islamic month of fasting. During this month, Muslims refrain from eating or drinking each day from dawn to sunset, in an act of worship to God. It is a month of spirituality accompanied by different cultural festivities throughout the Middle East. Huge stained glass lanterns light up the streets and long dinner tables piled with food are set up at sunset, where rich and poor are invited to break their fast and share the main meal of the day. Other non-Arab Muslim groups living in the region share some of the Islamic customs of the Arabs.

The **Turks** are a second group living in the region. They originally moved west from Central Asia to settle in the Anatolian Peninsula, and they converted to Islam. The Turks do not speak Arabic, but many of the word in Turkish come from Arabic. Turkish customs are similar to Islamic customs, as well as customs that came about from European influence.

Persians are a third group of people living in the area of Iran. Their history goes back to the Ancient Persian civilization. The language spoken by Persians is Farsi. The main religion of the Persians today is Islam and many of their customs are shared with other Muslim countries. Other customs and traditions relate to history and show a strong sense of pride and connection with their rich heritage. Persians traditionally live in the area of modern day Iran.

Another group that is a relative newcomer to the area are the **Jews** living in Israel. Israel was established by in 1948 as a nation for the Jews from all over the world. Jews have had lived in Palestine since ancient times along with people of other faiths, but they did not have a designated Jewish nation. The call for the establishment of a Jewish State dates back to the turn of the century. In the wake of the Holocaust after World War II, the newly established United Nations passed a resolution that divided Palestine and created a Jewish State and a Palestinian State. Within the resolution, Great Britiain agreed to leave the territory known as the British Mandate of Palestine. The Jews that had fled Europe migrated to Israel, and many more Jews joined them from all over the world. This has become an area of great conflict in the region, since the Palestinian Arabs living in Palestine had been displaced by the Jews. This conflict has yet to be resolved. The official languages in Israel are Hebrew and Arabic. English is widely used and spoken as well. Israeli customs come from a variety of cultures, as do the Israeli people. Other customs celebrate different aspects of the Jewish faith. In a short time, the people of Israel have been built a strong economy that depends on farming and industry. There is also a vibrant high-tech industry in Israel.

The **Berbers** were the first group that can be traced to inhabit North Africa. They are the oldest ethnic group in Morocco and Algeria, and when this area was conquered by the Arabs, they converted to Islam. Many people still speak Berber today.

Other non-Arab groups in the region include the **Kurds**, who speak a Kurdish language that is close to Farsi. Kurds have long wanted to establish their own independent nation, but have not met acceptance from the governments of the countries where they live (parts of Syria, Iran, Iraq and Turkey). There are also non-Muslim groups in the Middle East, both Arab and non-Arab, in Lebanon, Egypt, and other countries in the region.

Most of the above groups are intermingled in different areas in the Middle East. As a result of the colonial period, European languages have become second languages for many of the people. English as a second language is taught in the schools of Egypt, Isarel, and the Arabian Peninsula. French is a second language in Lebanon and North Africa. Large cities have grown in almost every Middle Eastern country and there are many signs of westernization, blended with the traditional aspect of each nation, creating unique cultures.

Skill 11.3 **Demonstrate knowledge of the historical development of the three major religions that originated in the Middle East, the importance of the Ottoman Empire to North Africa/Southwest Asia, the effects of the colonial period on the development of North Africa/Southwest Asia, independence movements in the region, major challenges in Southwest Asia during the twentieth century, and efforts by North African/Southwest Asian nations and individuals to address these challenges**

The Middle East and North Africa have been home to some of the world's earliest known civilizations, and cradle to the three major religions followed by most people in the world. The three religions of Judaism, Christianity and Islam are believed to come from the same divine source, God, and followers of these faiths follow similar practices and hold similar beliefs and concepts of the world. Following is an account of how the religious books of each religion relate how each faith originated and grew.

The origin of the three religions can be traced back to a man named Abraham, who lived in Mesopotamia (Iraq) and moved to the land of Canaan (present day Israel). God instructed Abraham to spread His teachings of worshipping God and adopting moral behavior. Abraham had a son named Isaac, and a grandson named Israel (Jacob), the ancestor of all the Israelites or the Jews. Famine in Canaan forced the Israelites to move to Egypt, where they settled. After many years, a new Pharaoh came to power in Egypt, and he persecuted the Jews, killing many and enslaving the rest. A baby named Moses was born to a Jewish family, and he was adopted by Pharaoh's daughter. Moses grew up to be a strong righteous man.

The Bible relates that Moses once killed an Egyptian man, whom he saw beating a Jewish slave. Moses fled from Egypt to Midian (the Sinai Peninsula), and there, God instructed him to go back to Egypt and spread His teachings of monotheism, and virtue. Moses tried to approach the Pharaoh and demanded the release of Jewish slaves, but was rejected. G-d would inflict ten plagues on Egypt, and the Jews fled. Religious books relate the story of a miraculous escape where God parted the sea to allow Moses and his followers to escape, and the Pharaoh and his army drowned in their pursuit. The Jews lived in the Sinai Desert as nomads, for forty years, and Moses continued to spread the teachings of God. These teachings are compiled into the Torah, the one of the sacred books of the Jews, and they include the Ten Commandments. They instruct people to worship only God (monotheism) and to be honest and moral. The other two are the writings of the Prophets and the Additional Writings. These three books make up the Old Testament in the Christian Bible. After the death of Moses, the Jews settled in Canaan, and they had several other leaders who spread the teachings of God, including David and Solomon. Today, there are approximately 13 million people who follow the Jewish faith.

Christianity also originated in the land of Canaan, in Bethlehem. There, a baby named Jesus was born to a woman named Mary. Jesus was always interested in the teachings of Judaism, at a time when many of the people had grown away from those teachings, and great sectarianism existed. God appointed Jesus to teach the people His laws of worship and morality. Jesus was also endowed with miraculous powers of healing the sick and restoring sight to the blind. Jesus had 12 students who helped him spread his teachings, and those laws are compiled in the New Testament. The Old Testament and the New Testament are what makes up The Bible, the sacred book for Christians. The followers of Jesus increased and since the Roman Empire controlled the area, the leaders of the empire felt threatened that Jesus was gaining power. Jesus was arrested and crucified. However, Christian teachings continued to be spread by his followers and students, and reached many parts of the world.

Christianity and Judaism were not widely practiced in Arabia. The Arabians there practiced polytheism, where they worshipped different gods and idols of their own making. In 570 AD, a baby named Muhammad was born in Mecca. His ancestry is traced back to one of Abraham's sons, Ishmael. Mecca was on a famous trade route to different parts of Asia, and it was a center for polytheism, where the idols of different tribes were placed at a shrine named the Kaaba, and people from all over Arabia came to worship their idols. This boosted the economy for the Meccans and they made great wealth as a result of this yearly pilgrimage, as well as placing them in a position of great power among the Arabs. As Muhammad grew up and practiced trade, he became known for his honesty and hard work. At the age of 40, Muhammad was appointed to be God's messenger and, spread the teachings of monotheism and morality to the people.

As Islam spread, the powerful people of Mecca were disturbed. They were concerned that the teachings of monotheism and brotherhood in Islam would interfere with their income and upset the balance of power. Muslims in Mecca were persecuted and they were forced to move to Medina, another town in Arabia about 200 miles away. There, Islam spread and grew strong, and the Muslims were able to return to Mecca 13 years later in a victory where no blood was shed. The teachings of Islam are compiled in the Quran, the holy book for the Muslims.

At the dawn of Islam, the Byzantine Empire had been the center for Christianity and its capital was Constantinople. Slowly, Islam began to spread to this empire. In the 1300s the Turks,a Muslim group from central Asia, moved to Anatolia and within a century and a half, they came to power and renamed the city of Constantinople to Istanbul, the capital of the Ottoman Empire. The Ottomans controlled the entire area of the Middle East, and they were great supporters of science, the arts and architecture, and they believed in religious freedom. They developed a thriving trade with Europe and many European influences spread in the empire.

In 1922, the Ottoman Empire gave way to European colonization, and most countries in the region became colonies of Europe. Even though the people in the area resented colonization, western influences in education, government and culture spread. At the end of the period of colonization, all of the countries were given independence. Answering the need to create a Jewish State in the Middle East and in reaction to the persecution of Jews in Europe during World War II, the United Nations partitioned Palestine into two states, a national homeland for the Jews in its former colony, and a Palestinian State. The Jews immediatlely accepted the resolution, and the surrounding Arab states rejected it. Jews from all over the world immigrated to Palestine. At this time, the inhabitants of Palestine had been Palestinian Arabs consisting of Jews, Christians and Muslims. These people did not accept the sudden loss of their land to the Jews. Most of the Arabs in the region felt that way too.

However, the nation of Israel was stronger and has been supported by the U.S. Israelis were able to make a home there and occupy some of the lands that were not patitioned to them by the UN, displacing many of the Palestinians. This has been the cause of several wars and tensions in the region, and has yet to be resolved.

Another important factor that has shaped the development of the Middle East is the discovery of great amounts of oil reserves in the Arabian Peninsula in the 1960s. This led to a great surge of international trade, wealth, modernization and westernization. Standards of living for the countries of the Persian Gulf improved and their nations were able to hold important positions in influencing world economy.

In 1990, Iraq invaded the small nation of Kuwait in an attempt to take over some of its oil. The U.S. intervened and Iraq was quickly defeated in the Gulf War, but U.S. military presence in the region continued long past the war. This angered many people in the region, and they saw the war as an excuse the Americans use to secure their grasp on the oil rich countries. In September 2001, terrorists attacked several locations in the U.S. homeland, killing thousands of innocent civilians. In response, the U.S. invaded Afghanistan, in an effort to root out the terrorists. The nations of the Middle East were outraged by this and saw U.S. policy as being uncalled for. An entire people were being bombed in order to punish a small number of terrorists, who may or may not be hiding in Afghanistan. More recently, the U.S. invaded Iraq, claiming that Iraq owned weapons of mass destruction. Even though no weapons were found, U.S. invasion of Iraq continued. These military actions by the U.S., along with the U.S. continued support of Israel are causing most people in the Middle East to feel that the U.S. policy in the Middle East is extreme and unjust. Middle Eastern governments have had a growing problem in maintaining credibility in the eyes of their people. People believe that the governments are not sufficiently expressing their concerns and are trying to appease the United States because it is a superpower.

Skill 11.4   Recognize the effects of location, climate, physical characteristics, the distribution of natural resources, and population size on the development of North Africa/Southwest Asia

The location of the Middle East has long made it a crossroads of trade and civilizations, connecting Africa, Asia and Europe. In the desert areas and most of the Arabian Peninsula, the weather is hot and dry. People have settled along the coasts, and nomads continue to live in the desert, moving their settlements from place to place. Other places such as Turkey and Iran receive sufficient rain to support a farming industry. In Egypt, the population is densely concentrated around the banks of the river Nile, where both farmland and water are available.

Remnants of historical civilizations in some areas such as Egypt, Israel, Iraq and Iran make them popular tourist destinations. In addition, the mountains of Iran provide good skiing activity. More recently, the Red Sea on the coast of Egypt has been gaining popularity for scuba diving.

Until the discovery of oil in the Middle East, there were no significant natural resources as water and farmland were limited. The discovery of oil has been the cause of great development in all areas of life for many countries in the Arabian Peninsula. These countries have been able to afford great wealth and prosperity for their people and have very high living standards. Other countries in the region do not have a wealth of oil and are struggling to support their growing populations. Cairo, Egypt is one of the largest, most densely populated cities in the world. Most people live on the banks of the Nile, where farmland and water supply used to be plentiful. However, the exploding population and the use of valuable farmland for buildings and roads have caused a shortage both in farmland and water. Egypt is suffering from widespread unemployment and increasing poverty and the government is constantly being criticized for not being able to improve conditions for the people.

The political tensions in the region have taken a toll on its development and prosperity. The Israeli-Palestinian conflict casts a shadow over the political stability of the region, and the wars in Kuwait, Iraq, Lebanon and tensions in Syria have placed a constant drain on the resources of these countries and affected the tourism industry in particular.

Skill 11.5 **Recognize the effects of human-environment interaction on the development of North Africa/Southwest Asia and the approaches North African/Southwest Asian countries have taken to address these and other environmental problems**

The region of North Africa and southwest Asia is challenged with several environmental problems, some due to modernization and development. Most areas do not receive enough rain and farmland has to be watered by expensive methods of irrigation. The oil industry has spurred rapid development in the oil producing countries, but oil spills and air pollution problems have increased. In 1990, Iraq set fire to the oilfields of Kuwait, burning off millions of gallons of oil and creating air conditions that have caused many respiratory illnesses.

Other countries such as Egypt have undergone a population explosion that has created numerous environmental concerns. There is shortage of clean water and farmland has been taken over to build houses, factories and roads. There have been lax laws to protect the environment from industrial waste, and as a result, Cairo is one of the most polluted cities in the world. The city of Cairo is extremely crowded and some people are living in areas that do not have access to water and electricity. Poverty is also increasing in other parts of North Africa. Governments are trying to address environmental problems, especially those caused by industries polluting the environment, but too much damage has already been done, and the success of government attempts to remedy the problems has been limited.

Skill 11.6 **Demonstrate knowledge of the basic structure of North African/Southwest Asian governments and analyze the effects of ethnic conflicts and civil wars on North African/Southwest Asian governments**

There are two main kinds of governments in the Middle East. Most countries of the Arabian Peninsula, Jordan and Morocco have been monarchies throughout their history. These monarchies are led by kings or emirs who have significant power. Other monarchies have been replaced by republics in recent history. Egypt founded a republic in 1952 after a peaceful revolution. Tunisia's monarchy was also replaced after a revolution, and the Republic of Iran was founded in 1979 after the Islamic Revolution drove the Shah (king) out of Iran and put a republic government in power.

Most of the governments in the Middle East, whether monarchies or republics have authoritarian regimes. Kings or presidents have unlimited power and are able to override legislature and issue impromptu laws. In many countries, only one political party is permitted, and in others with multiple parties, the party supporting the government is allowed more freedom and power. Recently, there has been a movement toward more democracy. Some true elections have been held in several places, such as Iran.

Legislature in the countries of the Middles East consists of Islamic law or sharia and other laws or adaptations specific to each country and culture. Countries that were colonies of Europe have adopted a blend of Islamic and western law.

Israel is the only nation in the region whose government is democratic in the western sense of the word. There are multiple parties, real elections, the president has limited power, and the affairs of the country are run by the parliament. The United States has had close ties with Israel almost since its independence. Palestinians living in the West Bank do not have the right to vote in elections like Israeli citizens. Conflict in Israel exists because the Palestinians do not accept the existence of a Jewish country and consider them as a foreign occupation. Actions from Palestinian forces have included suicide bombings, car bombings, kidnappings, and other military actions. Israel also has engaged in the conflict by engaging in preemptive strikes.

Political tensions, wars and civil wars have placed pressure on the governments and resources of all the governments in the Middle East. The major issue is the Israeli-Palestinian conflict, and more recently the American presence in Iraq, seen by many as a foreign invasion. There is general dissatisfaction with the performance of the governments, both domestically and in foreign policy. Within countries, people in several areas are suffering from poor living standards, unemployment and growing poverty. Governments have not been effective in addressing these problems. People are also feeling oppressed by the growing power of Israel, supported by the U.S. The people of the region feel that the U.S. is turning a blind eye to the injustices performed by Israel against the Arabs. American military action in Iraq has fanned these feelings. Governments are under continuous pressure from their people to take a bolder stand against the U.S. and indicate their support to the Arabs more clearly. The governments are not able to do that because they receive substantial financial aid and political support from the U.S. As dissatisfaction and loss of hope among the people grow as a result of government inaction, social problems are increasing, including drug abuse, crime, and for a few, falling prey to the ideas of terrorism.

Skill 11.7 **Identify major features of the different types of economic systems found in North Africa/Southwest Asia, recognize the involvement of North Africa/Southwest Asia in international trade and analyze factors that have influenced economic growth in various parts of the region**

The countries of the Arabian Peninsula originally made their living from fishing and pearl diving. The sudden discovery of oil in their land brought large scale development and great wealth to them and placed them in a powerful position in world economy. The oil rich countries joined together to form the **OPEC (Organization of the Petroleum Exporting Countries)** which would allow them to sell their oil to the world and agree on its price. Today, this region of the Middle East produces and exports most of the oil in the world and has undergone great modernization in all aspects.

Other countries in the region have little or no oil and have much lower living standards. The people of these countries often seek employment in the oil producing countries in order to raise their living standards. Egypt has enough oil to meet its own needs, but not enough to make it a wealthy country, with respect to the size of its population. Egypt has a sizeable farming industry, as well as tourism and trade of certain hand made goods. Israel is not rich in oil, but it has a well developed economy, and depends on huge U.S. financial aid. Israel depends on farming and high tech industry as its sources of income.

Political instability, wars and incidents of terrorism in the region have placed a strain on the economy and have discouraged foreign investments.

Skill 11.8 **Demonstrate familiarity with major literary, artistic, and musical forms of the peoples of North Africa/Southwest Asia**

There are various forms of art and literature that are popular in the Middle East. **Storytelling** is an important form of preserving the heritage of nations, and it is especially practiced in countries with rich civilizations, such as Iran, Iraq, Syria and Egypt. Storytelling takes several forms such as eloquent prose, poetry and drama. A famous group of tales called *One Thousand and One Nights* tells short stories that have rich cultural content from all over the region. **Poetry** is another respected form of art, and the Arabs were once known for their beautiful poetry and expression, which gave them some prestige among their neighbors. Calligraphy is a decorative style of writing practiced by the Muslims.

Calligraphers are talented artists who devote many years to learning how to form the elegant strokes of calligraphy. Some copies of the Quran are written in calligraphy and often paintings and wall decorations consist of short quotes from the Quran, written in calligraphy.

Another form of art seen in the buildings is Islamic architecture, which combines elements of elegant design with decorative aspects characteristic of the palaces and dwellings of early Muslim civilizations.

Iran and Turkey are famous for beautiful handmade **rugs** which are very valuable antiques and decorative items. Also, pottery and metal crafts using copper and silver are age old crafts. Craftsmen spend their lives creating such products and souvenirs which are sold in traditional stores and bazaars.

References for Skills 11.1 to 11.8

World Regions: Adventures in Time and Place. McGraw-Hill, 1998.

COMPETENCY 12.0   UNDERSTAND MAJOR HISTORICAL, SOCIAL, ECONOMIC, AND POLITICAL DEVELOPMENTS IN SOUTHERN AND EASTERN ASIA AND THE GEOGRAPHIC FACTORS INFLUENCING THEM.

Skill 12.1   Demonstrate knowledge of the location and characteristics of the major physical and political features of Southern and Eastern Asia

Asia is the largest continent geographically and the most populated. Southern Asia consists of Bangladesh. British Indian Ocean Territory, Bhutan, India, Maldives, Nepal, Pakistan, Sri Lanka, Afghanistan, Iran, and Tibet. South Asia contains largely struggling economies depending on agriculture and natural resources to support the economy. **India** is the largest and most diverse economy in the region with the **second highest population** in the world. The climate of the area is a challenge mostly tropical and arid. Governments varies from the republic form of government in countries like India, Nepal, Bangladesh, Sri Lanka, Maldives and Pakistan, a theocratic republic in Iran and an Islamic republic in Afghanistan.

Eastern Asia contains some of the world largest economies including People's Republic of China, Hong Kong, Macau, Taiwan, Japan, Mongolia, Democratic People's Republic of Korea (north) and Republic of Korea (south). All but Mongolia and North Korea are diverse and thriving economies. Mongolia is rich in natural resources. North Korea struggles economically. Much of the region is tropical, although Japan, Taiwan and Korea have large coastlines. China is the largest country geographically in the region and is largely mountainous. China has administrative oversight over Hong Kong and Macau. Taiwan maintains greater independence but is an area claimed by China. The government of the region is largely democratic excepted for Communist China and North Korea.

Southeastern Asia is a densely populated area, and includes Cambodia, Laos, Malaysia, Burma, Singapore, Thailand, Vietnam, Brunei, East Timor, Indonesia, and the Philippines. A number of the countries including Cambodia, Vietnam, and Laos are recovering from civil wars. Cambodia and Vietnam are Communist countries; Burma is a military controlled communist country; Thailand, Brunei and Malaysia are constitutional monarchies; and Singapore, Indonesia, East Timor, and Philippines are democracies. The region has a tropical climate and struggling economies. Malaysia, Singapore, and Thailand are the most advanced economies in Southeast Asia.

Throughout Asia poverty remains high and the region struggles with a variety of health and environmental problems.

Skill 12.2 **Identify the major ethnic groups of Southern and Eastern Asia, including indigenous groups and peoples from other regions of the world, and demonstrate knowledge of their areas of settlement, religions, customs, and traditions**

See also Skill 12.3

Asia is a diverse region ethnically. In Southern Asia each country has diverse ethnic groups. Bangladesh is primarily Bengali in origin. The Bengali culture developed in India. Portions of India also maintain the Bengali culture. Indo-Aryan is the dominant ethnic group in India and in various forms throughout the region tracing its origins to Iran. Southern India is dominated by Dravidians believed to come to India from the Middle East and migrated to Pakistan and Bangladesh. The culture of the region was influenced by European culture due to the colonization of the region. Half the population of Iran is Persian while the rest of the population is smaller ethnic groups including Azeri, Kurds and Turks.

Eastern Asia is largely Chinese in China, Taiwan, Hong Kong and Macau; Japanese in Japan; and Korean on the Korean peninsula. Ethnically the countries are very homogeneous. Southeast Asia is primarily Chinese and indigenous people such as Malay, Burman, and Khmer.

Major religions throughout the region include Muslim (Afghanistan, Indonesia, Pakistan, and Iran); Buddhism (Burma, Cambodia, Japan, South Korea, Taiwan, Thailand, and Sri Lanka); Christianity (Philippines, East Timor) and Hindu (India, Nepal). Taoism is a native Chinese religion with worship of more deities than almost any other religion. It teaches all followers to make the effort to achieve the two goals: happiness and immortality. Shinto is the native religion of Japan developed from native folk beliefs worshipping spirits and demons in animals, trees, and mountains. According to its mythology, deities created Japan and its people, which resulted in worshipping the emperor as a god. Shinto was strongly influenced by Buddhism and Confucianism but never had strong doctrines on salvation or life after death.

While countries tend to have a dominant religion, other religions are present in the country and can account for a large number of people. For instance, while 82% of India population is **Hindi** and 13% **Muslim**, means over 130 million Muslims live in India, one of the largest concentrations in the world. China and North Korea are officially atheistic. Much of the region is very traditional in customs adhering strictly to religious teachings. In India, the **caste system,** which establishes a hierarchal society, remains in practice. Additionally, while contact with western society has begun to change Asian culture, traditional views of women-dress, habits-particular outside of cosmopolitan areas remain common practices.

Skill 12.3 **Demonstrate knowledge of the origins and spread of Hinduism and Buddhism, important trade and technological developments in China, why China ceased to trade with other parts of the world in the fifteenth century and Chinese reaction to later European efforts to force relations with China, European colonialism in southern and eastern Asia, and major developments in southern and eastern Asia during the twentieth century**

Hinduism is the world third largest religion and is considered the oldest religion. . It is believed to have developed as early as 4000 BC in India and has spread throughout the region and globally. **Brahman** is the supreme deity of the religion. Hinduism recognizes various gods which represent different aspects of Brahman, and believes in the concept of reincarnation of the soul. The goal of life is to achieve an oneness with God, Nirvana. Actions in one life prescribe the lesson plan for the next life. Achieving a unity with God can be achieved through yoga or paths including love, meditation, wisdom or action. Vedas, Upanishads and Bhagavad-Gita are among the supreme texts of the religion.

Buddha was a Hindu, born of a royal family who lived during 5 BC. Buddha's teachings have developed into a major world religion. Having grown out of Hinduism, many of the principles of Hinduism were adopted in Buddhism. Buddhists recognize the four noble truths – the existence of suffering, caused by desire, and suffering can be stopped by following the Eightfold Path. The Eightfold Path prescribes a way of life which includes right views, actions, speech, conduct, livelihood, effort, thoughts and meditation. Buddha's teachings framed the beliefs of the religion. The Vinaya Pitaka, Sutra Pitaka and Abhidharma Pitaka are the supreme texts of the religion. Buddhism spread throughout the region to China, Korea, Japan and ultimately globally.

China is considered by some historians to be the oldest, uninterrupted civilization in the world and was in existence around the same time as the ancient civilizations founded in **Egypt**, **Mesopotamia**, and the **Indus Valley**. The Chinese studied nature and weather; stressed the importance of education, family, and a strong central government; followed the religions of Buddhism, Confucianism, and Taoism; and invented such things as gunpowder, paper, printing, and the magnetic compass.

China began building the Great Wall; practiced crop rotation and terrace farming; increased the importance of the silk industry, and developed caravan routes across Central Asia for extensive trade. Also, they increased proficiency in rice cultivation and developed a written language based on drawings or pictographs (no alphabet symbolizing sounds as each word or character had a form different from all others). Ancient China was a land in constant turmoil.

Tribes warred with one another almost from the first, with the **Great Wall of China** being a consolidation of walls built to keep out invaders. The Great Wall was built at the direction of China's emperor, and the idea of an emperor or very strong "government of one" was the rule of law until the twentieth century. Chinese people became very proficient at producing beautiful artworks and exporting them, along with silk, to the rest of the world along the **Silk Road**.

During the fifteenth century China developed a fleet of vessels which successfully traded as far as Africa. Some believe the Chinese may have sailed to North America before Columbus. Fearing a shift of power because of the success of the trading fleets, the emperor was convinced by advisors to destroy the fleet because the trade threatened Chinese culture. This led to isolationist policies that would keep China closed to the rest of the world.

Europe began searching for alternative routes to the Silk Road to the east. A common belief was that by sailing west from Europe a ship could reach the Far East. Many explorers followed this quest. During the early sixteenth century **Ferdinand Magellan**, sailing for Portugal led a fleet around the tip of Africa and ultimately led to Portuguese control of the Indian Ocean and the colonization of Macau. Portugal also developed a presence in Japan. Soon, other European countries followed. Spain claimed the Philippines, the Dutch claimed Indonesia and Taiwan, the British annexed Burma and parts of India and Hong Kong, and the French claimed Indochina including Laos, Vietnam, Cambodia and part of China. Thailand or Siam was pressured from both the British and the French.

The presence of European ultimately led to China developing trading partnerships. Much of the silver mined in Mexico and South America between the sixteenth and nineteenth century was sent to China in exchange for silk and other items. Later the silver commodity was replaced with tobacco. The British also used opium as a trading commodity and began trading opium with China, despite a ban on the use of opium by the China government. This led to mass addictions and problems in China. Ultimately two opium wars between the British and Chinese forced China to legalize the importation of opium and to cede areas to Britain.

The civilization in **Japan** borrowed much of their culture from China. It was the last of these classical civilizations to develop. Although they used, accepted, and copied Chinese art, law, architecture, dress, and writing, the Japanese refined these into their own unique way of life, including incorporating the religion of Buddhism into their culture. Early Japanese society focused on the emperor and the farm, in that order. The Sea of Japan protected Japan from more than Chinese invasion, including the famous Mongol invasion that was blown back by the "divine wind." The power of the emperor declined as it was usurped by the era of the Daimyo and his loyal soldiers, the **Samurai**.

Japan flourished economically and culturally during many of these years, although the policy of isolation the country developed kept the rest of the world from knowing such things. Buddhism and local religions were joined by Christianity in the sixteenth century, but it wasn't until the mid-nineteenth century that Japan rejoined the world community.

A period of Japanese isolation ended with **Admiral Matthew Perry's** arrival in Japan in 1853 to force trade and diplomacy. In the later 1800s, Japan's growing military strength led to their desire to expand borders. Japan annexed Taiwan and other islands following the Sino-Japanese war in 1894. In 1898, Japan defeated Russia and claimed part of the Manchurian peninsula. Additional land was taken from Russia following a second war in 1904-05. In 1910, Korea became part of Japan. Japanese imperialism continued through World War II. During the 1930s Japan claimed all of Manchuria, invaded both China and Indochina. Japan developed an alliance with Germany and Italy. The United States pressure for economic sanctions against Japan ultimately led to the Japanese attack on Pearl Harbor which in turn, led to the United States' entry in World War II. Japan surrendered following the dropping of two atomic bombs on Hiroshima and Nagasaki.

Following the war, the Japanese military was disbanded and democratic reforms were introduced. The United States protected Japan through the post war years. Japan focused on building its manufacturing capacity and industry, as opposed to military industry. This has led to the development of one of the largest economies in the world.

The spread of communism throughout Asia began following World War II. Mao Tse-Tung led the Chinese revolutionaries in defeat the military controlled Nationalist government of Chiang Kai-Shek. The Nationalist Government moved to Taiwan following their defeat in 1949. Mao ruled China till his death in 1976. The United States and other countries did not recognize the government of Taiwan as the Chinese government until the 1970s. While China remains Communist, in recent years it has adopted a more market based economy which has led to rapid economic growth in the country.

Following World War II, a series of military conflicts developed. The Soviet Union regained control of Manchuria and agreed with the United States to divide control of Korea. The Soviet Union was responsible for the North and the United States for the South, pending negotiations on reunification of the country. An agreement was never reached. North Korea developed a Communist regime, while the South adopted a republic form of government. In 1950 North Korea crossed the 38th parallel which divided the country and attacked the South. South Korea supported by the United States and the United Nations was able push the North back, despite having the support of both Russia and China. An armistice agreement was negotiated. Korea remains a divided country today.   South Korea economically has flourished while the North remains challenged.

Asian countries gained their independence from foreign control in the aftermath of World War II. The United States controlled the Philippines following Spain's defeat in the Spanish-American war until 1946 when the country was given its independence. Indonesia gained its independence from the Netherlands. An agreement was reached to divide French Indochina into North and South Vietnam. North Vietnam supported by the Soviet Union and China developed a Communist State. Vietnam won its initial independence from France during the 1950s. During the late 1950s the north attempted to foster rebellion in the south and supported the sending of guerrilla rebels to the south. The United States came to the aid of the South. War continued through 1973 when a cease-fire was agreed to and the United States troops left South Vietnam. Ultimately the South was defeated by the North. Conflict also broke out in Cambodia and Laos leading to the creation of communist regimes. Cambodia has since adopted a democratic form of government.

India gained its independence from Great Britain in 1947. India was partitioned into India and Pakistan. Pakistan initially was a country divided into East and West Pakistan separated by India. A revolution in 1971 in East Pakistan led to the establishment of Bangladesh. Tensions remain between India and Pakistan over land claims.

Afghanistan after a long civil war won its independence from the Soviet Union. Recently following the September 11 attack on the World Trade Center, the United States invaded the country and restored a republic form of government. Afghanistan was harboring terrorists. Afghanistan continues to be the world's largest producer of opium.

Skill 12.4 Recognize the effects of location, climate, physical characteristics, the distribution of natural resources, and population size on the development of southern and eastern Asia

Forty percent of Asians live in urbanized area, some of the most densely populated cities in the world. The Asian cities of Singapore, Beijing, Tokyo, Calcutta, Shanghai, Hong Kong, Delhi, Karachi, Jakarta, Tehran, Bangkok, Bombay, Lahore, Dacca, Bangalore, Wuhan, Tianjin, Canton, Chongqing, Shenyang, Busan, Hyderabad, Yokohama, Seoul, Pyongyang, Ahmadabad, and Chennai are in the top fifty most populated cities in the world. Only New York City and Los Angeles of the United States cities are in the top fifty. There has been a large migration from rural areas to cities which has challenged the capacity of the urban centers to meet the needs of the community not just in jobs, but housing, sewage, food and health care. The availability of inexpensive labor has led to the development of industrial and manufacturing companies throughout the region which has exploded foreign trade.

Portions of the region such as Pakistan, Afghanistan, Iran, and Mongolia are desert or arid making the development of land for agriculture or grazing difficult. Herding of goats, sheep and camels is common in areas less conducive to agriculture. Much of Asia is devoted to agriculture. Many small farmers are not able to produce an adequate supply of food products to support their family. As subsistence farmers, the entire family works the land. Rice and grains are staple crops of the region. The tropic location allows for year round growing. Meat products are less available.

Large scale farming is often encouraged to allow for exporting. Items such as rubber, coffee, tea and sugar are produced for export. The Communist countries followed the Soviet Union model of state-owned farms or collectives. Fishing is also common. As timber is exploited, deforestation became a problem throughout the region.

The area is also rich in natural resources. China, Mongolia, and India have a variety of mineral deposits. Oil production occurs in China and offshore in Vietnam and Malaysia. Some of the highest mountains are located in the region in the Himalayans mountain range. Mount Everest, the highest mountain in the world is located in the Himalayas.

Some countries such as Afghanistan, North Korea, Vietnam, Laos, and Cambodia continue to struggle economically.

Skill 12.5   Recognize the effects of human-environment interaction on the development of southern and eastern Asia and the approaches the countries of southern and eastern Asia have taken to address these and other environmental problems

Air and water pollution is a common in Asian countries. Particularly in urban centers, air pollution from automobiles and industrial activity is a major problem. Air pollution in overpopulated urban centers from increasing automobile use has led to efforts to restrict automobiles and development of mass transit approaches. Forest fires and increased use of fossil fuels in industrial production has led to greater pollution throughout the region. Rapid industrialization has contributed to the rapidly growing environmental problems throughout Asia. A haze is common to most cities.

Water is a major resource of the region. Water pollution and declining water tables is a problem as well. Pollution is primarily caused by chemicals from industrialization and poor sanitation practices. In larger urban centers, adequate water and sanitation for the population challenges the cities. Water pollution from the increased use of pesticides and other chemicals is common. Food and water borne diseases is a concern throughout the region. Shortage of water is also a frequent occurrence. Water pollution can also impact the quality of marine life and thus food production of the area.

The growth of Asian pollution is forcing greater attention to environmental regulation. Japan, a successful example has been successful in reducing pollution throughout industrial regulation, improved transportation and personal regulation. Greater global attention is being focused on the Asia pollution problem because of the negative effect it is having on the planet. World organizations provide technical expertise as well as resources to help address the problem. Control and regulation of automobiles is becoming more common in larger cities.

Skill 12.6 Demonstrate knowledge of the basic structure of the governments of southern and eastern Asia

Largely, the governments of the region adopted various models from European examples. The republic is the dominant form where power of government is limited and a central government is elected by the citizens of the country. Countries following this form of government include East Timor, India, Indonesia, Iran (although Iran is a theocratic republic), Afghanistan (an Islamic republic), South Korea, Pakistan, Sri Lanka, Singapore. Countries tend to have the three branches of government Executive, Legislative and Judicial. Several countries, such as Bangladesh and Mongolia, have a parliamentarian form of government where the dominate party in the legislative branch selects the Prime Minister of the country. Several countries have constitutional monarchies including Bhutan, Brunei, Cambodia (combined with a multiparty democracy), Japan (combined with a parliamentary government), Malaysia and Thailand. Taiwan has a multiparty democracy. China, North Korea, Laos and Vietnam are communist states controlled by a dictator or the Communist Party structure. Macau and Hong Kong under China's control have limited democracy. Burma's government is controlled by the military.

Skill 12.7 Identify major features of the different types of economic systems found in southern and eastern Asia, recognize the involvement of these regions in international trade and the importance of the Pacific Rim in trade and economic development, and analyze factors that have influenced economic growth in various parts of these regions

A number of countries are struggling economies depending on international aid to sustain the economy. These economies include Afghanistan, Bangladesh, East Timor, North Korea (has limited foreign aid), Laos (developing a free market approach), Nepal, Pakistan, Sri Lanka and Vietnam.

Burma is resource rich in oil, gas and timber but has been slow to develop the private investment needed to advance. Cambodia is recovering from years of war and is beginning to encourage investment and textile exports.

The largest economy in the region, China has shifted from a centralized state-controlled system common to communist regimes to a more market-oriented approach which has successfully developing trade to fuel growth. Foreign investment has expanded in China in recent years. Both Macau and Hong Kong are under the administrative control of China and have been able to maintain their free market systems which promote exports.

Successful free market systems include some of the largest economies in the world. Japan, Singapore, Taiwan and North Korea are highly industrialized and diversified. Additionally Philippines, India, Indonesia, Brunei, Thailand and Indonesia are strong free market economies which have the infrastructure in place to foster economic growth.

While the economic growth is bright for many countries, the large population and the high degree of poverty throughout the region is a challenge which will require international support to address.

Skill 12.8   Demonstrate familiarity with major literary, artistic, and musical forms of the peoples of southern and eastern Asia

Asian **art** forms have been shaped by the belief and traditions of the **religions** of the region-Islam, Hinduism and Buddhism. As elsewhere, the development of art and literature was supported by the noble class. Asian art takes various forms from metal-bronze and silver-sculpture to painting of a variety of forms. The themes of art are often drawn from religious history and great religious figures like Buddha. Portraits of country rulers' are common. Some of the earliest forms of paintings where done on **scrolls** or **silk**. In China and Japan, screens and fans decorated with art was popular. In addition to religious themes, landscape themes are common. Music and dance developed traditionally as part of special events and ceremonies. Special puppet theaters and shadow play are part of the art of the region. Instruments made from bamboo, bronze and other materials have been found and dated back hundreds of years, BCE.

COMPETENCY 13.0 UNDERSTAND MAJOR HISTORICAL, SOCIAL, ECONOMIC, AND POLITICAL DEVELOPMENTS IN AUSTRALIA AND OCEANIA AND THE GEOGRAPHIC FACTORS INFLUENCING THEM.

Skill 13.1 Demonstrate knowledge of the location and characteristics of the major physical and political features of Australia and Oceania

Australia and Oceania are located mostly in the Southern Hemisphere in the eastern part of the Pacific Ocean. The region is made up mostly of islands. The continent of Australia is the largest landmass in the region, with New Guinea and the islands of New Zealand as the largest islands.

Australia is the smallest continent in the world, and is the only continent that is also a single country. It is bordered on the east by the Pacific Ocean and on the west by the Indian Ocean. The major land areas of Australia include a wide plateau in the western part of the country that covers two thirds of the continent. In the central part of the continent are the Central Lowlands, a large flat region that was formerly the bed of an ancient sea. These lowlands cover about one quarter of the continent. The Eastern Highlands run along the eastern coast of Australia and include rugged, mountainous terrain. Between the highlands and the ocean coast is a strip of coastal lowlands where most of Australia's population lives. Sydney, Australia's largest city is on the southeastern Pacific Coast. The capital is Canberra.

Oceania is a term used to refer to the large island-populated region of the South Pacific, including the countries of Indonesia, Papua New Guinea, and New Zealand. Many smaller island nations are also considered part of Oceania.

Indonesia is one of the world's most populous countries and is made up of thousands of islands. It is located north of Australia. Jakarta the capital and largest city in Indonesia, is also one of the most densely populated areas of the world. Jakarta has a population of over 23 million people and is part of an even larger megalopolis.

Off the northeastern coast of Australia is the Island of New Guinea, which is divided into Papua, a province of Indonesia, and Papua New Guinea, an independent country formerly controlled by Australia. The country of New Zealand is southeast of Australia and is made up of two long, narrow, mountainous islands. Auckland is the capital of New Zealand, and the largest city in the country.

Oceania also contains several smaller island nations as well as islands that are territories or parts of other countries outside the region. Hawaii, for instance, although an American state, is culturally and geographically closely related to Oceania.

Skill 13.2   Identify the major ethnic groups of Australia and Oceania, including indigenous groups and peoples from other regions of the world, and Demonstrate knowledge of their areas of settlement, religions, customs, and traditions

Australia and New Zealand were colonized by Europeans beginning in the eighteenth century and most of the current residents of these countries are of European descent. The native populations of these countries were largely disregarded or displaced by European settlers and their numbers declined. Their cultures survived among the remaining indigenous inhabitants and in recent years Australia and New Zealand have taken steps to protect the cultures of indigenous peoples.

The indigenous people of Australia, sometimes called Aborigines, are a diverse people who lived in all areas of the continent. Prior to European contact, those on the coast and outlying islands relied heavily on fishing and subsistence agriculture for food, growing sugar cane, taro and sweet potato. They also domesticated the dingo and pigs. Indigenous Australians living in the interior sections of the continent were primarily hunter-gatherers and were semi-nomadic, moving from place to place over the course of the year. Some tribes returned to the same places every year and archaeological evidence shows that some of these places were used for thousands of years.

Indigenous Australians used wooden and stone weapons such as spears and the boomerang or throwing stick to hunt birds, kangaroo, and other animals. Insects and grubs were also a regular part of their diet. They often used fire to clear large areas of brush to improve hunting and encourage new plant growth, but they did not engage in any crop cultivation.

Indigenous Australian populations declined sharply after European settlement owing largely to disease and displacement. They currently make up less than 3% of the Australian population. The native people of New Zealand are known collectively as Maori. The Maori lived in small settlements centered on small plots of cultivated land and fishing. The Maori culture is a significant part of the history in New Zealand, and the Maori language is still spoken. There are presently approximately 600,000 people identifying themselves as Maori in New Zealand.

Many of the native people of the island of Papua still live in small villages as they have for thousands of years. The government of Papua New Guinea has passed legislation allowing these villages to have control over their traditional lands and has made efforts to protect this way of life. Some tribes of Papua sometimes practiced ritual cannibalism, which is now outlawed.

Indonesia is an ethnically diverse country with a strong nationalistic sentiment and a widely spoken common language, Indonesian. Islam is the dominant religion in Indonesia and it is the most populous Islamic nation in the world.

Skill 13.3 **Demonstrate knowledge of the reasons for British colonization of Australia, the effects of European diseases on the indigenous peoples of Australia and Oceania, and major developments in Australia and Oceania during the twentieth century**

In the eighteenth century, Britain regularly sent convicted prisoners out of the country to one of its colonies. Following the loss of the American colonies in the Revolutionary War, Britain needed to find another location to send convicts. As the Industrial Revolution started and urbanization resulted in denser populations and higher unemployment, Britain's prisoner situation grew more urgent.

Captain James Cook had visited Australia on his voyage in 1770, and the continent was chosen as the site of a new penal colony, to be established at Botany Bay near the southeastern coast. The first ship arrived in January 1788. The settlement was eventually established nearby at Sydney Cove. The colony had a rough start, but eventually gained a foothold, and Britain began to send more and more prisoners to Australia, about one-third of them Irish.

The arrival of Europeans had a similar impact on the indigenous people as it had in other colonial regions. Native peoples had little resistance to the diseases brought by the Europeans and fell victim in large numbers. Venereal disease became another problem in Australia's native population, affecting the birth rate. As European settlement expanded throughout Australia and Oceania, natives were usually displaced from their traditional lands by force, by treaty or by bargain.

Beginning in the early years of the twentieth century, nationalistic sentiment began to grow in Japan, as it sought to position itself as a world power. After joining World War I to fight against Germany and its allies, the Japanese navy began taking over German-controlled settlements in Oceania. Following the war, Japan was given control of these former German territories. During World War II, much of the fighting between Japan and the United States took place in Oceania, with New Zealand and Australia providing troops and strategic locations for the Allied effort.

Following the end of World War II, some of the countries of Oceania and the region were placed under control of the traditional colonial powers in the area, such as France and England, while some were placed under control of the countries that had emerged as major powers following the war, such as the U.S. and the Soviet Union. As tension between Soviet Russia and the U.S. rose and colonialism collapsed, the region became instable. The Korean War in the 1950s and the Viet Nam War in the 1960s and 1970s were results of this instability.

Skill 13.4   Recognize the effects of location, climate, physical characteristics, the distribution of natural resources, and population size on the development of Australia and Oceania

The former British colonies of Australia and New Zealand were very remote from the mother country, and were established much later than other British colonies such as those in America. These factors plus difficult conditions encountered by the early settlers resulted in relatively slow population growth in these two countries.

The populations of Australia and New Zealand today are very concentrated around urban areas, leaving wide expanses of land available for farming, ranching, forestry and mining. The relatively small populations of these countries make for lower domestic demand for these products, allowing them a competitive advantage over more populous countries in the world market. What was once a disadvantage in location because of its remoteness from Europe is now an advantage in its proximity to Asia.

Indonesia was an early destination for European traders because of valuable commodities such as nutmeg and cloves. The Dutch were the most successful in creating a near monopoly in the spice trade through the Dutch East India Company and established their colonial power over the region. This extensive trade activity brought people from all over the world to the islands, and Indonesia retains this wide diversity today.

The relative isolation of the thousands of smaller inhabited islands in Oceania allowed early native peoples to live largely without extensive contact with larger civilizations. These islands often had only enough natural resources to support a small population and so did not become targets for European or Asian trade or colonization. As the world economy has grown leaving almost no corner of the globe untouched, some of these small populations have been able to develop markets for tourism. Some populations are dwindling as new generations choose to leave for larger population centers.

Skill 13.5   Recognize the effects of human-environment interaction on the development of Australia and Oceania and the approaches the countries of Australia and Oceania have taken to address these and other environmental problems

The large majority of Australia's population lives along the eastern and southeastern coastline, between the Great Dividing Ridge and the sea. The desert climate of the interior, or "**Outback,**" of Australia was forbidding to the first European settlers, who chose the milder and more advantageously placed coastal regions for settlement.

The result is a dense concentration of Australia's population in urban areas, which impacted the environment by concentrating the use of resources and creating pollutants that enter the air, land and water. Australia's government has addressed these issues by encouraging "sustainable" cities through the use of clean power sources such as solar power and the production of household appliances that use less power and water.

Australia has also taken steps to reduce the production of ozone-depleting substances and greenhouse gases associated with global warming. One of the possible effects of global warming is a rise in sea level as more polar ice melts because of higher average temperatures. This is an especially crucial issue for Australia and Oceania where most of the population lives in coastal areas.

Global warming and the warming of the ocean water have an affect on the many coral reefs through the region. **Coral reefs** are large ridges of coral that develop along coastal edges that support a wide variety of organisms. Water temperature is very important to the survival of coral reefs. If the water stays warm for too long, the coral becomes "bleached" and dies.

Human activity also affects coral reefs by altering water quality. Pollutants from industrial and agricultural activity enter the sea and can be toxic to the coral or other species of plants and animals that live along the reef.

The largest coral reef on the planet is the **Great Barrier Reef** in the Coral Sea northeast of Australia. Australia has several industrial and agricultural areas along the coast opposite the reef that have been associated with changing water quality. As a result, Australia has taken steps to regulate water quality to ensure that pollution levels do not become dangerous for the survival of the reef system. Large portions of the reef have been set aside as reserve areas, where tourism and scientific exploration are important activities.

Skill 13.6   Demonstrate knowledge of the basic structure of the governments of Australia and Oceania and Australia's relationship to the United Kingdom

The Commonwealth of Australia was formed in 1901 out of six self-governing British colonies. With the passage of the Australian Constitution, each colony became a state in the new nation: New South Wales, Queensland, South Australia, Tasmania, Victoria and Western Australia. The mainland of Australia also includes two territories, the Northern Territory and the Australian Capital Territory. The constitution created a constitutional monarchy with a federal system of states sharing a common central government. The government is based on the ideal of the separation of powers, with separate executive, legislative and judicial branches.

The reigning monarch of England is the executive the Australian government, currently Queen Elizabeth II. Australia does not officially refer to her as the head of state, but as the Queen of Australia. A Governor General, whom she appoints on the recommendation of the Prime Minister, represents her in Australia.

The Prime Minister is the leader of the party that holds a majority of the House of Representatives and is the actual executive leader of the government. The Prime Minister appoints a cabinet of members of Parliament to lead the various governmental departments. The 150 seats in the House of Representatives are apportioned based on population and are filled by popular election. The Australian legislature also has an elected Senate of 76 members, which is made up of an equal number of Senators from each state, plus a smaller number elected from the territories.

Each state has its own sovereign parliament, as well, which cannot encroach upon the authority of the federal parliament or other state parliaments. Territories also have their own legislatures, which can be overruled by the federal parliament.

The High Court of Australia is the country's highest court. It has both appellate jurisdiction, hearing cases appealed from lower courts, and original jurisdiction, hearing cases that originate in the High Court. The High Court reviews legislation and can declare laws unconstitutional.

The government of New Zealand is similar to that of Australia and other former British Colonies in having a federal parliament led by a Prime Minister. New Zealand also recognizes the reigning monarch of Great Britain as the chief executive of the government, but vests actual power in an elected parliament. New Zealand differs from Australia in having only one legislative house, the House of Commons.

The government of Indonesia has undergone major reforms in recent years. Its basic structure is similar to parliamentary systems, but with an elected president and vice president. The legislature is called the People's Consultative Assembly and is made up of two houses, the Regional Representatives Council and the People's Representative Council. Indonesia has an independent Supreme Court, whose members are appointed by the president. The smaller island nations of Oceania have varying forms of government, often based on the forms imposed upon them by former colonial powers. Many small island territories have local governments but are still subject to the laws and government of the larger countries that claim them.

Skill 13.7 **Identify major features of the different types of economic systems found in Australia and Oceania, recognize the involvement of the region in international trade and the importance of the Pacific Rim in trade and economic development, and analyze factors that have influenced economic growth in various parts of the region**

Australia has a Western-style free market economy that relies heavily on service industries and export. Australia has a wealth of natural resources that it exports, including minerals, coal and natural gas. Agricultural products such as grain and wool are also important exports. Because Australia's exports are mainly raw commodities, the economy is subject to fluctuations in world prices. However, Australia has an advantage over other countries because its population is quite small compared to the size of the country. This places a lower domestic demand on these products, allowing Australia to compete in the world market.

New Zealand's economy is also heavily reliant on trade. New Zealand's principal exports are agricultural, including dairy, meat, fish, wool and forest products. New Zealand's economy has traditionally been tied closely to Great Britain's because of the trade concessions Great Britain extended to its dominions. In recent years, however, economic reforms and international agreements have allowed New Zealand to compete in global trade.

The country of Indonesia has a market-based economy that has significant government involvement in the form of state-owned industries and price controls. It is a significant exporter of **oil**. During the 1970s, revenue from oil exports spurred tremendous growth in the Indonesian economy. This growth outpaced Indonesia's regulatory and legal systems' ability to sustain the economy, and it entered into crisis in the 1980s and 1990s. In recent years, Indonesia has entered into agreements with international regulatory programs that have stabilized its economy and poised it for growth again.

The abundance of natural materials in Australia and Oceania have made the region an important part of the world economy. Extensive access to the sea to transport these materials worldwide has also contributed to the importance of trade within the domestic economies of the region. Proximity to growing Asian markets such as India and South Korea, as well as established economic powers like China and Japan, have aided the region in establishing a significant trade presence. The region is located along the Pacific Rim, which refers to the countries located around the edges of the Pacific Ocean, including the United States. Pacific Rim trade grew rapidly in the 1990s and is a large part of the world economy.

Skill 13.8   Demonstrate familiarity with major literary, artistic, and musical forms of the peoples of Australia and Oceania

The literary tradition of the indigenous people of Australia and Oceania is primarily oral, passed down from generation to generation without being written. Artistic forms of the Maori of New Zealand and the indigenous people of Australia are decorative and highly stylized, usually carved in wood or inscribed in stone. These decorations adorn their houses, canoes and tools. Their traditional music involves both voice and instruments, including the **didgeridoo** of Australia, an ancient wind instrument that creates a complex droning sound and requires mastering a special breathing technique to play. Early Portuguese explorers brought stringed instruments to some islands in Oceania, and these have become part of some musical traditions, such as the ukulele in Hawaii. Dance is an important part of many Polynesian cultures, as well, using stylized moves to convey meaning as in the Hawaiian hula tradition.

Indonesia has always been a diverse region with a wide variety of cultural influences. Wood and stone carvings have a long tradition in the region, with religious subjects taken from Buddhism, Hinduism, Confucianism and Islam. Indonesia also has a long tradition of dance, which is connected to the traditions of India and Thailand. The traditional music of Indonesia is played on the **gamelan**, a collection of drums, gongs and xylophones played by several musicians together. Drama and theater are also important parts of Indonesian culture. One popular form of drama uses elaborate shadow puppets to perform historical dramas.

The culture of modern Australia and New Zealand is closely associated with the western, English-speaking world and in particular the United Kingdom. Several internationally popular film actors and musicians have come from the region, and films and novels depicting the culture and people have been well received. The traditions of the indigenous peoples of Australia and New Zealand have had an influence on popular art and music of those countries. In literature, the English language has been enriched by the adoption of some of the native expressions and words that originated in the region.

DOMAIN III.   **GEORGIA STUDIES AND SOCIAL SCIENCE SKILLS**

COMPETENCY 14.0   **UNDERSTAND MAJOR DEVELOPMENTS IN GEORGIA HISTORY AND GEORGIA'S ROLE IN THE HISTORY OF THE UNITED STATES.**

Skill 14.1   **Locate major physical regions and features of Georgia and recognize the effects of climate and geography on the development of Georgia**

The geography of Georgia can be divided into six major regions:

The **Atlantic Coastal Plain** makes up the eastern part of the lower half of the state, bordering on the Atlantic Ocean. Rivers in this coastal plain drain into the Atlantic mainly through the Savannah River and its tributaries.

The **East Gulf Coastal Plain** makes up the western half of the lower part of the state. Rivers in this region drain into the Gulf of Mexico. The Suwannee River is the primary river of this region. The Okefenokee Swamp is partly in the East Gulf Coastal Plain and partly in the Atlantic Coastal Plain, at the southern end of the regions.

The **Piedmont** is a hilly region that cuts across the middle part of Georgia. It extends from the foot of the mountainous regions in the north to the edge of the coastal plains where the elevation drops rapidly, creating rapids and waterfalls where it is crossed by rivers. The Chattahoochee River runs from the northern elevations through the Piedmont.

The **Blue Ridge** mountain range extends into the northeastern corner of the state. These peaks rise to between 2,000 and 5,000 feet and are heavily forested. Georgia's highest point, Mount Etonah (4,784 ft.) is located in this region.

The **Appalachian Ridge and Valley Region** is in the northwest corner of the state. This region includes fertile valley plains between the sandstone ridges of the Appalachian system. A small portion of the **Appalachian Plateau** borders on this region in the extreme northwest. This plateau is about 2,000 feet above sea level.

Since the time of the earliest native settlements, Georgia's rivers have been the sites of its primary settlements. The first European settlement was made on the Savannah River near the Atlantic Coast, chosen for its access to the sea. The Europeans called the natives they found living in Georgia the Creek Indians after the site of their villages along the tributaries to the Savannah. Atlanta, Georgia's largest city and capital, is situated along the Chattahoochee River in the northern part of the state, relying on the river and its related tributaries for industry, drinking water and power.

Georgia's climate is mild in the winter and hot and humid in the summer, making it a good region for crop production, especially cotton. Cotton became the base of Georgia's economy and growth during the eighteenth and nineteenth centuries.

Skill 14.2   Demonstrate knowledge of Native American cultures of the southeastern United States and analyze the effects of European exploration and settlement on native groups in Georgia.

The Mississippian Culture was an early Native American culture that thrived throughout much of the eastern part of North America from approximately 800 to 1500 A.D. From this culture, which was centered on mound building and maize cultivation, many of the tribes and related cultures that were encountered by the first Europeans to explore the east coast of North America descended.

In the region that is now Georgia, the Cherokee and the Creek tribes were the primary groups that inhabited the area from the sixteenth century on.

The Cherokee lived partly in the southern Appalachian Mountains in what is now northern Georgia. They were an agricultural people who raised corn, beans and squash. They lived in numerous villages made up of 30 to 60 houses around a large counsel house.

The Creek were a confederacy of related tribes named after a group that lived mainly along the Ocmulgee River, which runs through the center of present day Georgia. The tribes were linked culturally and shared the same language, Muskogean. Like the Cherokee, the Creek were agricultural people who lived in villages.

In 1540, Hernando De Soto was the first European to describe the Native Americans living in the Georgia region. As European settlement in the new world advanced, they brought significant changes to the Native American groups in Georgia. New trade opportunities introduced European goods into Native communities, but sometimes also aggravated tensions between different tribes. Horses and firearms changed how warfare was waged. Natives were exposed to European diseases against which they had no natural defenses. Smallpox in particular became epidemic among Native Americans, decimating their populations.

Exposure to Europeans also brought advances to the Native American tribes. After being exposed to the Western system of writing, Sequoyah, a Cherokee man, invented an alphabet to represent the spoken Cherokee language, spurring the development of schools and widespread literacy among the tribe. The alphabet is still used today.

Skill 14.3   Identify major events of the colonial period of Georgia history

During the seventeenth century, the east coast of North America was rapidly settled by European colonists in the north and by the Spanish in the south. In 1670, the British colony of South Carolina was founded directly north of Spanish controlled Florida, creating a tense frontier in what is now Georgia. Military conflict followed until the Spanish missions were withdrawn in 1704 and the area occupied by Yamasee Native Americans friendly to the British.

Relations grew sour between the Yamasee and the British in 1715 over the fur trade, however, and the Yamasee began attacking British colonists. The colonists responded with force and the Yamasee were driven out of the area to Florida. This largely depopulated the coast region between Charleston, the capital of British Carolina, and St, Augustine, the capital of Spanish Florida.

In the early 1730s, James Oglethorpe, a British Member of Parliament, was engaged in a campaign of prison reform in England. English citizens who fell into debt could be thrown into debtor's prisons under deplorable conditions, where they were usually mistreated and often died. Oglethorpe presented a plan to colonize the newly available land in North America with some of these debtors to give them an opportunity to escape the horrors of prison and start over in the New World.

King George II approved Oglethorpe's scheme, and on June 9, 1732, granted a royal charter to him and a group of 20 other philanthropists to found a colony in North America. These 21 trustees called the new colony Georgia in honor of the king.

In the end, the first people chosen to go to the new colony were not debtors, but were chosen by the trustees based on their skills and professions and potential usefulness in the new colony. The first group of 114 people, including Oglethorpe, sailed from England on the *Anne* in November 1732, arriving in Charleston two months later. Oglethorpe scouted ahead into the Georgia region and selected a bluff on the Savannah River to build the first settlement, called Savannah.

Oglethorpe and the trustees wished to avoid duplicating England's strict class system in the new colony, which they felt had led to the practice of imprisoning debtors. They implemented a series of rules in the colony that prohibited slavery and required each man to work his own land. Identical houses were built on equal sized lots to emphasize the equality of all.

The peaceful agrarian community that was envisioned by Oglethorpe grew happily for a time, but positioned as it was on the British frontier with the Spanish, the realities of potential warfare occupied the colony's attentions. Oglethorpe successfully petitioned the British government to grant him military authority in the area and to provide him with a regiment of British troops to defend the frontier. He unsuccessfully attempted to capture St. Augustine, spurring a series of battles between the Spanish and British allied troops under Oglethorpe. The British emerged victorious after holding the line at the Battle of Bloody Marsh in 1742, after which the Spanish did not try to invade Georgia again.

Skill 14.4   **Demonstrate knowledge of Georgia's role in the American Revolution, analyze the strengths and weaknesses of the Georgia Constitution of 1777, and demonstrate knowledge of Georgia's role in the framing and adoption of the U.S. Constitution.**

As dissatisfaction with taxation increased in the northern colonies, similar rumblings began in Georgia, which joined the other colonies in 1765 in renouncing the Stamp Act. Georgia had prospered under its royal charter, however, and many Georgians believed that they needed British protection from neighboring Native Americans.

When news of the Battle of Lexington and Concord reached Georgia, patriotic resolve was strengthened and in May 1775, a group of patriots raided the arsenal at Savannah and took a supply of British gunpowder. Georgian colonists set up their own government shortly thereafter and joined the association of colonies in enforcing a ban on trade with the British. While British Governor James Wright was still the official authority in Georgia, the provincial government founded in July 1775 gave executive authority to a Council of Safety, which held the real power.

Wright was eventually expelled in 1776, after being held hostage by the colonists as British warships approached Savannah. Without a governor, provincial congress was convened at Augusta in April 1776, and a set of Rules and Regulations were adopted outlining a simple structure of government. Three delegates were sent to the Second Continental Congress in Philadelphia in time to sign the Declaration of Independence in July.

Three months later, a convention was called in Savannah to provide for a more permanent form of government in Georgia. The result of this convention was Georgia's first constitution, the Constitution of 1777. The new constitution created a single elected assembly that in turn chose a governor. This constitution was remarkable for its time in granting voting rights to a wide group of citizens, although only white men were allowed to vote. The Georgia Constitution also provided for future amendments by state convention. This provision, which was not included in all state constitutions at the time, eventually became common practice throughout the United States.

The Constitution of 1777 lacked many of the internal balances of political power that would be included in the United States Constitution, however, and serious movements began in 1788 to redraft it.

Following the American victory in the Revolutionary War, Georgia engaged with the rest of the new states in the debate over a federal constitution. Along with its southern neighbors, Georgia opposed a strong central government advocated by the Federalists, fearing the concentration of political power in the northern states. The Bill of Rights, the first ten amendments to the U.S. Constitution that spell out limits on governmental authority, were included in the proposed Constitution to ensure the rights of the states. In this way, Georgia and the other southern states greatly influenced the shape of the Constitution. Georgia ratified the U.S. Constitution in January 1788.

Skill 14.5   Recognize major social, religious, economic, and political developments in Georgia between 1789 and 1840.

In 1785, the Georgia General Assembly set aside a tract of land to be used for the establishment of a college or seminary. In 1798, a portion of the land was sold to raise funds to establish a university, and in 1799 the **University of Georgia** was officially founded. Classes began in 1801. The University of Georgia was the first state-chartered university in the United States.

Baptists have been present in Georgia since the first colonists arrived in 1733. At about that time, the Methodist denomination was developing in England and the American colonies during what is called the **First Great Awakening**. This protestant religious movement in the colonies emphasized a personal involvement in one's church and personal responsibility for sin and salvation. In Georgia, as elsewhere, protestant denominations gained in membership throughout the eighteenth century. The **Second Great Awakening** was a similar wave of religious zeal that moved through Georgia and the rest of the country in the early nineteenth century. Methodist and Baptist churches in particular saw huge growth. The Civil War cooled this revival in the North, but in the South, religious involvement was strengthened.

The **Yazoo land fraud** was a corrupt scheme involving several Georgia politicians, including Governor George Mathews, where public land was sold to private companies for extremely low prices. These companies included many state legislators as stockholders. When the details of the scheme became known, a scandal ensued which resulted in the election of reformer Jared Irwin as Governor. In 1796 Irwin nullified the act that had sold the land.

Before the invention of the cotton gin in 1793, cotton in Georgia was mainly grown only along the seaboard. The kind of cotton that would grow in these areas could be easily cleaned of seeds because of its long fibers. The **cotton gin** was a device that could clean the short-fiber cotton that grew better inland. Its invention suddenly opened up large areas of potential farmland in Georgia.

The rapid growth of cotton farming required an expansion of the available labor, which came from slavery. As cotton production expanded, so did the Georgia economy's reliance on slave labor. This increased reliance on slavery heightened Georgia's concern with the growing abolitionist movement in the North and would directly contribute to its eventual secession.

The expansion of cotton farming also resulted in the displacement of the **Cherokee** and **Creek** peoples who inhabited desirable potential planting ground. The Cherokee and Creek were eventually forced out of Georgia and relocated to the Indian Territory in present day Oklahoma.

Skill 14.6   Demonstrate knowledge of Georgia's role in the Civil War and the effects of Reconstruction on Georgia.

When the anti-slavery candidate Abraham Lincoln was elected President in 1860, many southern states began to seriously consider the issue of seceding from the Union. The issue of whether slavery should be perpetuated in the growing country by allowing it in new territories had been a contentious matter for decade. The southern slave states were concerned that the federal government had been taken over by abolitionists, and that the complete abolition of slavery was not far away.

The white male voters of Georgia were overwhelmingly opposed to abolition, as their livelihoods depended on the labor of slaves. They differed somewhat on the question of **secession**; however, with some in favor of immediate secession after the election of Lincoln, and some in favor of using secession as a bargaining chip to gain assurance from the federal government that it would make no attempt to abolish slavery in the states. On January 19, 1861, a state convention called to consider the question of secession.

Georgians played a prominent role in the drafting and adoption of the Constitution of the Confederate States in Alabama. Georgian Alexander Stephens served as the first Vice President under Confederate President **Jefferson Davis.**

Considered safely within the boundaries of the Confederate States, Georgia was the location of considerable Confederate military operations such as munitions factories and the Andersonville prison camp. Georgia was not safe from attack, however, and in 1864, General William Sherman embarked on a campaign that cut a path of destruction through Georgia. Sherman captured Atlanta on September 2, 1864, and burned the entire city. Sherman continued on to the capital, Milledgeville, and finally to Savannah.

Following the surrender of the southern states, the federal government adopted a system of reconstruction in the south. **Reconstruction** required former Confederate states to adopt new constitutions in order to be readmitted into the Union. Georgia was one of the last states to surrender, and the last state to be readmitted. This was partly because the terms of readmission had changed after the death of Lincoln, requiring Georgia to hold two conventions on a new constitution.

The post-reconstruction government abolished slavery and granted voting rights to all men, black and white. At first, many whites boycotted elections, allowing many blacks to participate in the government for a time.

Skill 14.7   Demonstrate knowledge of important political, economic, and social changes that occurred in Georgia between 1877 and 1918.

"**New South**" is a term sometimes used to describe the South after the Civil War, and refers to South that is based on industry and no longer dependent on slave labor. In Georgia, Henry Grady is closely associated with the New South movement in the 1880s, which sought to bring northern investment and industry to the state, particularly in the Atlanta region.

The New South was an ideal more than a reality for Georgia farmers, who found themselves stressed by falling cotton prices after the Civil War. The growing Populist movement in the 1890s blamed the entrenched Democratic Party for many of the farmer's woes, and mounted a challenge to the party. Georgia populists sought to include blacks in the movement and called for prison reform. By the turn of the century, **Populism** as a movement had largely faded from Georgia politics, but it had lasting effects.

Jim Crow laws were laws enacted after the Civil War, which resulted in the segregation of whites and blacks, with blacks being forced to use inferior facilities. During Reconstruction, southern states were forced to adopt protections for free black citizens. Once the Reconstruction governments were replaced with "Redeemer" governments, laws were enacted that required separate schools and public facilities for blacks and whites, thereby replacing the Black Codes that had been in effect prior to the Civil War.

Jim Crow laws had the effect of denying voting rights to many black citizens by requiring the payment of a **poll tax**. The all white Democratic Party also discouraged black participation in politics and elections. Despite these prejudices, many blacks prospered following the war, especially in the growing industrial center of Atlanta. As the white elite witnessed the emergence of a black economic elite in Atlanta, some argued that allowing blacks to vote had caused them to think of themselves as equal to whites and that the vote should be taken away from blacks.

Tension grew between the races, eventually erupting in violence in Atlanta in 1906. Unsubstantiated reports circulated that black men had attacked four white women. A mob of white men and boys gathered and raided black neighborhoods, destroying black businesses and killing several people. The state militia was called in to control the mob, which eventually subsided. As a result of the riot, even further restrictions were placed on black voting rights.

Skill 14.8 Demonstrate knowledge of the effects of World Wars I and II in Georgia and the major economic and political developments of the interwar period.

World War I greatly impacted Georgia, which became the location of several military training camps. Thousands of troops from all over the country passed through Georgia on their way to war. In 1918, the troop ship *Otranto* sunk tragically, killing almost 400 men. 130 of them were from Georgia.

When President Wilson instituted the draft, many white Georgians tried to prevent black men from being called into service, especially landowners who employed black sharecroppers. Not wanting to lose their labor force, they would sometimes not deliver draft notices, or prevent blacks from registering. As a result, many blacks were arrested and jailed for evading the draft.

Agriculture was not only threatened by the potential loss of farm labor. The boll weevil is an insect that affects cotton. It began its spread northward from Mexico in the late nineteenth century and reached Georgia around 1915. Within 10 years, the number of acres planted in cotton in Georgia halved because of the pest. The boll weevil forced farmers to diversify their crops, leading to the rise of peanut farming, which became an important agricultural product.

Eugene Talmadge began his career in state politics as the Commissioner of Agriculture in 1926. Outspoken and opinionated, Talmadge won popular support of the rural community and rapidly became a polarizing influence in the Democratic Party. He was elected governor in 1932 and re-elected in 1934. After unsuccessful bids for the U.S. Senate, Talmadge was again elected governor in 1940.

Talmadge was a forceful leader who would bypass legislative action and remove appointees who disagreed with his views. Talmadge removed faculty members from the state university system whom he thought wanted to integrate the schools or held the belief of racial equality. As a result of his raid on the system, the university lost its accreditation. The more moderate Ellis Arnall challenged Talmadge in the gubernatorial race of 1942, promising to restore accreditation, and won. Talmadge was re-elected governor in 1946, but died before taking office.

Talmadge was a major opponent of President Franklin Roosevelt's New Deal, a series of public programs beginning in 1933 designed to assist Depression-wracked Americans and promote economic recovery. Talmadge and others saw the New Deal as the federal government interference with local affairs, but the program, which provided farm subsidies, built new infrastructure and provided direct assistance to poor Georgians was popular among the people. President Roosevelt himself was popular in Georgia, having adopted Warm Springs as a second home during his time in office.

The New Deal did help many poor southerners, but failed to bring the dramatic turnaround that had been hoped for in the South. It was World War II and the related boom in war industry transformed Georgia's economy. Defense contractors found a large and willing labor force in Georgia, and shipbuilding and aircraft manufacturing became important industries, employing hundreds of thousands of people. With many men away in the military, women entered the workforce in large numbers for the first time. Black workers also benefited from the labor shortage, entering positions that had formerly been reserved for white men. Segregation was still enforced, however.

Skill 14.9   Analyze major political developments in Georgia since World War II.

New methods of agriculture kept farming a viable endeavor once again, but Georgia was no longer entirely dependent on agriculture. The City of Atlanta made an early commitment to developing air travel in 1925 with the establishment of an airfield. The airfield grew throughout the twentieth century, and under the administration of Mayor Maynard Jackson was transformed into the **Hartsfield International Airport,** a huge building project that opened in 1980. Later, renamed the airport to Hartsfield-Jackson International Airport. It is currently the busiest airport in the world.

Ellis Arnall was elected Governor of Georgia in 1942 at the age of 35. Arnall made several significant reforms, including the elimination of poll taxes and the lowering of the voting age. He also proposed checks to the power of the governor, feeling that Eugene Talmadge had abused his power previously. Arnall left office in 1947, and ran again in 1966 against the segregationist Lester Maddox. Maddox emerged the victor in that race and served as governor until 1971.

Herman Talmadge was the only son of former Governor Eugene Talmadge. He ran his father's successful campaign for Governor in 1946, and was briefly appointed Governor by the legislature when his father died before taking office. Herman Talmadge was himself elected Governor in 1948. Talmadge worked to bring industry to Georgia and supported segregation. He served as Governor until 1954, when he ran for the U.S. Senate and was elected. Talmadge served in the Senate until 1981.

Between Reconstruction and the 1960s, the Democratic Party dominated Georgia politics. Republicans had been installed by the federal government during reconstruction. They were quickly replaced by Democrats after the federal troops that supported the Republican state governments were withdrawn. The civil rights era began drawing sharp lines between old line Democrats and more moderate Democrats, sometimes splitting the vote and allowing Republicans to gain footholds.

Another change in Georgia politics in the 1960s was the end of the county unit system of conducting state primaries. Under this system, all of a county's unit votes were awarded to the candidate that received the most individual votes within that county. This system favored rural counties, and allowed for the election of candidates who had actually lost the popular vote, as was the case in the 1946 primary where Eugene Talmadge won the primary for Governor. Primary politics were important in Georgia. Because of the dominance of the Democratic Party, winning the primary virtually ensured winning the general election. The U.S. Supreme Court declared the county unit system illegal in 1963.

In 1962, Jimmy Carter was elected to the Georgia legislature after challenging fraudulent returns in his election. He went on to serve as Governor of Georgia and was elected President of the United States in 1976, defeating President Gerald Ford.

Dr. Martin Luther King, Jr., was born in Atlanta in 1929. He studied sociology and theology in college and became a Baptist pastor in Montgomery, Alabama in 1953. In 1955, in Montgomery, Alabama, **Rosa Parks**, a black woman, was arrested for refusing to give her bus seat to a white man, as was required under the segregation laws of the time. King organized a boycott of Montgomery buses, which lasted over a year. During this time, King was himself arrested and his home was bombed. The matter eventually reached the United States Supreme Court, which ruled that segregation of public transportation was illegal.

King became a national spokesman for civil rights for African Americans and non-violent protest of segregation. Through organized protests and powerful public speeches, King brought national attention to the issue of civil rights culminating in 1963 with the **March on Washington**. The March was an organized demonstration by several African American organizations calling for an end to segregation and legal discrimination. The demonstration was successful in influencing the passage of the **Civil Rights Act of 1964.** Dr. King continued to speak out against violence and in opposition to the U.S. involvement in Viet Nam. Dr. King was assassinated in 1968.

Maynard Jackson was the first African American mayor of Atlanta. The grandson of prominent civil rights leader John Wesley Dobbs, Jackson brought a commitment to civil rights to his office. He implemented an affirmative action program that increased the number of city contracts with African American businesses and introduced public involvement in neighborhood planning. Jackson also undertook to reform the Atlanta Police Department to provide more opportunity for black advancement.

Andrew Young was a key aid to Dr. King during the growth of the civil rights movement. Young organized voter registration drives and encouraged political participation among African Americans. Following Dr. King's assassination, Young ran for Congress and became one of the first black congressmen in the twentieth century, where he continued to advocate for improvement in civil rights legislation. Young succeeded Maynard Jackson as Mayor of Atlanta.

COMPETENCY 15.0 UNDERSTAND THE GEORGIA STATE CONSTITUTION, THE STRUCTURE OF GEORGIA STATE GOVERNMENT, AND THE ROLE OF CITIZENS AND LOCAL GOVERNMENTS IN GEORGIA.

Skill 15.1 Demonstrate knowledge of the basic structure and principles of the Georgia State Constitution

The most recent Georgia Constitution became law on July 1, 1983, after having been ratified by Georgia voters the prior year. This is the tenth Constitution for Georgia. The first constitution was adopted in 1777. The original constitution of the state established the basic structure of state government which continues today. Following the example of the U.S. Constitution, Georgia adopted a structure based on separations of powers where each body, the legislative, executive and judicial branch, of government has specific responsibilities and where checks and balances are in place to protect against a branch of government from abusing its power. Checks and balances include the ability of the Court system to decide on the constitutionality of laws passed by the General Assembly and the General Assembly right to impeach an executive or judicial officer, including the Governor. Similarly the Governor has the ability to veto any legislation passed by the General Assembly.

The concept of popular sovereignty, or majority rule, is a concept common to democracies. Those who are governed consent to the process and government can use powers spelled out in the constitution. This can be contrasted to the traditional system of Medieval Europe – **the divine right of kings** – where the power of a King to govern was derived from God, not citizens of the country. Part of the debate leading to the Civil War involved the concept of **popular sovereignty** being a State or National decision. Confederate States believed that it was the State ability to set laws including slavery laws and even secede from the Union.

Skill 15.2 Recognize the rights and responsibilities of Georgia citizens, demonstrate knowledge of voting requirements and the electoral process in Georgia, and examine the role of political parties in Georgia government

The Georgia Constitution establishes a Bill of Rights for citizens of the State. Specific rights include:

- The right to life, liberty and property except as deprived by law;
- Requires the Government to protect citizens and property equally;
- Right to worship according to individual conscience;
- Freedoms of religion, speech and press;
- Requirement that testimony against anyone must be free from libel;
- Right to keep and bear arms;

- No retroactive laws may be passed;
- Right to trial by jury and court trial;
- Protection against illegal searches and seizures;
- Right to the benefit of legal counsel;
- Protection from self-incriminating testimony;
- Protection from the loss of life and liberty due to double jeopardy-being tried twice for the same offense (except in the case of a mistrial or after conviction); and
- And several rights common to modern society.

Georgia citizens are required to obey the laws of the community, state, and national governments. Additionally, citizens may be required or asked to participate in the military or serve on a jury. Obeying all laws includes the payment of all taxes and fees required to support government operations.

Citizens have both a right and responsibility to vote for elected officials. Voting by citizens is a primary responsibility in a democracy. To qualify to vote a Georgia citizen must be at least 18 years of age, have not been convicted of a felony and register to vote. Persons who are determined to be mentally incompetent are not eligible to register. All elections are by secret ballot. Georgia election law does not provide for Party registration. In the primary election a voter may choose to vote the Democratic, Republican or Nonpartisan ballot. This choice may change with each primary election. The law provides that should a run-off election be required, the voter must vote within the same group as voted in the primary. Provision also allows for absentee ballot voting.

Skill 15.3 Explain the origins, functions, purposes, and differences of county and city governments in Georgia

Historically, counties in Georgia have provided a variety of services to the region. Counties were the center of government, the local court system and formed the boundaries for electing public officials. The initial State Constitution recognized only 8 counties. The 1983 Constitution establishes the maximum number of counties at 159, the number of counties at the time. County governments in Georgia manage many important services for the local area including:

- Voter registration and election management;
- County Court system;
- Official record site for wills and deeds;
- Public services including transportation, libraries, fire protection and police; and
- Management of local building codes, planning and zoning.

Counties also manage a variety of programs for the State Government. A county is managed by a Commissioner or a Board of Commissioners. Additional positions include the Sheriff, the chief law enforcement official in the county, various record keeping officials and judges. The judge for the probate court also manages wills, deeds, and marriage licenses. The tax commissioner is responsible for collection of taxes to support county operations. Counties have the power to set local law and the ability to take property through eminent domain to allow for the development of an area.

Similarly, cities in Georgia manage local affairs through a variety of forms. Similar to county governments, cities manage local affairs in areas of transportation, land use, public safety, streets, roads, water and other public utilities, planning and zoning. A weak mayor-council system of government establishes the mayor as the chief executive officer of the city but the role can be more ceremonial. The council can dominate the policymaking process and the management role. In other cities mayor and council share these roles.

The strong mayor-council approach is the opposite where the mayor is the chief executive officer with strong power and authority. The mayor typically has ability to appoint both committees and key city officials.

The council-manager form of government establishes council as the legislative body for the city and hires a manager to oversee the affairs of the city reporting to council. The mayor is a ceremonial position. The manager has authority over city operations and staffing.

Special purpose bodies may be created with the authority to tax and charge fees. These special purpose bodies have jurisdiction over their area of specialization. Examples include school districts, library systems, local authorities and community development entities.

Skill 15.4   Recognize the qualifications, terms, election, and duties of members of the General Assembly, the governor, and the lieutenant governor

The General Assembly is charged by the Georgia Constitution as the legislative branch of the state. The General Assembly is divided into two bodies, the Senate and the House of Representatives. The State Constitution provides that the Senate shall consist of no more than 56 members and the State House of Representatives will consist of not less than 180 delegates. Both State Senators and State Representatives are elected from designated districts within the state. The General Assembly approves the geographic distribution of districts following each decennial census. To qualify for the Senate, a resident of the State must be a United States citizen and a citizen of Georgia for at least two years, reside in the district for at least a year and must be at least 25 years of age. To qualify for the House of Representatives, a resident must be at least 21 years of age, reside in the district for at least a year, a citizen of Georgia for two years at least and a citizen of the United States. Members of the General Assembly may not be on active duty of the United States armed forces or have a civil appointment. They are elected by the eligible voters of the district and serve a term of two years.

A **quorum** is required consisting of a majority of the members of each house of the General Assembly to conduct business. The Assembly is charged by the State Constitution with enacting laws which are consistent with both the State and National Constitutions. The constitution identifies specific powers of the General Assembly to include the authority to establish laws for:

- Land use to conserve natural resources;
- Establishing a state militia;
- Establishing guidelines for participation in federal and state programs by municipalities and jurisdictions and the ability to of municipalities to condemn property;
- Laws regarding the operation of the State in emergencies;
- The promotion of tourism in the state; and
- Regulation of tractor and motor vehicles.

The General Assembly will also authorize state programs and appropriate funds for various initiatives through the annual budget process. The Governor and the Lieutenant Governor are elected by the voters to a four-year term. The Governor may be elected for a maximum of two four-year terms. To qualify for either office requires U.S. citizenship for at least 15 years and 6 year residency requirement in the state. Additionally both officials must be at least 30 years of age. The Governor is the Chief Executive of the State enforcing laws and serving as the Commander in Chief of the state military. The Governor may assign specific duties to the Lieutenant Governor who will succeed to the Governorship upon the resignation, death, or disability of the Governor. The Governor may veto any law passed by state legislature. Once vetoed, the General Assembly may overrule the Governor with a two-third majority vote.

Skill 15.5   Describe the organization of the General Assembly and the executive branch with emphasis on major policy areas of state programs

The Lieutenant Governor serves as the President of the Senate. The Senate will elect a President Pro-Tempore to be the presiding officer of the Senate. The House elects both a Speaker of the House and a Speaker Pro-Tempore. The party in control of the Senate and the House will appoint a Majority Leader and a Majority Whip. The leader will manage the operations of the party caucus as well as serve as spokesperson and the whip will communicate with members seeking to gain support for key votes. The party out of controlling power in the Senate or House will appoint a minority leader and minority whip both with similar roles for the caucus.

Each House will establish committees which work on legislation, budget and appropriations. Much of the work of the General Assembly takes place in committees. Each party will appoint representatives to committees. They deal with various function and policy areas of state government such as economic development, children and youth, agriculture, banking, health and human services. The appropriation committee is important in managing the annual budget process.

In addition to the Governor and Lieutenant Governor several other officials are elected in a statewide race including Secretary of State, Attorney General, Commissioner of Agriculture, State School Superintendent, Commissioner of Insurance and the Commissioner of Labor. Additionally, the Governor may appoint officials to positions recognized by law and adopted by the General Assembly. Various departments oversee specific functions of state government such as administrative services, corrections, public safety, transportation, community affairs and other policy areas.

Skill 15.6   Recognize the steps in the legislative process by which a bill becomes law in Georgia

The General Assembly as the legislative branch of Georgia government is responsible for the enactment of laws for the State. Any member of the General Assembly may introduce a bill or a resolution to change or amend State law. Bills may have a sponsor or multiple cosponsors. Each body of the General Assembly will designate specific committees to review proposed legislation. Each year the General Assembly convenes for a session which usually lasts at least sixty days starting on the second Monday of January. The General Assembly may also be called into session at other times in the case of emergency. Once a bill is introduced, it is assigned to a committee to review and recommend action. While the General Assembly is in session for only a few months a year, work continues in the committee throughout the year. Committees review the bill and may invite testimony on the legislation. Often the bill is amended in Committee before presentation for a vote in the House or Senate. The Committee must vote to send a bill to the floor for consideration.

Often, because of time or interest, a bill is not reviewed by the Committee and is considered to have "died in Committee". Once a bill is voted out of Committee, it is sent to the next full session for a floor vote. The bill is read and debated. Members have the opportunity to speak in support or opposition to the bill. Amendments may be offered from other members and must be voted on by a majority in order to pass. Members will ultimately be asked to vote in favor or opposition to the bill. If the bill successfully passes the House or Senate, it is sent to the other House for consideration and goes through a similar process of Committee review. The bill must pass both Houses in some form. Should the bills differ, they are sent to a "conference" committee composed of representatives from both Houses who negotiate the differences before a final vote in both houses. It is common for a bill, especially bills which involve appropriations, to go to a conference.

Once the bill passes both Houses of the General Assembly, the Bill goes to the Governor for signature. The governor may sign the bill and it becomes law or vetoes the bill and sends it back to the General Assembly. If the governor does nothing within 40 days, the bill automatically becomes law.

Skill 15.7   Demonstrate knowledge of the court system in Georgia and how judges are selected

The judicial branch of government in Georgia includes the various courts of magistrate, probate, juvenile, state, superior, court of appeals and the Supreme Count. The General Assembly establishes the jurisdiction and responsibilities for the lower court and also municipal courts. Superior court jurisdiction over felony cases, title to land, equity and divorce is established by the State Constitution. Both the Court of Appeal and the Supreme Court are appellate courts hearing appeals on lower court decisions. Additionally the Supreme Court has jurisdiction over constitutional issues and election issues.

Superior and State Court judges are elected to four year terms. Judges on the Supreme Court and the Court of Appeals are elected to six year terms. Other judges are elected locally within the area they have jurisdiction.

Skill 15.8   Compare the juvenile justice system to the adult justice system in Georgia

Juvenile Court in Georgia is created to deal with offenses by children under age 18. Juvenile Court has jurisdiction in cases such as truancy, substance abuse, and criminal behavior. Juveniles can be tried as adults in certain cases such as murder, rape, aggravated assault, involuntary manslaughter, and armed robbery. Juvenile Court does not include jury trial and sentences are shorter term than adult sentences. Additionally Superior Court proceedings where juveniles are tried as adults are open to the general public. As with adults, juveniles have a right to an attorney. Juveniles sentenced as adults serve time within the prison system as opposed to juvenile facilities. Juvenile court protects the confidentiality and records of the juvenile. In many ways the Juvenile process follows the process for adults. An intake process occurs. The juvenile can be taken into custody, at which time the parents are notified. There is a preliminary or dispositional hearing to determine if probable cause exists for the case to proceed to court. The next step is for the adjudicatory hearing to be held to determine the case. Finally a dispositional hearing is held to determine sentencing or treatment. The juvenile system is a faster process than the adult system of justice.

COMPETENCY 16.0   UNDERSTAND SOCIAL SCIENCE RESOURCES, TOOLS, AND RESEARCH PROCEDURES.

Skill 16.1   Recognize the characteristics and uses of various social-science reference resources.

Reference sources can be of great value and by teaching students how to access these first, they will later have skills that will help them access more in—depth databases and sources of information.

Encyclopedias are reference materials that appear in book or electronic form and can be considered general or specific. General encyclopedias peripherally cover most fields of knowledge; specific encyclopedias cover a smaller amount of material in greater depth. Encyclopedias are good first sources of information for students. While their scope is limited, they can provide a quick introduction to topics so that students can get familiar with the topics before exploring the topics in greater depth.

Almanacs provide statistical information on various topics. Typically, these references are rather specific. They often cover a specific period of time. One famous example is the *Farmer's Almanac*. This annual publication summarizes among many other things weather conditions for the previous year among many other things.

Bibliographies contain references for further research. Bibliographies are usually organized topically. They point people to the in-depth resources they will need for a complete review of a topic.

Databases, typically electronic, are collections of material on specific topics. For example, teachers can go online and find many databases of science articles for students in a variety of topics.

The Internet and other research resources provide a wealth of information on thousands of interesting topics for students preparing presentations or projects. Using search engines like Google and Yahoo!, student can search multiple Internet resources or databases on one subject search. Students should have an outline of the purpose of a project or research presentation that includes:

- Purpose - identify the reason for the research information.
- Objective - having a clear thesis for a project will allow the students opportunities to be specific on Internet searches.
- Preparation - when using resources or collecting data, students should create folders for sorting through the information. Providing labels for the folders will create a system of organization that will make construction of the final project or presentation easier and less time consuming.

- Procedure - organized folders and a procedural list of what the project or presentation needs to include will create A+ work for students and A+ grading for teachers.
- Visuals or artifacts - choose data or visuals that are specific to the subject content or presentation. Make sure that poster boards or Power Point presentations can be visually seen from all areas of the classroom. Teachers can provide laptop computers for Power Point presentations.

When a teacher models and instructs students in the proper use of search techniques, the teacher can minimize wasted time in preparing projects and wasted paper from students who print every search. In some school districts, students are allowed a minimum number of printed pages per week. Since students have Internet accounts for computer usage, the monitoring of printing is easily done by the school's librarian and teachers in classrooms.

Having the school's librarian or technology expert as a guest speaker in classrooms provides another method of sharing and modeling proper presentation preparation using technology. Teachers can also appoint technology experts from the students in a classroom to work with students on projects and presentations. In high schools, technology classes provide students with upper-class teacher assistants who fill the role of technology assistants.

Internet usage agreements define a number of criteria of technology use that a students must agree to in order to have access to school computers. Students must exercise responsibility and accountability in adhering to technology usage during the school day. Students who violate any parts of the computer usage agreement are subject to have all access to school computers or other educational technology denied or blocked, which, for the student needing to print a paper using the school computer and printer, could make the difference in handing assignments in on time or receiving a lower grade for late assignments.

Atlases are visual representations of geographic areas. Often they serve different functions. Some atlases demonstrate geologic attributes, while others emphasize populations of various areas.

An **atlas** is a collection of maps usually bound into a book and contain geographic features, political boundaries, and perhaps social, religious and economic statistics. Atlases can be found at most libraries but they are widely available on the Internet. The United States Library of Congress holds more than 53,000 atlases, most likely the largest and most comprehensive collection in the world.

Finally, periodical guides categorize articles and special editions of journals and magazines to help archive and organize the vast amount of material that is put in periodicals each year.

Statistical **surveys** are used in social sciences to collect information on a sample of the population. With any kind of information, care must be taken to accurately record information so the results are not skewed or distorted.

Opinion Polls are used to represent the opinions of a population by asking a number of people a series of questions about a product, place, person, event or perhaps the president and then using the results to apply the answers to a larger group or population. Polls, like surveys are subject to errors in the process. Errors can occur based on who is asked the question, where they are asked, the time of day or the biases one may hold in relevance to the poll being taken.

Skill 16.2   Distinguish between primary and secondary sources and analyze the advantages and limitations of each

Primary sources include the following kinds of materials:

1. Documents that reflect the immediate and everyday concerns of people. They should be understood the context in which it was produced.
2. Do not read history blindly; but be certain that you understand both explicit and implicit referenced in the material.
3. Read the entire text you are reviewing; do not simply extract a few sentences to read.
4. Although anthologies of materials may help you identify primary source materials, the full original text should be consulted.

Secondary sources include the following kinds of materials:

- Books written on the basis of primary materials about the period of time,
- Books written on the basis of primary materials about persons who played a major role in the events under consideration,
- Books and articles written on the basis of primary materials about the culture, the social norms, the language, and the values of the period,
- Quotations from primary sources,
- Statistical data on the period,
- The conclusions and inferences of other historians, and
- Multiple interpretations of the ethos of the time.

Guidelines for the use of secondary sources:

- Do not rely upon only a single secondary source.
- Check facts and interpretations against primary sources whenever possible.
- Do not accept the conclusions of other historians uncritically.
- Place greatest reliance on secondary sources created by the best and most respected scholars.
- Do not use the inferences of other scholars as if they were facts.
- Ensure that you recognize any bias the writer brings to his/her interpretation of history.
- Understand the primary point of the book as a basis for evaluating the value of the material presented in it to your questions.

Skill 16.3   Demonstrate knowledge of basic map characteristics, characteristics of different map projections, the problem of cartographic distortion, and the advantages and disadvantages of various standard map projections

Refer to Skill 17.2 for further discussion on map characteristics.

Skill 16.4   Apply research skills and procedures used in the social sciences

Formulating meaningful questions is a primary part of any research process and providing students with a wide variety of resources promotes this ability by making them aware of a wide array of social studies issues. Encouraging the use of multiple resources also introduces diverse viewpoints and different methods of communicating research results. This promotes the ability to judge the value of a resource and the appropriate ways to interpret it, which supports the development of meaningful inquiry skills.

In measuring the social significance of an event or issue, one of the first questions to ask is how many people are affected. Wide sweeping events such as wars, natural disasters, revolutions, etc., are significant partly because they can change the way of life for many people in a short time.

Sometimes significant changes take place over long periods of time, however, so it is also important to look at long-term effects of an event or phenomenon, following the chain of causes and effects. In this way, sometimes events that seem insignificant at the time they occur, or which affect only a small number of people, can be linked directly to large societal changes.

The scientific method is the process by which researchers over time endeavor to construct an accurate (that is, reliable, consistent and non-arbitrary) representation of the world. Recognizing that personal and cultural beliefs influence both our perceptions and our interpretations of natural phenomena, standard procedures and criteria minimize those influences when developing a theory.

The **scientific method** has four steps:

1. Observation and description of a phenomenon or group of phenomena.
2. Formulation of a hypothesis to explain the phenomena.
3. Use of the hypothesis to predict the existence of other phenomena or to predict quantitatively the results of new observations.
4. Performance of experimental tests of the predictions by several independent experimenters and properly performed experiments.

While the researcher may bring certain biases to the study, it's important that bias not be permitted to enter into the interpretation. It's also important that data that doesn't fit the hypothesis not be ruled out. This is unlikely to happen if the researcher is open to the possibility that the hypothesis might turn out to be null. Another important caution is to be certain that the methods for analyzing and interpreting are flawless. Abiding by these mandates is important if the discovery is to make a contribution to human understanding.

The phenomena that interest social scientists are usually complex. Capturing that complexity more fully requires the assessment of simultaneous co-variations along the following dimensions: the units of observation, their characteristics, and time. This is how behavior occurs. For example, to obtain a richer and more accurate picture of the progress of school children means measuring changes in their attainment over time together with changes in the school over time. This acknowledges that changes in one arena of behavior are usually contingent on changes in other areas. Models used for research in the past were inadequate to handle the complexities suggested by multiple co-variations. However, the evolution of computerized data processing has taken away that constraint.

While descriptions of the research project and presentation of outcomes along with analysis must be a part of every report, graphs, charts, and sometimes maps are necessary to make the results clearly understandable.

COMPETENCY 17.0   UNDERSTAND THE INTERPRETATION AND
ANALYSIS OF INFORMATION RELATED TO SOCIAL
SCIENCE TOPICS.

Skill 17.1   Interpret social science evidence and information

Primary sources include the following kinds of materials:

Documents that reflect the immediate, everyday concerns of people: memoranda, bills, deeds, charters, newspaper reports, pamphlets, graffiti, popular writings, journals or diaries, records of decision-making bodies, letters, receipts, snapshots, etc.

Theoretical writings reflect care and consideration in composition attempt to convince or persuade. The topic will generally be deeper and more pervasive values than is the case with "immediate" documents. These may include newspaper or magazine editorials, sermons, political speeches, philosophical writings, etc.

Narrative accounts of events, ideas, trends, etc. written with intention by someone contemporary with the events described.

Statistical data, although useful, statistics may be misleading.

Literature and nonverbal materials, novels, stories, poetry and essays from the period, as well as coins, archaeological artifacts, and art produced during the period. Guidelines for the use of primary resources:

1. Be certain that you understand how language was used at the time of writing and that you understand the context in which it was produced.
2. Do not read history blindly; but be certain that you understand both explicit and implicit referenced in the material.
3. Read the entire text you are reviewing; do not simply extract a few sentences to read.
4. Although anthologies of materials may help you identify primary source materials, the full original text should be consulted.

Secondary sources include the following kinds of materials:

- Books written on the basis of primary materials about the period of time,
- Books written on the basis of primary materials about persons who played a major role in the events under consideration,
- Books and articles written on the basis of primary materials about the culture, the social norms, the language, and the values of the period,
- Quotations from primary sources,
- Statistical data on the period,
- The conclusions and inferences of other historians, and
- Multiple interpretations of the ethos of the time.

Guidelines for the use of secondary sources:

- Do not rely upon only a single secondary source.
- Check facts and interpretations against primary sources whenever possible.
- Do not accept the conclusions of other historians uncritically.
- Place greatest reliance on secondary sources created by the best and most respected scholars.
- Do not use the inferences of other scholars as if they were facts.
- Ensure that you recognize any bias the writer brings to his/her interpretation of history.
- Understand the primary point of the book as a basis for evaluating the value of the material presented in it to your questions.

Skill 17.2 Use maps to analyze various geographic and other social science phenomena.

Physical locations of the earth's surface features include the four major hemispheres and the parts of the earth's continents in them. **Political locations** are the political divisions, if any, within each continent. Both physical and political locations are precisely determined in two *ways:* (1) Surveying determines boundary lines and distance from other features. (2) Exact locations are precisely determined by imaginary lines of **latitude (parallels)** and **longitude (meridians).** The intersection of these lines at right angles forms a grid, making it possible to pinpoint an exact location of any place using any two grid coordinates.

The process of putting the features of the Earth onto a flat surface is called **projection**. All maps are really map projections. There are many different types. Each one deals in a different way with the problem of distortion. Map projections are made in a number of ways. Some are done using complicated mathematics. However, the basic ideas behind map projections can be understood by looking at the three most common types:

(1) **Cylindrical Projections** - These are done by taking a cylinder of paper and wrapping it around a globe. A light is used to project the globe's features onto the paper. Distortion is least where the paper touches the globe. For example, suppose that the paper was wrapped so that it touched the globe at the equator, the map from this projection would have just a little distortion near the equator.

However, in moving north or south of the equator, the distortion would increase as you moved further away from the equator. The best known and most widely used cylindrical projection is the **Mercator Projection.** It was first developed in 1569 by Gerardus Mercator, a Flemish cartographer.

(2) **Conical Projections** - The name for these maps come from the fact that the projection is made onto a cone of paper. The cone is made so that it touches a globe at the base of the cone only. It can also be made so that it cuts through part of the globe in two different places. Again, there is the least distortion where the paper touches the globe. If the cone touches at two different points, there is some distortion at both of them. Conical projections are most often used to map areas in the **middle latitudes.** Maps of the United States are most often conical projections. This is because most of the country lies within these latitudes.

(3) **Flat-Plane Projections** - These are made with a flat piece of paper. It touches the globe at one point only. Areas near this point show little distortion. Flat-plane projections are often used to show the areas of the north and south poles. One such flat projection is called a **Gnomonic Projection**. On this kind of map all meridians appear as straight lines, Gnomonic projections are useful because any straight line drawn between points on it forms a Great-Circle Route.

Great-Circle Routes can best be described by thinking of a globe and when using the globe the shortest route between two points on it can be found by simply stretching a string from one point to the other. However, if the string was extended in reality, so that it took into effect the globe's curvature, it would then make a great-circle. A great-circle is any circle that cuts a sphere, such as the globe, into two equal parts. Because of distortion, most maps do not show great-circle routes as straight lines, Gnomonic projections, however, do show the shortest distance between the two places as a straight line, because of this they are valuable for navigation. They are called Great-Circle Sailing Maps.

To properly analyze a given map one must be familiar with the various parts and symbols that most modern maps use. For the most part, this is standardized, with different maps using similar parts and symbols, these can include:

The Title - All maps should have a title, just like all books should. The title tells you what information is to be found on the map.

The Legend - Most maps have a legend. A legend tells the reader about the various symbols that are used on that particular map and what the symbols represent, (also called a *map key).*

The Grid - A grid is a series of lines that are used to find exact places and locations on the map. There are several different kinds of grid systems in use however most maps do use the longitude and latitude system, known as the **Geographic Grid System**.

Directions - Most maps have some directional system to show which way the map is being presented. Often on a map, a small compass will be present, with arrows showing the four basic directions, north, south, east, and west.

The Scale - This is used to show the relationship between a unit of measurement on the map versus the real world measure on the Earth. Maps are drawn to many different scales. Some maps show a lot of detail for a small area. Others show a greater span of distance, whichever is being used one should always be aware of just what scale is being used. For instance the scale might be something like 1 inch = 10 miles for a small area or for a map showing the whole world it might have a scale in which 1 inch = 1,000 miles. The point is that one must look at the map key in order to see what units of measurements the map is using.

Maps have four main properties. They are: (1) the size of the areas shown on the map, (2) The shapes of the areas, (3) Consistent scales, and (4) Straight line directions. A map can be drawn so that it is correct in one or more of these properties. No map can be correct in all of them.

Equal areas - One property which maps can have is that of equal areas. In an equal area map, the meridians and parallels are drawn so that the areas shown have the same proportions as they do on the Earth. For example, Greenland is about 118th the size of South America, thus it will be show as 118th the size on an equal area map. The **Mercator projection** is an example of a map that does not have equal areas. In it, Greenland appears to be about the same size of South America. This is because the distortion is very bad at the poles and Greenland lies near the North Pole.

Conformal Map - A second map property is conformal, or correct shapes. There are no maps which can show very large areas of the earth in their exact shapes. Only globes can really do that, however Conformal Maps are as close as possible to true shapes. The United States is often shown by a Lambert Conformal Conic Projection Map.

Consistent Scales - Many maps attempt to use the same scale on all parts of the map. Generally, this is easier when maps show a relatively small part of the earth's surface. For example, a map of Florida might be a Consistent Scale Map. Generally maps showing large areas are not consistent-scale maps. This is because of distortion. Often such maps will have two scales noted in the key. One scale, for example, might be accurate to measure distances between points along the Equator. Another might be then used to measure distances between the North Pole and the South Pole.

Maps showing physical features often try to show information about the elevation or **relief** of the land. **Elevation** is the distance above or below the sea level. The elevation is usually shown with colors, for instance, all areas on a map which are at a certain level will be shown in the same color.

Relief Maps - Show the shape of the land surface, flat, rugged, or steep. Relief maps usually give more detail than simply showing the overall elevation of the land's surface. Relief is also sometimes shown with colors, but another way to show relief is by using **contour lines**. These lines connect all points of a land surface which are the same height surrounding the particular area of land.

Thematic Maps - These are used to show more specific information, often on a single **theme**, or topic. Thematic maps show the distribution or amount of something over a certain given area in topics of interest such as population density, climate, economic information, cultural, political information, etc.

We use **illustrations** of various sorts because it is often easier to demonstrate a given idea visually instead of orally. Sometimes it is even easier to do so with an illustration than a description. This is especially true in the areas of education and research because humans are visually stimulated. It is a fact that any idea presented visually in some manner is always easier to understand and to comprehend than simply getting an idea across verbally, by hearing it or reading it. Throughout this document, there are several illustrations that have been presented to explain an idea in a more precise way. Sometimes these will demonstrate some of the types of illustrations available for use in the arena of political science. Among the more common illustrations used in political science are various types of **maps, graphs and charts**.

Photographs and globes are useful as well, but as they are limited in what kind of information that they can show, they are rarely used. Unless, as in the case of a photograph, it is of a particular political figure or a time that one wishes to visualize.

Although maps have advantages over globes and photographs, they do have a major disadvantage. This problem must be considered as well. The major problem of all maps comes about because most maps are flat and the Earth is a sphere. It is impossible to reproduce exactly on a flat surface an object shaped like a sphere. In order to put the earth's features onto a map they must be stretched in some way. This stretching is called **distortion.**

Distortion does not mean that maps are wrong; it simply means that they are not perfect representations of the Earth or its parts. **Cartographers,** or mapmakers, understand the problems of distortion. They try to design them so that there is as little distortion as possible in the maps.

To apply information obtained from **graphs** one must understand the two major reasons why graphs are used:

1. To present a model or theory visually in order to show how two or more variables interrelate.

2. To present real world data visually in order to show how two or more variables interrelate.

Most often used are those known as **bar graphs** and **line graphs**. Graphs themselves are most useful when one wishes to demonstrate the sequential increase, or decrease of a variable or to show specific correlations between two or more variables in a given circumstance.

Most common is the **bar graph** because it has an easy to see and understand way of visually showing the difference in a given set of variables. However it is limited in that it can not really show the actual proportional increase, or decrease, of each given variable to each other. (In order to show a decrease, a bar graph must show the "bar" under the starting line, thus removing the ability to really show how the various different variables would relate to each other).
Thus in order to accomplish this, one must use a **line graph**. Line graphs can be of two types: a **linear** or **non-linear** graph. A linear line graph uses a series of straight lines; a non-linear line graph uses a curved line. Though the lines can be either straight or curved, all of the lines are called **curves**.

A line graph uses a number line or **axis.** The numbers are generally placed in order, equal distances from one another, the number line is used to represent a number, degree or some such other variable at an appropriate point on the line. Two lines are used, intersecting at a specific point. They are referred to as the X-axis and the Y-axis. The Y-axis is a vertical line the X-axis is a horizontal line. Together they form a **coordinate system.** The difference between a point on the line of the X-axis and the Y-axis is called the **slope** of the line, or the change in the value on the vertical axis divided by the change in the value on the horizontal axis. The Y-axis number is called the **rise** and the X-axis number is called the **run**, thus the equation for slope is:

SLOPE = <u>RISE</u> - (Change in value on the vertical axis)
　　　　　RUN - (Change in value on the horizontal axis)

The slope tells the amount of increase or decrease of a given specific variable. When using two or more variables one can plot the amount of difference between them in any given situation. This makes presenting information on a line graph more involved. It also makes it more informative and accurate than a simple bar graph. Knowledge of the term slope and what it is and how it is measured helps us to describe verbally the pictures we are seeing visually. For example, if a curve is said to have a slope of "zero", you should picture a flat line. If a curve has a slope of "one", you should picture a rising line that makes a 45-degree angle with the horizontal and vertical axis lines.

The preceding examples are of **linear** (straight line) curves. With **non-linear** curves (the ones that really do curve) the slope of the curve is constantly changing, so as a result, we must then understand that the slope of the non-linear curved line will be at a specific point. How is this done? The slope of a non-linear curve is determined by the slope of a straight line that intersects the curve at that specific point. In all graphs, an upward sloping line represents a direct relationship between the two variables. A downward slope represents an inverse relationship between the two variables. In reading any graph, one must always be very careful to understand what is being measured, what can be deduced and what cannot be deduced from the given graph.

To use **charts** correctly, one should remember the reasons one uses graphs. The general ideas are similar. It is usually a question as to which, a graph or chart, is more capable of adequately portraying the information one-wants to illustrate. One can see the difference between them and realize that in many ways graphs and charts are interrelated. One of the most common types is the **Pie-chart** because it is easy to read and understand, even for the lay person. You can see pie-charts used often, especially when one is trying to illustrate the differences in percentages among various items, or when one is demonstrating the divisions of a whole.

Demography is the branch of science of statistics most concerned with the social well being of people. **Demographic tables** may include: (1) Analysis of the population on the basis of age, parentage, physical condition, race, occupation and civil position, giving the actual size and the density of each separate area. (2) Changes in the population as a result of birth, marriage, and death. (3) Statistics on population movements and their effects and their relations to given economic, social and political conditions. (4) Statistics of crime, illegitimacy and suicide. (5) Levels of education and economic and social statistics.

Such information is also similar to that area of science known as **vital statistics** and as such is indispensable in studying social trends and making important legislative, economic, and social decisions. Such demographic information is gathered from census, and registrar reports and the like, and by state laws such information, especially the vital kind, is kept by physicians, attorneys, funeral directors, member of the clergy, and similar professional people.

Skill 17.3   Interpret graphic presentations of social science materials and evaluate the appropriateness of alternative graphic formats for conveying social science information.

Information can be gained looking at a map that might take hundreds of words to explain otherwise. Maps reflect the great variety of knowledge covered by social sciences. To show such a variety of information, maps are made in many different ways. Because of this variety, maps must be understood in order to make the best sense of them. Once they are understood, maps provide a solid foundation for social science studies.

To apply information obtained from **graphs** one must understand the two major reasons why graphs are used:

1.   To present a model or theory visually in order to show how two or more variables interrelate.
2.   To present real world data visually in order to show how two or more variables interrelate.

Most often used are those known as **bar graphs** and **line graphs**. (Charts are often used for similar reasons and are explained in the next section).

Graphs themselves are most useful when one wishes to demonstrate the sequential increase, or decrease of a variable or to show specific correlations between two or more variables in a given circumstance.

Most common is the **bar graph**, because it is easy to see and understandable way of visually showing the difference in a given set of variables. However it is limited in that it can not really show the actual proportional increase, or decrease, of each given variable to each other. (In order to show a decrease, a bar graph must show the "bar" under the starting line, thus removing the ability to really show how the various different variables would relate to each other).

Thus in order to accomplish this one must use a **line graph**. Line graphs can be of two types: a **linear** or **non-linear** graph. A linear line graph uses a series of straight lines; a non-linear line graph uses a curved line. Though the lines can be either straight or curved, all of the lines are called **curves**.

To use **charts** correctly, one should remember the reasons one uses graphs. The general ideas are similar. It is usually a question as to which, a graph or chart, is more capable of adequately portraying the information one wants to illustrate. One can see the difference between them and realize that in many ways graphs and charts are interrelated. One of the most common types, because it is easiest to read and understand, even for the lay person, is the **pie-chart**.

You can see pie-charts used often, especially when one is trying to illustrate the differences in percentages among various items, or when one is demonstrating the divisions of a whole.

Posters: The power of the political poster in the 21st century seems trivial considering the barrage of electronic campaigning, mudslinging, and reporting that seems to have taken over the video and audio media in election season. Even so, the political poster has been a powerful propaganda tool, and it has been around for a long time. For example, in the 1st century AD, a poster that calls for the election of a Satrius as quinquennial has survived to this day. Nowhere have political posters been used more powerfully or effectively than in Russia in the 1920s in the campaign to promote communism. Many of the greatest Russian writers of that era were the poster writers. Those posters would not be understood at all except in the light of what was going on in the country at the time.

However, today we see them primarily at rallies and protests where they are usually hand-lettered and hand-drawn. The message is rarely subtle. Understanding the messages of posters requires little thought as a rule. However, they are usually meaningless unless the context is clearly understood. For example, a poster reading "Camp Democracy" can only be understood in the context of the protests of the Iraq War near President George W. Bush's home near Crawford, Texas. "Impeach" posters are understood in 2006 to be directed at President Bush, not a local mayor or representative.

Cartoons: The political cartoon (aka editorial) presents a message or point of view concerning people, events, or situations using caricature and symbolism to convey the cartoonist's ideas, sometimes subtly, sometimes brashly, but always quickly. A good political cartoon will have wit and humor, which is usually obtained by exaggeration that is slick and not used merely for comic effect. It will also have a foundation in truth; that is, the characters must be recognizable to the viewer and the point of the drawing must have some basis in fact even if it has a philosophical bias. The third requirement is a moral purpose.

Using political cartoons as a teaching tool enlivens lectures, prompts classroom discussion, promotes critical thinking, develops multiple talents and learning styles, and helps prepare students for standardized tests. It also provides humor. However, it may be the most difficult form of literature to teach. Many teachers who choose to include them in their social studies curricula caution that, while students may enjoy them, it's doubtful whether they are actually getting the cartoonists' messages.

The best strategy for teaching such a unit is through a subskills approach that leads students step-by-step to higher orders of critical thinking. For example, the teacher can introduce caricature and use cartoons to illustrate the principles. Students are able to identify and interpret symbols if they are given the principles for doing so and get plenty of practice, and cartoons are excellent for this. It can cut down the time it takes for students to develop these skills, and many of the students who might lose the struggle to learn to identify symbols may overcome the roadblocks through the analysis of political cartoons. Many political cartoons exist for the teacher to use in the classroom and they are more readily available than ever before.

A popular example of an editorial cartoon that provides a way to analyze current events in politics is the popular comic strip "Doonesbury" by Gary Trudeau. For example, in the time period prior to the 2004 presidential election, Alex, the media savvy teenager does her best for political participation. In January she rallies her middle school classmates to the phones for a Deanathon and by August she is luring Ralph Nader supporters into discussions on Internet chat rooms. Knowledgeable about government, active in the political process, and willing to enlist others, Alex has many traits sought by the proponents of civics education.

We use **illustrations** of various sorts because it is often easier to demonstrate a given idea visually instead of orally. Sometimes it is even easier to do so with an illustration than a description. This is especially true in the areas of education and research because humans are visually stimulated. It is a fact that any idea presented visually in some manner is always easier to understand and to comprehend than simply getting an idea across verbally, by hearing it or reading it. Among the more common illustrations used are various types of **maps, graphs and charts**.

Photographs and globes are useful as well, but as they are limited in what kind of information that they can show and are rarely used. Unless, as in the case with photographs, it is of a particular political figure or a time that one wishes to visualize.

Although maps have advantages over globes and photographs, they do have a major disadvantage. This problem must be considered as well. The major problem of all maps comes about because most maps are flat and the Earth is a sphere. It is impossible to reproduce exactly on a flat surface an object shaped like a sphere. In order to put the earth's features onto a map they must be stretched in some way. This stretching is called **distortion.**

Distortion does not mean that maps are wrong it simply means that they are not perfect representations of the Earth or its parts. **Cartographers,** or mapmakers, understand the problems of distortion. They try to design them so that there is as little distortion as possible in the maps.

Bibliography

Adams, James Truslow. (2006). "The March of Democracy," Vol 1. "The Rise of the Union". New York: Charles Scribner's Sons, Publisher.

Barbini, John & Warshaw, Steven. (2006). "The World Past and Present." New York: Harcourt, Brace, Jovanovich, Publishers.

Berthon, Simon & Robinson, Andrew. (2006. "The Shape of the World." Chicago: Rand McNally, Publisher.

Bice, David A. (2006). "A Panorama of Florida II". (Second Edition). Marceline, Missouri: Walsworth Publishing Co., Inc.

Bram, Leon (Vice-President and Editorial Director). (2006). "Funk and Wagnalls New Encyclopedia." United States of America.

Burns, Edward McNall & Ralph, Philip Lee. (2006. "World Civilizations Their History and Culture" (5th ed.). New York: W.W. Norton & Company, Inc., Publishers.

Dauben, Joseph W. (2006). "The World Book Encyclopedia." Chicago: World Book Inc. A Scott Fetzer Company, Publisher.

De Blij, H.J. & Muller, Peter O. (2006). "Geography Regions and Concepts" (Sixth Edition). New York: John Wiley & Sons, Inc., Publisher.

Encyclopedia Americana. (2006). Danbury, Connecticut: Grolier Inc, Publisher.

Heigh, Christopher (Editor). (2006). "The Cambridge Historical Encyclopedia of Great Britain and Ireland." Cambridge: Cambridge University Press, Publisher.

Hunkins, Francis P. & Armstrong, David G. (2006). "World Geography People and Places." Columbus, Ohio: Charles E. Merrill Publishing Co. A Bell & Howell Company, Publishers.

Jarolimek, John; Anderson, J. Hubert & Durand, Loyal, Jr. (2006). "World Neighbors." New York: Macmillan Publishing Company. London: Collier Macmillan Publishers.

McConnell, Campbell R. (2006). "Economics-Principles, Problems, and Policies" (Tenth Edition). New York: McGraw-Hill Book Company, Publisher.

Millard, Dr. Anne & Vanags, Patricia. (2006). "The Usborne Book of World History." London: Usborne Publishing Ltd., Publisher.

Novosad, Charles (Executive Editor). (2006). "The Nystrom Desk Atlas." Chicago: Nystrom Division of Herff Jones, Inc., Publisher.

Patton, Clyde P.; Rengert, Arlene C.; Saveland, Robert N.; Cooper, Kenneth S. & Cam, Patricia T. (2006). "A World View." Morristown, N.J.: Silver Burdette Companion, Publisher.

Schwartz, Melvin & O'Connor, John R. (2006). "Exploring A Changing World." New York: Globe Book Company, Publisher.

"The Annals of America: Selected Readings on Great Issues in American History 1620-1968." (2006). United States of America: William Benton, Publisher.

Tindall, George Brown & Shi, David E. (2006). "America-A Narrative History" (Fourth Edition). New York: W.W. Norton & Company, Publisher.

Todd, Lewis Paul & Curti, Merle. (2006). "Rise of the American Nation" (Third Edition). New York: Harcourt, Brace, Jovanovich, Inc., Publishers.

Tyler, Jenny; Watts, Lisa; Bowyer, Carol; Trundle, Roma & Warrender, Annabelle (2006) 'The Usbome Book of World Geography." London: Usbome Publishing Ltd., Publisher.

Willson, David H. (2006). "A History of England." Hinsdale, Illinois: The Dryder Press, inc., Publisher

Sample Essay Question

Discuss the emergence, expansion, and evolution of Islam

Islam is a monotheistic faith that traces its traditions to Abraham and considers the Jewish patriarchs and prophets, especially Moses, King Solomon and Jesus Christ as earlier "Prophets of God".

Mohammed was born in 570 CE in a small Arabian town. Around 610, **Mohammed** came to some prominence through a new religion called **Islam** or submission to the will of God and his followers were called **Moslems.** His first converts were members of his family and his friends. As the new faith began to grow, it remained a secret society. But when they began to make their faith public, they met with opposition and persecution from the pagan Arabians who feared the loss of profitable trade with the pilgrims who came to the Kaaba every year. In 622, Mohammed and his close followers fled persecution in Mecca and found refuge in **Medina.** His flight is called the **Hegira**. Mohammed took advantage of feuds between Jews and Arabs and became the ruler, making it the capital of a rapidly growing state.

Islam changed significantly. It became a fighting religion and Mohammed became a political leader. The group survived by raiding caravans on the road to Mecca and plundering nearby Jewish tribes. It attracted many converts from Bedouin tribes. By 630, Mohammed conquered Mecca and made it the religious center of Islam, toward which all Moslems turned to pray. By taking over the sacred city, Mohammed made it easier for converts to join the religion. By the time of his death in 632, most of the people of Arabia had become adherents of Islam.

Mohammed left behind a collection of revelations (**surahs**) he believed were delivered by the angel Gabriel. The **Quran** was reputedly dictated to Muhammad as the Word of God and published in a book called the **Koran.** The revelations were never dated or kept in any kind of order. After Mohammed's death they were organized by length in diminishing order. The Koran contains Mohammed's teachings on moral and theological questions, his legislation on political matters, and his comments on current events. Five basic principles of Islam are: Allah, Pray five times a day facing Mecca, Charity, fasting during Ramadan and Pilgrimage to Mecca.

The Islamic armies spread their faith by conquering the Arabian Peninsula, Mesopotamia, Egypt, Syria and Persia by 650 CE and expanding to North Africa and most of the Iberian Peninsula by 750 CE. During this period of expansion, the Muslim conquerors established great centers of learning in the Middle East.

Sample Test

1. **The end to hunting, gathering, and fishing of prehistoric people was due to:**
   (Average) (Skill 1.1)

   A. Domestication of animals

   B. Building crude huts and houses

   C. Development of agriculture

   D. Organized government in villages

2. **The English explorer who gave England its claim to North American was:**
   (Average) (Skill 1.3)

   A. Raleigh

   B. Hawkins

   C. Drake

   D. Cabot

3. **The first European to see Florida and sail along its coast was:**
   (Average) (Skill 1.3)

   A. Cabot

   B. Columbus

   C. Ponce de Leon

   D. Narvaez

4. **Maps as a rule are:**
   (Skill 1.4) (Easy)

   A. All subject to some sort of distortion

   B. Always entirely accurate

   C. Not very useful in political science studies

   D. Usually difficult to understand

5. **Florida was originally settled by:**
   (Easy) (Skill 1.5)

   A. Italy

   B. Great Britain

   C. Spain

   D. France

6. **Which one of the following is not a reason why Europeans came to the New World?**
   (Average) (Skill 1.5)

   A. To find resources in order to increase wealth

   B. To establish trade

   C. To increase a ruler's power and importance

   D. To spread Christianity

7. **Of the thirteen English colonies, it can be said that settlers came for all but the following reasons:**
(Easy) (Skill 1.6)

A. Religious freedom

B. The chance to own slaves

C. Political freedom

D. Ownership of land

8. **The year 1619 was a memorable for the colony of Virginia. Three important events occurred resulting in lasting effects on US history. Which one of the following is not one of the events?**
(Average) (Skill 1.6)

A. Twenty African slaves arrived.

B. The London Company granted the colony a charter making it independent.

C. The colonists were given the right by the London Company to govern themselves through representative government in the Virginia House of Burgesses

D. The London Company sent to the colony 60 women who were quickly married, establishing families and stability in the colony.

9. **In an indirect democracy:**
(Average) (Skill 2.1)

A. All the people together decide on issues

B. People elect representatives to act for them

C. Democracy can never really work

D. Government is less efficient than a direct democracy

10. **Which of the following is not associated with the Revolutionary War?**
(Average) (Skill 2.1)

A. Stamp Act

B. Louisiana Purchase

C. Quartering Act

D. Townsend Act

11. France decided in 1777 to help the American colonies in their war against Britain. This decision was based on: (Rigorous) (Skill 2.1)

    A. The naval victory of John Paul Jones over the British ship "Serapis"

    B. The survival of the terrible winter at Valley Forge

    C. The success of colonial guerilla fighters in the South

    D. The defeat of the British at Saratoga

12. The Declaration of Independence owes much to the philosophy of: (Average) (Skill 2.3)

    A. Vladimir Lenin

    B. Karl Marx

    C. Thomas Hobbes

    D. John Locke

13. Which of the following is an important idea expressed in the Declaration of Independence? (Rigorous) (Skill 2.3)

    A. People have the right to change their government

    B. People should obey the government authority

    C. A monarch is a bad thing

    D. Indirect democracy is best

14. The term that describes the division of government function is: (Easy) (Skill 2.4)

    A. Free enterprise

    B. Constitutional Prerogative

    C. Checks and Balances

    D. Separation of Powers

15. In the U.S., checks and balances refers to: (Easy) (Skill 2.4)

    A. The ability of each branch of government to "check" or limit the actions of the others

    B. Balance of payments

    C. International law

    D. The federal deficit

16. **There is no doubt of the vast improvement of the U.S. Constitution over the weak Articles of Confederation. Which one of the four accurate statements below is a unique yet eloquent description of the constitution?**
(Easy) (Skill 2.4)

    A.   The establishment of a strong central government in no way lessened or weakened the individual states.

    B.   Individual rights were protected and secured.

    C.   The Constitution is the best representation of the results of the American genius for compromise.

    D.   Its flexibility and adaptation to change gives it a sense of timelessness.

17. **The political document that was the first to try to organize the newly independent American colonies was the:**
(Easy) (Skill 2.4)

    A.   Declaration of Independence

    B.   Articles of Confederation

    C.   The Constitution

    D.   The Confederate States

18. **Give the correct order of the following:**
(Rigorous) (Skill 2.4)

    A.   The Constitution, the Declaration of Independence, the Articles of Confederation

    B.   The Declaration of Independence, the Constitution, the Articles of Confederation

    C.   The Declaration of Independence, the Articles of Confederation, the Constitution

    D.   The Articles of Confederation, the Declaration of Independence, the Constitution

19. **In the United States government, the power of taxation and borrowing is:**
(Average) (Skill 2.5)

    A.   Implied or suggested

    B.   Concurrent or shared

    C.   Delegated or expressed

    D.   Reserved

20. **In the United States government, power or control over public education, marriage, and divorce is:**
     (Rigorous) (Skill 2.5)

     A.   Implied or suggested

     B.   Concurrent or shared

     C.   Delegates or expressed

     D.   Reserved

21. **The Judiciary refers to:**
     (Easy) (Skill 2.5)

     A.   The President

     B.   Congress

     C.   The legal system

     D.   The system of states' rights

22. **Under the brand new Constitution, the most urgent of the many problems facing the new federal government was that of:**
     (Average) (Skill 2.4, 2.5)

     A.   Maintaining a strong army and navy

     B.   Establishing a strong foreign policy

     C.   Raising money to pay salaries and war debts

     D.   Setting up courts, passing federal laws, and providing for law enforcement officers

23. **In the United States government, power or control over public education, marriage, and divorce is:**
     (Easy) (Skill 2.5)

     A.   Implied or suggested

     B.   Concurrent or shared

     C.   Delegated or expressed

     D.   Reserved

24. **The Executive branch refers to:**
     (Easy) (Skill 2.5)

     A.   The Senate

     B.   The Legislature

     C.   Congress

     D.   The President and Vice-President

25   **Which of the three branches of government is responsible for taxation?**
     (Average) (Skill 2.5)

     A.   Legislative

     B.   Executive

     C.   Judicial

     D.   Congressional

26. **To "impeach" a President means to:**
(Average) (Skill 2.5)

   A.   Bring charges against a President

   B.   Remove a President from office

   C.   Re-elect the President

   D.   Override his veto

27. **In the US government, the power of coining money is:**
(Rigorous) (Skill 2.5)

   A.   Implied or suggested

   B.   Concurrent or shared

   C.   Delegated or expressed

   D.   Reserved

28. **The US government's federal system consists of:**
(Average) (Skill 2.5)

   A.   Three parts, the Executive, the Legislative, and the Judiciary

   B.   Three parts, the Legislative, the Congress, and the Presidency

   C.   Four parts, the Executive, the Judiciary, the courts, and the Legislative

   D.   Two parts, the Government and the governed

29. **The power to declare war, establish a postal system, and coin money rests with which branch of the government?**
(Rigorous) (Skill 2.5)

   A.   Presidential

   B.   Judicial

   C.   Legislative

   D.   Executive

30. **The highest appellate court in the United States is the:**
(Rigorous) (Skill 2.5)

   A.   National Appeals Court

   B.   Circuit Court

   C.   Supreme Court

   D.   Court of Appeals

31. **In the United States, the right to declare war is a power of:**
(Rigorous) (Skill 2.5)

   A.   The President

   B.   Congress

   C.   The Executive Branch

   D.   The States

32. **The source of authority for national, state, and local governments in the US is:**
(Average) (Skills 2.5, 2.6)

   A. The will of the people

   B. The US Constitution

   C. Written laws

   D. The Bill of Rights

33. **The Bill of Rights says that any rights it does not mention are:**
(Rigorous) (Skill 2.6)

   A. Reserved to the federal government

   B. Not important

   C. Judged by the Supreme Court

   D. Reserved to the states or to the people

34. **The Bill of Rights was mostly written by:**
(Average) (Skill 2.6)

   A. Thomas Jefferson

   B. James Madison

   C. George Washington

   D. Alexander Hamilton

35. **The Orders in Council:**
(Rigorous) (Skill 3.1)

   A. Prohibited the Declaration of Independence

   B. Prohibited American ships from entering French ports

   C. Gave Americans representation in Parliament

   D. Imposed a tax on American goods entering England

36. **Which one of the following was not a reason why the United States went to war with Great Britain in 1812?**
(Rigorous) (Skill 3.2)

   A. Resentment by Spain over the sale exploration, and settlement of the Louisiana Territory

   B. The westward movement of farmers because of the need for more land

   C. Canadian fur traders were agitating the northwestern Indians to fight American expansion

   D. Britain continued to seize American ships on the high seas and force American seamen to serve aboard British ships

37. **Colonial expansion by Western European powers in the 18th and 19th centuries was due primarily to:** (Average) (Skill 3.2)

    A.   Building and opening the Suez Canal

    B.   The Industrial Revolution

    C.   Marked improvements in transportation

    D.   Complete independence of all the Americas and loss of European domination and influence

38. **It can be reasonably stated that the change in the United States from an agricultural country into an industrial power was due to all of the following except:** (Rigorous) (Skill 3.2)

    A.   Tariffs on foreign imports

    B.   Millions of hardworking immigrants

    C.   An increase in technological developments

    D.   The change from steam to electricity for powering industrial machinery

39. **From about 1870 to 1900 the settlement of America's "last frontier", the West, was completed. One attraction for settlers was free land but it would have been to no avail without:** (Easy) (Skill 3.2)

    A.   Better farming methods and technology

    B.   Surveying to set boundaries

    C.   Immigrants and others to seek new land

    D.   The railroad to get them there

40. **Historians state that the West helped speed up the Industrial Revolution. Which one of the following statements was not a reason for this?**
(Average) (Skill 3.2)

   A. Food supplies for the ever increasing urban populations came from farms in the West

   B. A tremendous supply of gold and silver from western mines provided the capital needed to built industries

   C. Descendants of western settlers, educated as engineers, geologists, and metallurgists in the East, returned to the West to mine the mineral resources needed for industry

   D. Iron, copper, and other minerals from western mines were important resources in manufacturing products

41. **The belief that the United States should control all of North America was called:**
(Rigorous) (Skill 3.2)

   A. Westward Expansion

   B. Pan Americanism

   C. Manifest Destiny

   D. Nationalism

42. **Democracy is defined as:**
(Easy) (Skill 3.3)

   A. Rule for a few elite

   B. Rule by a monarch

   C. Rule by the people either directly or through representatives

   D. Rule by a dictator

43. **A number of women worked hard in the first half of the 19th century for women's rights but decisive gains did not come until after 1850. The earliest accomplishments were in:**
(Average) (Skill 3.5)

   A. Medicine

   B. Education

   C. Writing

   D. Temperance

44. **Which one of the following events did not occur during the period known as the "Era of Good Feeling?"**
(Average) (Skill 3.6)

   A. President Monroe issued the Monroe Doctrine

   B. Spain ceded Florida to the United States

   C. The building of the National Road

   D. The charter of the second Bank of the United States

45. Which of the following was not a provision of the Compromise of 1850? (Rigorous) (Skill 3.6)

A. Admission of California as a free state

B. end of slave trading in Washington D.C.

C. Approval of the Louisiana Purchase

D. Creation of New Mexico and Utah territories

46. The principle of "popular sovereignty" allowing people in any territory to make their own decision concerning slavery was stated by; (Average) (Skill 3.6)

A. Henry Clay

B. Daniel Webster

C. John C. Calhoun

D. Stephen A. Douglas

47. The three-day Battle of Gettysburg was the turning point of the Civil War for the North leading to victory. The battle in the West reinforcing the North's victory and sealing the South's defeat was the day after Gettysburg at: (Rigorous) (Skill 3.7)

A. Perryville

B. Vicksburg

C. Stones River

D. Shiloh

48. The post-Civil War years were a time of low public morality, greed, graft, and dishonesty. Which one of the reasons listed would not be accurate? (Rigorous) (Skill 4.1)

A. The war itself because of the money and materials needed to carry on the War

B. The very rapid growth of industry and big business after the War

C. The personal example set by President Grant

D. Unscrupulous heads of large impersonal corporations

49. **The Radical Republicans who pushed the harsh Reconstruction measures through Congress after Lincoln's death lost public and moderate Republican support when they went too far:**
(Rigorous) (Skill 4.1)

A. In their efforts to impeach the President

B. By dividing ten southern states into military-controlled districts

C. By making the ten southern states give freed African Americans the right to vote

D. Sending carpetbaggers into the South to build up support for Congressional legislation

50. **What event sparked a great migration of people from all over the world to California?**
(Average) (Skill 4.2)

A. The birth of Labor Unions

B. California statehood

C. The invention of the automobile

D. The gold rush

51. **The American concept of Manifest Destiny means:**
(Average) (Skill 4.2)

A. America has a right to spread throughout the North American continent from coast to coast

B. The United States should respect the right of native peoples encounters in its push westward

C. The rest of the world powers should stay out of this part of the world

D. America should strive to be the dominant world power

52. **The American labor union movement started gaining new momentum:**
(Rigorous) (Skill 4.3)

A. During the building of the railroads

B. After 1865 with the growth of cities

C. With the rise of industrial giants such as Carnegie and Vanderbilt

D. During the war years of 1861-1865

53. **Potential customers for any good or service are not only called consumers but can also be called a:**
(Average) (Skill 4.3)

A. Resource

B. Base

C. Commodity

D. Market

54. **The Panic of 1893:**
(Rigorous) (Skill 4.5)

A. Resulted in several bank failures

B. Was a fear of a British invasion

C. Was the South panicking about the end of slavery

D. Was the result of invasion by Mexico

55. **"Walk softly and carry a big stick" is a statement associated with:**
(Average) (Skill 4.5)

A. Franklin Roosevelt

B. Theodore Roosevelt

C. George Washington

D. Thomas Hobbes

56. **After the Civil War, the US adapted an attitude of isolation from foreign affairs. But the turning point marking the beginning of the US becoming a world power was:**
(Average) (Skill 4.5)

A. World War I

B. Expansion of business and trade overseas

C. The Spanish-American War

D. The building and financial of the Panama Canal

57. **The Fourteen Points was proposed by:**
(Rigorous) (Skill 4.6)

A. President Wilson

B. President Roosevelt

C. The King of England

D. President Washington

58. **The international organization established to work for world peace at the end of the First World War was the:**
(Average) (Skill 4.6)

A. United Earth League

B. Confederate States

C. United Nations

D. League of Nations

59. Nineteenth century imperialism by Western European nations had important and far-reaching effects on the colonial peoples they ruled. All four of the following are the result of this. Which one was most important and had lasting effects on key 20th century events?
(Rigorous) (Skill 4.6)

A. Local wars were ended

B. Living standards were raised

C. Demands for self-government and feelings of nationalism surfaced

D. Economic developments occurred

60. Which of the following did not contribute to the Stock Market Cash in 1929?
(Average) (Skill 5.1)

A. Uneven distribution of wealth

B. Speculative investments

C. Buying on Margin

D. World War I

61. The New Deal involved:
(Rigorous) (Skill 5.2)

A. Financing stock market speculation

B. Programs to relieve the suffering of the Depression and to stimulate the economy

C. A new monetary system

D. A new pact with England

62. Which of the following was not a New Deal program?
(Rigorous) (Skill 5.2)

A. Public Works Administration

B. Bretton Woods System

C. National Recovery Administration

D. Works Progress Administration

63. Which of the following was not a leading figure during World War II?
(Easy) (Skill 5.3)

A. Hitler

B. Stalin

C. Tojo

D. Castro

64. **Of all the major causes of World Wars I and II, the most significant one is considered to be:**
(Rigorous) (Skill 5.3)

   A. Extreme nationalism

   B. Military buildup and aggression

   C. Political unrest

   D. Agreements and alliances

65. **Of all the major causes of World Wars I and II, the most significant one is considered to be:**
(Rigorous) (Skill 5.3)

   A. Extreme nationalism

   B. Military buildup and aggression

   C. Political unrest

   D. Agreements and alliances

66. **Who is not associated with World War II?**
(Average) (Skill 5.4)

   A. Hitler

   B. Tojo

   C. Queen Victoria

   D. Stalin

67. **The international organization established to work for world peace at the end of the Second World War is the:**
(Average) (Skill 5.4)

   A. League of Nations

   B. United Federation of Nations

   C. United Nations

   D. United World League

68. **Which one of the following would not be considered a result of World War II?**
(Average) (Skill 5.5)

   A. Economic depressions and slow resumption of trade and financial aid

   B. Western Europe was no longer the center of world power

   C. The beginnings of new power struggles not only in Europe but in Asia as well

   D. Territorial and boundary changes for many nations, especially in Europe

69. The U.S. doctrine that sought to keep Communism from spreading was:
(Average) (Skill 5.6)

    A. The Cold War

    B. Roll-back

    C. Containment

    D. Détente

70. The study of the ways in which different societies around the world deal with the problems of limited resources and unlimited needs and wants is in the area of:
(Easy) (Skill 6.1)

    A. Economics

    B. Sociology

    C. Anthropology

    D. Political Science

71. After World War II, the United States:
(Average) (Skill 6.3)

    A. Limited its involvement in European affairs

    B. Shifted foreign policy emphasis from Europe to Asia

    C. Passed significant legislation pertaining to aid to farmers and tariffs on imports

    D. Entered the greatest period of economic growth in its history

72. Who did not influence U.S. major political developments after 1960?
(Average) (Skill 6.3)

    A. John F. Kennedy

    B. Gerald Ford

    C. Harry S. Truman

    D. Lyndon B. Johnson

73. During the 1920s, the United States almost completely stopped all immigration. One of the reasons was:
(Rigorous) (Skill 6.4)

    A. Plentiful cheap unskilled labor was no longer needed by industrialists

    B. War debts from World War I made it difficult to render financial assistance

    C. European nations were reluctant to allow people to leave since there was a need to rebuild populations and economic stability

    D. The United States did not become a member of the League of Nations

74. The only Central American country with no standing army, a freely elected government, and considered the oldest democracy in the region is:
(Rigorous) (Skill 7.1)

A. Costa Rica

B. Belize

C. Honduras

D. Guatemala

75. One South American country quickly and easily gained independence in the nineteenth century from European control; was noted for the uniqueness of its political stability and gradual orderly changes. This most unusual Latin American country is:
(Rigorous) (Skill 7.1, 7.2)

A. Chile

B. Argentina

C. Venezuela

D. Brazil

76. The principle of zero in mathematics is the discovery of the ancient civilization found in:
(Rigorous) (Skill 7.2)

A. Egypt

B. Persia

C. Mayan

D. Babylon

77. Which political and social system contained the capital known as the richest capital in the new world?
(Rigorous) (Skill 7.2)

A. The Mayans

B. The Atacamas

C. The Incas

D. The Tarapacas

78. What was not a factor in the move for Latin American independence?
(Rigorous) (Skill 7.3)

A. The American Revolution

B. A war with Germany

C. The French Revolution

D. Napoleon's invasion of France

79. The United Provinces of Central America did not include:
(Rigorous) (Skill 7.3)

A. Mexico

B. El Salvado

C. Honduras

D. Nicaragua

80. **"First Nations" refers to:**
(Rigorous) (Skill 8.2)

   A.   Mexican Indian tribes

   B.   American Indian tribes

   C.   Canadian Indian tribes

   D.   Honduran Indian tribes

81. **Soil erosion is most likely to occur in large amounts in:**
(Rigorous) (Skill 8.6)

   A.   Mountain ranges

   B.   Deserts

   C.   Tropical rainforests

   D.   River valleys

82. **Which French Renaissance writer made contributions in the area of literature and philosophy?**
(Rigorous) (Skill 9.3)

   A.   Francois Rabelais

   B.   Desiderius Erasmus

   C.   Michel de Montaigne

   D.   Sir Francis Bacon

83. **The changing focus during the Renaissance when artists and scholars were less concerned with religion but centered their efforts on a better understanding of people and the world was called:**
(Easy) (Skill 9.3)

   A.   Realism

   B.   Humanism

   C.   Individualism

   D.   Intellectualism

84. **Who made important contributions in the area of anatomy during the Renaissance?**
(Rigorous) (Skill 9.3)

   A.   Vesalius

   B.   Servetus

   C.   Galen

   D.   Harvey

85. **In Western Europe, the achievements of the Renaissance were unsurpassed and made these countries outstanding cultural centers on the continent. All of the following were accomplishments except: (Rigorous) (Skill 9.3)**

    A.   Investment of the printing press

    B.   A rekindling of interest in the learning of classical Greece and Rome

    C.   Growth in literature, philosophy and art

    D.   Better military tactics

86. **Studies in astronomy, skills in mapping, and other contributions to geographic knowledge came from: (Rigorous) (Skill 9.3)**

    A.   Galileo

    B.   Columbus

    C.   Eratosthenes

    D.   Ptolemy

87. **The Age of Exploration begun in the 1400s was led by: (Average) (Skill 9.3)**

    A.   The Portuguese

    B.   The Spanish

    C.   The English

    D.   The Dutch

88. **The ideas and innovations of the period of the Renaissance were spread throughout Europe mainly because of: (Rigorous) (Skill 9.3)**

    A.   Extensive exploration

    B.   Craft workers and their guilds

    C.   The invention of the printing press

    D.   Increased travel and trade

89. **Who is considered to be the most important figure in the spread of Protestantism across Switzerland? (Rigorous) (Skill 9.3)**

    A.   Calvin

    B.   Zwingli

    C.   Munzer

    D.   Leyden

90. **The Protestant Reformation began in:**
    (Average) (Skill 9.3)

    A. Italy

    B. Germany

    C. England

    D. Ireland

91. **Which one of the following did not contribute to early medieval European civilization?**
    (Average) (Skill 9.3)

    A. The heritage from the classical cultures

    B. The Christian religion

    C. The influence of the German Barbarians

    D. The spread of ideas through trade and commerce

92. **The European Union does not include:**
    (Rigorous) (Skill 9.6)

    A. A Parliamentary System

    B. Common currency

    C. Dictatorship

    D. Uniform economic policies

93. **One difference between a presidential and a parliamentary system is, in a parliamentary system:**
    (Rigorous) (Skill 9.6)

    A. The Prime Minister is head of government while a president or monarch is head of state

    B. The President is head of government and the Vice-President is head of state

    C. The President pro-tempore of the Senate is head of state while the Prime Minister is head of government

    D. The President appoints the head of state

94. **Which of the following countries was not a part of the former Eastern Europe?**
    (Easy) (Skill 9.7)

    A. Romania

    B. Bulgaria

    C. France

    D. Albania

95. **The drought stricken region of Africa south of the Sahara and extending east and west from Senegal to Somalia is: (Average) (Skill 10.1)**

    A. The Kalahari

    B. The Namib

    C. The Great Rift Valley

    D. The Sahel

96. **Which of the following was not a group from Africa? (Easy) (Skill 10.2)**

    A. Inca

    B. Kushites

    C. Bantu

    D. Ibu

97. **Where was the Slave Coast located? (Rigorous) (Skill 10.3)**

    A. Libya

    B. Ivory Coast

    C. Mali

    D. Dahomey

98. **The Nile River: (Easy) (Skill 11.1)**

    A. Is the longest river in the world

    B. Flows through Europe

    C. Flows through Canada

    D. Flows through Mexico and the U.S.

99. **Which was not a religion of the Middle East? (Easy) (Skill 11.3)**

    A. Christianity

    B. Hinduism

    C. Islam

    D. Judaism

100. **The first ancient civilization to introduce and practice monotheism was the: (Rigorous) (Skill 11.3)**

    A. Sumerians

    B. Minoans

    C. Phoenicians

    D. Hebrews

101. Which one of the following is not an important legacy of the Byzantine Empire? (Rigorous) (Skill 11.3)

    A. It protected Western Europe from various attacks from the East by such groups as the Persians, Ottoman Turks, and Barbarians

    B. Its center was at Constantinople

    C. Its military organization was the foundation for modern armies

    D. It had been a center for Christianity

102. The Ottoman Empire resulted in: (Rigorous) (Skill 11.3)

    A. Free rule for the Middle East

    B. A free Israel

    C. Colonization of much of the Middle East

    D. Colonization of the Middle East by the British

103. The most populated continent is: (Easy) (Skill 12.1)

    A. South America

    B. Asia

    C. Australia

    D. Europe

104. The world religion which includes a caste system is: (Average) (Skill 12.3)

    A. Buddhism

    B. Hinduism

    C. Sikhism

    D. Jainism

105. The term Oceania refers to all except: (Average) (Skill 13.1)

    A. Indonesia

    B. New Zealand

    C. Papua New Guinea

    D. Hawaii

106. Which of the following geographic regions is not a part of the geography of Georgia? (Average) (Skill 14.1)

    A. The Atlantic Coastal Plain

    B. The Panhandle

    C. The Piedmont

    D. The Blue Ridge

107. Which tribes were part of the Native American cultures of the Southeastern U.S.? (Rigorous) (Skill 14.2)

   A.   Cherokee and Cree

   B.   Inca and Mayan

   C.   Hopi and Cherokee

   D.   Navajo and Hopi

108. The only colony not founded and settled for religious, political or business reasons was: (Average) (Skill 14.3)

   A.   Delaware

   B.   Virginia

   C.   Georgia

   D.   New York

109. Who received a charter to form Georgia? (Rigorous) (Skill 14.3)

   A.   Vasco da Gama

   B.   King George II

   C.   James Oglethorpe

   D.   John Cabot

110. The first ten amendments to the Constitution are called the: (Easy) (Skill 14.4)

   A.   Bill of Petition

   B.   Petition of Rights

   C.   Rights of Man

   D.   Bill of Rights

111. Georgia ratified the U.S. Constitution in: (Rigorous) (Skill 14.4)

   A.   1776

   B.   1788

   C.   1792

   D.   1783

112. The First Great Awakening refers to: (Average) (Skill 14.5)

   A.   The role of Catholicism in Georgia

   B.   A Protestant religious movement

   C.   The realization that slavery was wrong

   D.   The existence of the Ku Klux Klan

113. **Georgia's first constitution was adopted in:**
(Average) (Skill 14.4)

   A.   1776

   B.   1784

   C.   1779

   D.   1777

114. **The New South refers to:**
(Average) (Skill 14.7)

   A.   A new housing development

   B.   The South after the Civil War

   C.   The South before the Civil War

   D.   The South after World War I

115. **In the post World War II years, Georgia experienced all but the following:**
(Easy) (Skill 14.9)

   A.   Elimination of the poll tax

   B.   The re-establishment of the plantation system

   C.   The development of industry

   D.   Growth of cities

116. **Which of the following was not a Georgian?**
(Easy) (Skill 14.9)

   A.   Martin Luther King, Jr.

   B.   Rose Parks

   C.   Governor Eugene Talmadge

   D.   Senator Strom Thurmond

117. **An obligation identified with citizenship is:**
(Easy) (Skill 15.2)

   A.   Belonging to a political party

   B.   Educating oneself

   C.   Running for political office

   D.   Voting

118. **The Bill of Rights in the Georgia Constitution does not guarantee its citizens the right to:**
(Easy) (Skill 15.2)

   A.   Life, liberty and the pursuit of happiness

   B.   Freedom of Worship

   C.   To bear arms

   D.   To be free of taxation

119. **According to the State of Georgia Constitution, the Senate can consist of no more than:**
(Rigorous) (Skill 15.4)

   A.   56 members

   B.   93 members

   C.   100 members

   D.   38 members

120. **In the State of Georgia, a bill can be introduced by:**
(Average) (Skill 15.6)

   A.   The Governor only

   B.   A Senator only

   C.   A House member only

   D.   Any member of the General Assembly

120. **Which one of the following are called meridians?**
(Average) (Skill 17.2)

   A.   Elevation or altitude

   B.   Ocean currents

   C.   Latitude

   D.   Longitude

121. **Meridians, or lines of longitude, not only help in pinpointing locations but are also used for:**
(Easy) (Skill 17.2)

   A.   Measuring distance from the Poles

   B.   Determining direction of ocean currents

   C.   Determining the time around the world

   D.   Measuring distance on the equator

122. **Meridians, or lines of longitude, not only help in pinpointing locations but are also used for:**
(Easy) (Skill 17.2)

   A.   Measuring distance from the Poles

   B.   Determining direction of ocean currents

   C.   Determining exact locations

   D.   Measuring distance on the equator

123. **In which of the following disciplines would the study of physical mapping, modern or ancient, and the plotting of points and boundaries be least useful? (Easy) (Skill 17.2)**

    A.   Sociology

    B.   Geography

    C.   Archaeology

    D.   History

124. **The study of "spatial relationships and interaction" would be done by people in the field of: (Average) (Skill 17.2)**

    A.   Political Science

    B.   Anthropology

    C.   Geography

    D.   Sociology

125. **The name for those who make maps is: (Rigorous) (Skill 17.2)**

    A.   Haberdasher

    B.   Geographer

    C.   Cartographer

    D.   Demographer

Rigor Table

Easy %20	Average Rigor %40	Rigorous %40
4, 5, 7, 14, 15, 16, 17, 22, 23, 38, 41, 62, 69, 93, 95, 97, 98, 102, 109, 114, 115, 116, 117, 122, 123,	1, 2, 3, 6, 8, 9, 10, 12, 19, 20, 24, 25, 27, 31, 33, 36, 39, 42, 43, 45, 49, 50, 51, 52, 54, 55, 57, 59, 65, 66, 67, 68, 70, 71, 82, 86, 89, 90, 94, 103, 104, 105, 107, 111, 112, 113, 118, 120, 121, 124	11, 13, 18, 20, 26, 28, 29, 30, 32, 34, 35, 37, 40, 44, 46, 47, 48, 53, 56, 58, 60, 61, 63, 64, 72, 73, 74, 75, 76, 77, 78, 79, 80, 81, 83, 84, 85, 87, 88, 91, 92, 96, 99, 100, 101, 106, 108, 110, 119, 125

Answer Key

1.	C	41.	C	81.	C	121.	D
2.	D	42.	B	82.	B	122.	C
3.	A	43.	A	83.	A	123.	A
4.	A	44.	C	84.	D	124.	C
5.	C	45.	D	85.	D	125.	C
6.	B	46.	B	86.	A		
7.	B	47.	C	87.	C		
8.	B	48.	A	88.	A		
9.	B	49.	D	89.	B		
10.	B	50.	A	90.	D		
11.	D	51.	B	91.	C		
12.	D	52.	D	92.	A		
13.	A	53.	A	93.	C		
14.	D	54.	B	94.	D		
15.	A	55.	C	95.	A		
16.	C	56.	A	96.	D		
17.	B	57.	D	97.	A		
18.	C	58.	C	98.	B		
19.	C	59.	D	99.	D		
20.	B	60.	B	100.	C		
21.	D	61.	B	101.	C		
22.	C	62.	D	102.	B		
23.	D	63.	D	103.	B		
24.	A	64.	A	104.	D		
25.	A	65.	C	105.	B		
26.	C	66.	C	106.	A		
27.	A	67.	A	107.	C		
28.	C	68.	C	108.	C		
29.	C	69.	A	109.	D		
30.	B	70.	D	110.	B		
31.	A	71.	C	111.	B		
32.	D	72.	A	112.	D		
33.	B	73.	A	113.	B		
34.	B	74.	D	114.	B		
35.	A	75.	C	115.	D		
36.	B	76.	C	116.	D		
37.	A	77.	B	117.	D		
38.	D	78.	A	118.	A		
39.	C	79.	C	119.	A		
40.	C	80.	C	120.	D		

Rationale

1. **The end to hunting, gathering, and fishing of prehistoric people was due to:**
    (Average) (Skill 1.1)

    A.   Domestication of animals

    B.   Building crude huts and houses

    C.   Development of agriculture

    D.   Organized government in villages

    Answer: C – Development of agriculture

    Rationale: Although the domestication of animals, the building of huts and houses and the first organized governments were all very important steps made by early civilizations, it was the development of agriculture that ended the once dominant practices of hunting, gathering, and fishing among prehistoric people. The development of agriculture provided a more efficient use of time and for the first time a surplus of food. This greatly improved the quality of life and contributed to early population growth.

2. **The English explorer who gave England its claim to North American was:**
    (Average) (Skill 1.3)

    A.   Raleigh

    B.   Hawkins

    C.   Drake

    D.   Cabot

    Answer: D– Cabot

    Rationale: Sir Walter Raleigh (1554-1618) was an English explorer and navigator, who was sent to the New World in search of riches. He founded the lost colony at Roanoke, Virginia, and was later imprisoned for a supposed plot to kill the King for which he was later released. Sir John Hawkins (1532-1595) and Sir Francis Drake (1540-1596) were both navigators who worked in the slave trade, made some voyages to the New World, and commanded ships against and defeated the Spanish Armada in 1588. John Cabot (1450-1498) was the English explorer who gave England claim to North America.

3. **The first European to see Florida and sail along its coast was:**
   (Average) (Skill 1.3)

   A. Cabot

   B. Columbus

   C. Ponce de Leon

   D. Narvaez

   Answer: A – Cabot

   Rationale: (A) John Cabot (1450-1498) was the English explorer who gave England claim to North American and the first European to see Florida and sail along its coast. (B) Columbus (1451-1506) was sent by the Spanish to the New World and has received false credit for "discovering America" in 1492, although he did open up the New World to European expansion, exploitation, and Christianity. (C) Ponce de Leon (1460-1521), the Spanish explorer, was the first European to actually land on Florida. (D) Panfilo de Narvaez (1470-1528) was also a Spanish conquistador, but he was sent to Mexico to force Cortes into submission. He failed and was captured.

4. **Maps as a rule are:**
   (Skill 1.4) (Easy)

   A. All subject to some sort of distortion

   B. Always entirely accurate

   C. Not very useful in political science studies

   D. Usually difficult to understand

   Answer: A – All subject to some sort of distortion

   Rationale: Maps as a rule are all subject to some sort of distortion. Since they are representing a three-dimensional world in a two-dimensional representation, it will never be completely accurate. Even maps that are specifically designed to limit distortion still will lack total accuracy. Maps are still very helpful in most social science disciplines and generally designed to be understood easily using keys and symbols.

5.   **Florida was originally settled by:**
      (Easy) (Skill 1.5)

      A.   Italy

      B.   Great Britain

      C.   Spain

      D.   France

Answer: C. – Spain

Rationale: Florida was first explored by Ponce de Leon, the Spanish explorer searching for the Fountain of Youth in 1513. The Spanish settled Florida despite a lack of precious metals (such as those of Mexico or Peru) and strong resentment from the Native Americans already in the region, they felt that the strategic location of Florida was in itself a value. It was lost to the British in 1763 as part of the Treaty of Paris ending the Seven Years' War. Under the British, Florida was divided and stayed that way until the United States gained independence in the late 18th century.

6.   **Which one of the following is not a reason why Europeans came to the New World?**
      (Average) (Skill 1.5)

      A.   To find resources in order to increase wealth

      B.   To establish trade

      C.   To increase a ruler's power and importance

      D.   To spread Christianity

Answer: B – To establish trade

Rationale: The Europeans came to the New World for a number of reasons; often they came to find new natural resources to extract for manufacturing. The Portuguese, Spanish and English were sent over to increase the monarch's power and spread influences such as religion (Christianity) and culture. Therefore, the only reason given that Europeans did not come to the New World was to establish trade.

7. **Of the thirteen English colonies, it can be said that settlers came for all but the following reasons:**
    (Easy) (Skill 1.6)

    A. Religious freedom

    B. The chance to own slaves

    C. Political freedom

    D. Ownership of land

    Answer: B – The chance to own slaves

    Rationale: Settlers cam to the colonies looking for a better life and an end the lack of political and religious freedom They were also looking for the opportunity to own land. They did not immigrate for the purpose of being able to own slaves.

8. **The year 1619 was a memorable for the colony of Virginia. Three important events occurred resulting in lasting effects on US history. Which one of the following is not one of the events?**
    (Average) (Skill 1.6)

    A. Twenty African slaves arrived.

    B. The London Company granted the colony a charter making it independent.

    C. The colonists were given the right by the London Company to govern themselves through representative government in the Virginia House of Burgesses

    D. The London Company sent to the colony 60 women who were quickly married, establishing families and stability in the colony.

    Answer: B – The London Company granted the colony a charter making it independent.

    Rationale: In the year 1619, the Southern colony of Virginia had an eventful year including the first arrival of twenty African slaves, the right to self-governance through representative government in the Virginia House of Burgesses (their own legislative body), and the arrival of sixty women sent to marry and establish families in the colony. The London Company did not, however, grant the colony a charter in 1619.

9. **In an indirect democracy:**
    (Average) (Skill 2.1)

    A. All the people together decide on issues

    B. People elect representatives to act for them

    C. Democracy can never really work

    D. Government is less efficient than a direct democracy

    Answer: B – People elect representatives to act for them

    Rationale: In an indirect democracy people elect representatives to act for them. An example of an indirect democracy would be the United States government in which the people elect a president, vice-president, senators, and representatives to make decisions and run the government. An example of a direct democracy would be the government of the Greeks in Athens during the Classical Period, in which citizens represented themselves in their own government.

10. **Which of the following is not associated with the Revolutionary War?**
    (Average) (Skill 2.1)

    A. Stamp Act

    B. Louisiana Purchase

    C. Quartering Act

    D. Townsend Act

    Answer: B – Louisiana Purchase

    Rationale: The (A) Stamp Act was a tax on the colonists' use of newspapers, legal documents, and other printed matter. (C) The Quartering Act was passed in 1765 requiring the colonists to provide supplies and living quarters for the British troops. (D) The Townshend Acts passed in 1767 taxing lead, paint, paper, and tea brought into the colonies. All of these angered the colonists and were contributing factors to the revolution. The (B) Louisiana Purchase did not take place until the eighteen hundreds.

11. **France decided in 1777 to help the American colonies in their war against Britain. This decision was based on: (Rigorous) (Skill 2.1)**

    A.   The naval victory of John Paul Jones over the British ship "Serapis"

    B.   The survival of the terrible winter at Valley Forge

    C.   The success of colonial guerilla fighters in the South

    D.   The defeat of the British at Saratoga

Answer: D – The defeat of the British at Saratoga

Rationale: The defeat of the British at Saratoga was the overwhelming factor in the Franco-American alliance of 1777 that helped the American colonies defeat the British. Some historians believe that without the Franco-American alliance, the American Colonies would not have been able to defeat the British and American would have remained a British colony.

12. **The Declaration of Independence owes much to the philosophy of: (Skill 2.3)(Average)**

    A.   Vladimir Lenin

    B.   Karl Marx

    C.   Thomas Hobbes

    D.   John Locke

Answer: D – John Locke

Rationale: The Declaration of Independence owes much to the philosophy of the great enlightenment writer John Locke (1632-1704). Locke's empiricism and belief in the welfare of the middle class and their need to own property was a huge landmark in political philosophy. His work *Two Treatises on Civil Government* proved to be a huge influence on the formation of new governments such as the United States. His ideas about the right to life, liberty and property, which the founding fathers of the US changed to life, liberty and the pursuit of happiness to justify slavery and other injustices, was a cornerstone of the Declaration of Independence.

13. **Which of the following is an important idea expressed in the Declaration of Independence?**
(Rigorous) (Skill 2.3)

 A. People have the right to change their government

 B. People should obey the government authority

 C. A monarchy is a bad thing

 D. Indirect democracy is best

Answer: A – People have the right to change their government

Rationale: Although "people should obey their government", "monarchy is a bad thing", and "indirect democracy is best" may have very well been sentiments held by the authors of the Declaration of Independence. In the actual document the express statement is clearly that "people have the right to change their government", a sentiment that is still very important today.

14. **The term that describes the division of government function is:**
(Easy) (Skill 2.4)

 A. Free Enterprise

 B. Constitutional Prerogative

 C. Checks and Balances

 D. Separation of Powers

Answer: D – Separation of Powers

Rationale: (A) Free enterprise is the system of capitalism in which there is little or no government involvement in the economy and there is private control over the means of production. (C) Checks and balances is the system in place to prevent over-concentration of power in any one branch of government. The term (D) "separation of powers" best describes the division of government

15. **In the U. S., checks and balances refers to:**
    (Easy) (Skill 2.4)

    A. The ability of each branch of government to "check" or limit the actions of the others

    B. Balance of payments

    C. International law

    D. The federal deficit

    Answer: A – The ability of each branch of government to "check" or limit the actions of the others

    Rationale: In the United States, checks and balances refers to the ability of each branch of government (Executive, Legislative, and Judicial) to "check" or limit the actions of the others. Examples of checks and balances are: The Executive branch limits the Legislature by power of veto over bills and appointments in the court system. The Judicial branch limits the power of the Legislature by judicial review and the ability to rule laws unconstitutional and may also determine executive orders unconstitutional. The Legislature checks the Executive by power of impeachment.

16. **There is no doubt of the vast improvement of the U.S. Constitution over the weak Articles of Confederation. Which one of the four accurate statements below is a unique yet eloquent description of the Constitution?**
(Easy) (Skill 2.4)

A. The establishment of a strong central government in no way lessened or weakened the individual states.

B. Individual rights were protected and secured.

C. The Constitution is the best representation of the results of the American genius for compromise.

D. Its flexibility and adaptation to change gives it a sense of timelessness.

Answer: C – The Constitution is the best representation of the results of the American genius for compromise.

Rationale: The Constitution demands unquestioned respect and subservience to the federal government by all states and citizens. The U.S. Constitution was indeed a vast improvement over the Articles of Confederation and the authors of the document took great care to assure longevity. It clearly stated that the establishment of a strong central government in no way lessened or weakened the individual states. In the Bill of Rights, citizens were assured that individual rights were protected and secured. Possibly the most important feature of the new Constitution was its flexibility and adaptation to change which assured longevity.

Therefore, the only statement made that doesn't describe some facet of the Constitution is "The Constitution demands unquestioned respect and subservience to the federal government by all states and citizens." On the contrary, the Constitution made sure that citizens could critique and make changes to their government and encourages such critiques and changes as necessary for the preservation of democracy.

17. **The political document that was the first to try to organize the newly independent American Colonies was the:**
(Easy) (Skill 2.4)

   A.   Declaration of Independence

   B.   Articles of Confederation

   C.   The Constitution

   D.   The Confederate States

Answer: B – Articles of Confederation

Rationale: The political document that was the first to try to organize the newly independent American colonies was the deeply flawed but immensely important Articles of Confederation. As a precursor to the United States Constitution, the Articles of Confederation, presented to the Second Continental Congress in 1776 and ratified in 1781, proved ineffective in presenting the power of the central or federal government. Although the Articles of Confederation fostered a true national unity for the first time, its weakness in subordinating the federal government to the states, made it less respected than the Constitution, which was ratified in 1789.

18. **Give the correct order of the following:**
    (Rigorous) (Skill 2.4)

    A.   The Constitution, the Declaration of Independence, the Articles of Confederation

    B.   The Declaration of Independence, the Constitution, the Articles of Confederation

    C.   The Declaration of Independence, the Articles of Confederation, the Constitution

    D.   The Articles of Confederation, the Declaration of Independence, the Constitution

Answer: C – The Declaration of Independence, the Articles of Confederation, the Constitution

Rationale: The correct order of implementation of the doctrines listed below is:

1)   Declaration of Independence (July 4, 1776)

2)   The Articles of Confederation (March 1, 1781)

3)   The Constitution (April 30, 1789)

19. **Under the brand new Constitution, the most urgent of the many problems facing the new federal government was that of:**
(Average) (Skill 2.4, 2.5)

    A.   Maintaining a strong army and navy

    B.   Establishing a strong foreign policy

    C.   Raising money to pay salaries and war debts

    D.   Setting up courts, passing federal laws, and providing for law enforcement officers

Answer: C – Raising money to pay salaries and war debts

Rationale: Maintaining strong military forces, establishment of a strong foreign policy, and setting up a justice system were important problems facing the United States under the newly ratified Constitution. However, the most important and pressing issue was how to raise money to pay salaries and war debts from the Revolutionary War. Alexander Hamilton (1755-1804) then Secretary of the Treasury proposed increased tariffs and taxes on products such as liquor. This money would be used to pay off war debts and to pay for internal programs. Hamilton also proposed the idea of a National Bank.

20. **In the United States government, the power of taxation and borrowing is:**
(Average) (Skill 2.5)

    A.   Implied or suggested

    B.   Concurrent or shared

    C.   Delegated or expressed

    D.   Reserved

Answer: B – Concurrent or shared

Rationale: In the United States government, the power of taxation is concurrent or shared with the states. An example of this is the separation of state and federal income tax and the separate filings of tax returns for each.

21. **In the United States government, power or control over public education, marriage, and divorce is:**
(Rigorous) (Skill 2.5)

    A.   Implied or suggested

    B.   Concurrent or shared

    C.   Delegates or expressed

    D.   Reserved

Answer: D – Reserved

Rationale: In the United States government, power or control over public education, marriage, and divorce is reserved. This is to say that these powers are reserved for the people of the states to decide for themselves.

22. **The Judiciary refers to:**
(Easy) (Skill 2.5)

    A.   The President

    B.   Congress

    C.   The legal system

    D.   The system of states' rights

Answer: C – The legal system

Rationale: The Judiciary refers to the legal system of courts, judges, and due process. The President is part of the Executive branch and the Congress is part of the Legislative branch.

23. **The Executive branch refers to:**
(Easy) (Skill 2.5)

   A.   The Senate

   B.   The Legislature

   C.   Congress

   D.   The President and Vice-President

Answer: D – The President and Vice-President

Rationale: The Executive branch of government refers to the President and Vice-President. The Senate, Legislature, and Congress all refer to the Legislative branch.

24. **Which of the three branches of government is responsible for taxation?**
(Average) (Skill 2.5)

   A.   Legislative

   B.   Executive

   C.   Judicial

   D.   Congressional

Answer: A – Legislative

Rationale: The Legislative branch of government is responsible for taxation. The Congress is responsible for levying federal taxes while state legislatures determine the individual state's taxes. The Executive branch is often though to be responsible for taxation, as taxation is often a highly talked about issue in presidential campaigns, but it is in fact the Legislature that is responsible.

25.   To "impeach" a President means to:
       (Average) (Skill 2.5)

    A.   Bring charges against a President

    B.   Remove a President from office

    C.   Re-elect the President

    D.   Override his veto

Answer: A – Bring charges against a President

Rationale: Contrary to much popular understanding of impeachment, it means to bring charges against a President. It does not mean to remove or re-elect the President. Andrew Jackson and William Jefferson Clinton are the only two United States Presidents to have been impeached. Jackson and Clinton were both acquitted during hearings and remained in office. Richard M. Nixon resigned from office as the House of Representatives prepared impeachment proceedings.

26.   In the U.S. government, the power of coining money is:
       (Rigorous) (Skill 2.5)

    A.   Implied or suggested

    B.   Concurrent or shared

    C.   Delegated or expressed

    D.   Reserved

Answer: C – Delegated or expressed

Rationale: In the United States government, the power of coining money is delegated or expressed. Therefore, only the United States government may coin money, the states may not coin money for themselves.

27. **The United States government's federal system consists of:**
(Average) (Skill 2.5)

   A. Three parts, the Executive, the Legislative, and the Judiciary

   B. Three parts, the Legislative, the Congress, and the Presidency

   C. Four parts, the Executive, the Judiciary, the courts and the Legislative

   D. Two parts, the Government and the governed

Answer: A – Three parts, the Executive, the Legislative, and the Judiciary

Rationale: The United States government's federal system consists of three parts: the Executive, the Legislative, and the Judiciary. The Executive branch consists of the President, Vice-President, and Cabinet. The Legislative branch consists of the Senate and the House of Representatives, also known as Congress, and the Judiciary is made up of the courts and the judiciary. All three branches keep each other in line through a system of checks and balances.

28. **The power to declare war, establish a postal system, and coin money rests with which branch of the government:**
(Rigorous) (Skill 2.5)

   A. Presidential

   B. Judicial

   C. Legislative

   D. Executive

Answer: C – Legislative

Rationale: The power to declare war, establish a postal system, and coin money rests with the Legislative branch of the government. However, the President or Executive branch becomes the commander in chief and has strong influence over wartime activities. The President may veto Congress in its decision to go to war, although in our current political climate, more often it is the President who urges Congress to declare war.

29. **The highest appellate court in the United States is the:**
(Rigorous) (Skill 2.5)

    A.   National Appeals Court

    B.   Circuit Court

    C.   Supreme Court

    D.   Court of Appeals

Answer: C – Supreme Court

Rationale: The highest appellate court in the United States is the Supreme Court. There is also a federal circuit court of appeals and a state system that includes appellate courts and state supreme courts, but they are not as high as the United States Supreme Court.

30. **In the United States, the right to declare war is a power of:**
(Rigorous) (Skill 2.5)

    A.   The President

    B.   Congress

    C.   The Executive Branch

    D.   The States

Answer: B – Congress

Rationale: In the United States, the right to declare war is a power of the Congress or Legislative branch. After Congress declares war, the President and Executive branch are in control as the Commander in Chief of the military.

31.   **The source of authority for national, state, and local governments in the U.S. is:**
       (Average) (Skills 2.5, 2.6)

       A.   The will of the people

       B.   The US Constitution

       C.   Written laws

       D.   The Bill of Rights

       Answer: A – The will of the people

       Rationale: The source of authority for national, state, and local governments in the United States is the will of the people. Although the United States Constitution, the Bill of Rights, and the other written laws of the land are important guidelines for authority, they may ultimately be altered or changed by the will of the people.

32.   **The Bill of Rights says that any rights it does not mention are:**
       (Rigorous) (Skill 2.6)

       A.   Reserved to the federal government

       B.   Not important

       C.   Judged by the Supreme Court

       D.   Reserved to the states or to the people

       Answer: D – Reserved to the states or to the people

       Rationale: The Bill of Rights says that any rights it does not mention are reserved to the states or to the people. This means that just because a right is not listed specifically in the Bill of Rights does not necessarily mean that that right does not exist or that it may be violated.

33. **The Bill of Rights was mostly written by:**
    (Average) (Skill 2.6)

    A.   Thomas Jefferson

    B.   James Madison

    C.   George Washington

    D.   Alexander Hamilton

Answer: B – James Madison

Rationale: The Bill of Rights, along with the majority of the Constitution, was mostly written by James Madison. Thomas Jefferson wrote the Declaration of Independence. Washington and Hamilton were present at the Constitutional Convention of 1787 in Philadelphia and they were advocates of federalism or increasing the power of the federal government.

34. **The Orders in Council:**
    (Rigorous) (Skill 3.1)

    A.   Prohibited the Declaration of Independence

    B.   Prohibited American ships from entering French ports

    C.   Gave Americans representation in Parliament

    D.   Imposed a tax on American goods entering England

Answer: B – Prohibited American ships from entering French ports

Rationale: The Orders in Council was a series of measures by the British prohibiting American ships from entering any French ports, not only in Europe but also in India and the West Indies. This was a contributing factor to the outbreak of the War of 1812.

35. **Which one of the following was not a reason why the United States went to war with Great Britain in 1812?**
(Rigorous) (Skill 3.2)

    A.   Resentment by Spain over the sale exploration, and settlement of the Louisiana Territory

    B.   The westward movement of farmers because of the need for more land

    C.   Canadian fur traders were agitating the northwestern Indians to fight American expansion

    D.   Britain continued to seize American ships on the high seas and force American seamen to serve aboard British ships

Answer: A – Resentment by Spain over the sale, exploration, and settlement of the Louisiana Territory

Rationale: The United States went to war with Great Britain in 1812 for a number of reasons including the expansion of settlers westward and the need for more land, the agitation of Indians by Canadian fur traders in eastern Canada, and the continued seizures of American ships by the British on the high seas. Therefore, the only statement given that was not a reason for the War of 1812 was the resentment by Spain over the sale, exploration and settlement of the Louisiana Territory. In fact, the Spanish continually held more hostility towards the British than towards the United States. The War of 1812 is often considered to be the second American war for independence.

36. **Colonial expansion by Western European powers in the 18th and 19th centuries was due primarily to:**
(Average) (Skill 3.2)

    A.   Building and opening the Suez Canal

    B.   The Industrial Revolution

    C.   Marked improvements in transportation

    D.   Complete independence of all the Americas and loss of European domination and influence

Answer: B – The Industrial Revolution

Rationale: Colonial expansion by Western European powers in the late 18th and 19th centuries was due primarily to the Industrial Revolution in Great Britain that spread across Europe and needed new natural resources and therefore, new locations from which to extract the raw materials needed to feed the new industries.

37. **It can be reasonably stated that the change in the United States from an agricultural country into an industrial power was due to all of the following except:**
(Rigorous) (Skill 3.2)

   A. Tariffs on foreign imports

   B. Millions of hardworking immigrants

   C. An increase in technological developments

   D. The change from steam to electricity for powering industrial machinery

Answer: A – Tariffs on foreign imports

Rationale: It can be reasonably stated that the change in the United States from an agricultural country into an industrial power was due to a great degree of three of the reasons listed above. It was a combination of millions of hard-working immigrants, an increase in technological developments, and the change from steam to electricity for powering industrial machinery. The only reason given that really had little effect was the tariffs on foreign imports.

38. **From about 1870 to 1900 the settlement of America's "last frontier", the West, was completed. One attraction for settlers was free land but it would have been to no avail without:**
(Easy) (Skill 3.2)

   A. Better farming methods and technology

   B. Surveying to set boundaries

   C. Immigrants and others to seek new land

   D. The railroad to get them there

Answer: D – The railroad to get them there

Rationale: From about 1870 to 1900, the settlement for America's "last frontier" in the West was made possible by the building of the railroad. Without the railroad, the settlers never could have traveled such distances in an efficient manner.

39.   Historians state that the West helped speed up the Industrial Revolution. Which one of the following statements was not a reason for this?
(Average) (Skill 3.2)

A.   Food supplies for the ever increasing urban populations came from farms in the West

B.   A tremendous supply of gold and silver from western mines provided the Capital needed to built industries

C.   Descendants of western settlers, educated as engineers, geologists, and metallurgists in the East, returned to the West to mine the mineral resources needed for industry

D.   Iron, copper, and other minerals from western mines were important resources in manufacturing products

Answer: C – Descendants of western settlers, educated as engineers, geologists, and metallurgists in the East, returned to the West to mine the mineral resources needed for industry.

Rationale: The West helped to speed up the Industrial Revolution in a number of important and significant ways. First, the land yielded crops for the growing urban populations. Second, the gold and silver supplies coming out of the Western mines provided the capital needed to build industries. Also, resources such as iron and copper were extracted from the mines in the West and provided natural resources for manufacturing. The descendants of western settlers typically didn't become educated and then returned to the West as miners. The miners were typically working class with little or no education.

40. **The belief that the United States should control all of North America was called:**
(Rigorous) (Skill 3.2)

    A.   Westward Expansion

    B.   Pan Americanism

    C.   Manifest Destiny

    D.   Nationalism

Answer: C – Manifest Destiny

Rationale: The belief that the United States should control all of North America was called (B) Manifest Destiny. This idea fueled much of the violence and aggression towards those already occupying the lands such as the Native Americans. Manifest Destiny was certainly driven by sentiments of (D) nationalism and gave rise to (A) westward expansion.

41. **Democracy is defined as:**
(Easy) (Skill 3.3)

    A.   Rule for a few elite

    B.   Rule by a monarch

    C.   Rule by the people either directly or through representatives

    D.   Rule by a dictator

Answer: C – Rule by the people either directly or through representatives

Rationale: Democracy is loosely defined as "rule by the people," either directly or through representatives. Associated with the idea of democracy are freedom, equality, and opportunity. The basic concept of democracy existed in the 13 English colonies with the practice of independent self-government.

42. **A number of women worked hard in the first half of the nineteenth century for women's rights but decisive gains did not come until after 1850. The earliest accomplishments were in:**
(Average) (Skill 3.5)

   A.   Medicine

   B.   Education

   C.   Writing

   D.   Temperance

Answer: B – Education

Rationale: Although women worked hard in the early 19th century to make gains in medicine, writing, and temperance movements, the most prestigious accomplishments of the early women's movement was in the field of education. Women such as Mary Wollstonecraft (1759-1797), Alice Palmer (1855-1902), and of course Elizabeth Blackwell (1821-1910), led the way for women, particularly in the area of higher education.

43. **Which one of the following events did not occur during the period known as the "Era of Good Feeling?"**
(Average) (Skill 3.6)

   A.   President Monroe issued the Monroe Doctrine

   B.   Spain ceded Florida to the United States

   C.   The building of the National Road

   D.   The charter of the second Bank of the United States

Answer: A – President Monroe issued the Monroe Doctrine

Rationale: The so-called "Era of Good Feeling" describes the period following the War of 1812. This was during the Presidency of James Madison and focused the nation on internal national improvements such as the building of the second national bank (Charter for Bank of United States), construction of new roads (National Road), and the Treaty of Ghent, which ended the War of 1812 by forcing Spain to cede Florida to the United States. Of the possible answers, only the Monroe Doctrine (1823), which called for an end to any European occupation and colonization in the Americas, was not a part of the "Era of Good Feeling", it came a bit after.

44. **Which of the following was not a provision of the Compromise of 1850?**
(Rigorous) (Skill 3.6)

A.   Admission of California as a free state

B.   End of slave trading in Washington D.C.

C.   Approval of the Louisiana Purchase

D.   Creation of New Mexico and Utah territories

Answer: C – Approval of the Louisiana Purchase

Rationale: The Compromise of 1850 was the result of different factions wanting different things. Factions of Northerners advocated prohibition of slavery and Southerners favored slavery. A third faction arose supporting the doctrine of "popular sovereignty" which stated that people living in territories and states should be allowed to decide for themselves whether or not slavery should be permitted. In 1849, California applied for admittance to the Union and the furor began. The Compromise of 1850 resulted in the (A) admission of California as a free state, (B) the end of slave trading in Washington D.C and (d) Creation of New Mexico and Utah territories. (C) The Louisiana Purchase occurred earlier in the century.

45. The principle of "popular sovereignty" allowing people in any territory to make their own decision concerning slavery was stated by;
(Average) (Skill 3.6)

A. Henry Clay

B. Daniel Webster

C. John C. Calhoun

D. Stephen A. Douglas

Answer: D – Stephen A. Douglas

Rationale: (A) Henry Clay (1777-1852) and (B) Daniel Webster (1782-1852) were prominent Whigs whose main concern was keeping the United States one nation. They opposed Andrew Jackson and his Democratic party around the 1830s in favor of promoting what Clay called "the American System". (C) John C. Calhoun (1782-1850) served as Vice-President under John Quincy Adams and Andrew Jackson, and then as a state senator from South Carolina. He was very pro-slavery and a champion of states' rights. The principle of "popular sovereignty", in which people in each territory could make their own decisions concerning slavery, was the doctrine of (D) Stephen A. Douglas (1813-1861). Douglas was looking for a middle ground between the abolitionists of the North and the pro-slavery Democrats of the South. However, as the polarization of pro- and anti-slavery sentiments grew, he lost the presidential election to Republican Abraham Lincoln, who later abolished slavery.

46. **The three-day Battle of Gettysburg was the turning point of the Civil War for the North leading to victory. The battle in the West reinforcing the North's victory and sealing the South's defeat was the day after Gettysburg at:**
(Rigorous) (Skill 3.7)

A. Perryville

B. Vicksburg

C. Stones River

D. Shiloh

Answer: B – Vicksburg

Rationale: The Battle of Vicksburg was crucial in reinforcing the North's victory and sealing the south's defeat for a couple of reasons. First, the Battle of Vicksburg potentially gave the Union full control of the Mississippi River. More importantly, the battle split the Confederate Army and allowed General Grant to reach his goal of restoring commerce to the important northwest area.

47. **The post-Civil War years were a time of low public morality, greed, graft, and dishonesty. Which one of the reasons listed would not be accurate?**
(Rigorous) (Skill 4.1)

    A.   The war itself because of the money and materials needed to carry on the War

    B.   The very rapid growth of industry and big business after the War

    C.   The personal example set by President Grant

    D.   Unscrupulous heads of large impersonal corporations

Answer: C – The personal example set by President Grant

Rationale: The post-Civil War years were a particularly difficult time for the nation and public morale was especially low. The war had plunged the country into debt and ultimately into a recession by the 1890s. Racism was rampant throughout the South and the North where freed Blacks were taking jobs for low wages. The rapid growth of industry and big business caused a polarization of rich and poor, workers and owners. Many people moved into the urban centers to find work in the new industrial sector, jobs were typically low-wage, long hours, and poor working conditions. The heads of large impersonal corporations were arrogant in treating their workers inhumanely and letting morale drop to a record low. The heads of corporations showed their greed and malice towards the workingman by trying to prevent and disband labor unions.

48.   The Radical Republicans who pushed the harsh Reconstruction measures through Congress after Lincoln's death lost public and moderate Republican support when they went too far: (Rigorous) (Skill 4.1)

    A.   In their efforts to impeach the President

    B.   By dividing ten southern states into military-controlled districts

    C.   By making the ten southern states give freed African Americans the right to vote

    D.   Sending carpetbaggers into the South to build up support for Congressional legislation

Answer: A – In their efforts to impeach the President

Rationale: The public support and the moderate Republicans were actually being drawn towards the more radical end of the Republican spectrum following Lincoln's death during Reconstruction. Because many felt as though Andrew Johnson's policies towards the South were too soft and were running the risk of rebuilding the old system of white power and slavery. Even moderate Republicans in the North felt as though it was essential to rebuild the South but with the understanding that they must be abide by the Fourteenth and Fifteenth Amendment assuring Blacks freedom and the right to vote. The radical Republicans were so frustrated that the President would make concessions to the old Southerners that they attempted to impeach him. This turned back the support that they had received from the public and from moderates.

49.   What event sparked a great migration of people from all over the world to California? (Average) (Skill 4.2)

    A.   The birth of Labor Unions

    B.   California statehood

    C.   The invention of the automobile

    D.   The gold rush

Answer: D – The gold rush

Rationale: The answer is "The Gold Rush" (D). The discovery of gold in California created a lust for gold that quickly brought immigrants from the eastern United States and many parts of the world. To be sure, there were struggles and conflicts, as well as the rise of nativism. Yet this vast migration of people from all parts of the world began the process that has created California's uniquely diverse culture.

50.   **The American concept of Manifest Destiny means:**
      (Average) (Skill 4.2)

      A.   America had a right to spread throughout the American continent from coast to coast

      B.   The United States should respect the right of native peoples it encounters in its push westward

      C.   The rest of the world power should stay out of this part of the world

      D.   American should strive to be the dominant world power

Answer: A – America had a right to spread throughout the American continent from coast to coast

Rationale: The American concept of Manifest Destiny was a means of justifying expansion across the entire continent. Much like the other nationalistic movements that came before or since, Manifest Destiny put the needs and wants of those identifying themselves as Americans over the needs or wants of others. Manifest Destiny was a doctrine that justified the removal and extermination of many Native Americans already occupying lands in the West.

51.   **The American labor union movement started gaining new momentum:**
      (Rigorous) (Skill 4.3)

      A.   During the building of the railroads

      B.   After 1865 with the growth of cities

      C.   With the rise of industrial giants such as Carnegie and Vanderbilt

      D.   During the war years of 1861-1865

Answer: B – After 1865 with the growth of cities

Rationale: The American Labor Union movement had been around since the late 18th and early 19th centuries. The Labor movement began to first experience persecution by employers in the early 1800s. The American Labor Movement remained relatively ineffective until after the Civil War. In 1866, the National Labor Union was formed, pushing such issues as the eight-hour workday and new policies of immigration. This gave rise to the Knights of Labor and eventually the American Federation of Labor (AFL) in the 1890s and the Industrial Workers of the World (1905). Therefore, it was the period following the Civil War that empowered the labor movement in terms of numbers, militancy, and effectiveness.

52. **Potential customers for any good or service are not only called consumers but can also be called a:**
    (Average) (Skill 4.3)

    A. Resource

    B. Base

    C. Commodity

    D. Market

    Answer: D – Market

    Rationale: Potential customers for any product or service are not only customers but can also be called a market. A resource is a source of wealth; natural resources are the basis for manufacturing goods and services. A commodity is anything that is bought or sold, any product.

53. **The Panic of 1893:**
    (Rigorous) (Skill 4.5)

    A. Resulted in several bank failures

    B. Was a fear of a British invasion

    C. Was the South panicking about the end of slavery

    D. Was the result of invasion by Mexico

    Answer: A – Resulted in several bank failures

    Rationale: Panics refers to the banking systems, when depositors worry about the safety of their money and withdraw their funds from the bank. Since the banks only have a certain amount of cash on hand, when depositors wanted to withdraw more money than they had on hand the bank couldn't meet their demands. The panic would spread as more and more people tried to retrieve their money.

54. **"Walk softly and carry a big stick" is a statement associated with:**
(Average) (Skill 4.5)

   A. Franklin Roosevelt

   B. Theodore Roosevelt

   C. George Washington

   D. Thomas Hobbes

Answer: B – Theodore Roosevelt

Rationale: "Walk softly and carry a big stick" is a statement made by Theodore Roosevelt (1858-1919) in reference to his foreign policy, which was just as aggressive as his domestic policy. Roosevelt advocated for a new extension of the Monroe doctrine extending the idea all the way through South America. The statement also refers to Roosevelt's dealing with the Panama Canal situation, the open-door policy with China, and the formation of the Hague tribunal.

55. **After the Civil War, the US adapted an attitude of isolation from foreign affairs. But the turning point marking the beginning of the US becoming a world power was:**
(Average) (Skill 4.5)

   A. World War I

   B. Expansion of business and trade overseas

   C. The Spanish-American War

   D. The building and financial of the Panama Canal

Answer: C – The Spanish-American War

Rationale: The turning point marking the beginning of the United States becoming a super power was the Spanish-American War. This was seen as an extension of the Monroe doctrine, calling for United States dominance in the Western Hemisphere and removal of European powers in the region. The United States' relatively easy defeat of Spain in the Spanish-American War marked the beginning of a continuing era of dominance for the United States. In addition, in the post-Civil War era, Spain was the largest landowner in the Americas. Their easy defeat at the hands of the United States in Cuba, the Philippines, and elsewhere showed the strength of the United States across the globe.

56. The Fourteen Points was proposed by:
    (Rigorous) (Skill 4.6)

    A.   President Wilson

    B.   President Roosevelt

    C.   The King of England

    D.   President Washington

    Answer: A – President Wilson

    Rationale: The Fourteen Points was a proposal by President Wilson to end World War I. In these Points he had five points setting out general ideals; eight pertaining to immediately working to resolve territorial and political problems; and the fourteenth point counseled establishing an organization of nations to help keep world peace, the League of Nations.

57. The international organization established to work for world peace at the end of the First World War was the:
    (Average) (Skill 4.6)

    A.   United Earth League

    B.   Confederate States

    C.   United Nations

    D.   League of Nations

    Answer: D – League of Nations

    Rationale: The (B) Confederate States were those that seceded from the Union bringing about the Civil War. The (B) United Nations was established following World War II as an international organization for world peace. The (D) League of Nations was formed at the end of World War I to work towards world peace. The many shortcomings of the League of Nations, including a lack of membership of powerful nations, led to a need for a new international organization, the United Nations, to help end and keep the peace after World War II.

58. **Nineteenth century imperialism by Western Europe nations had important and far-reaching effects on the colonial peoples they ruled. All four of the following are the results of this. Which one was the most important and had lasting effects on key twentieth century events?**
(Rigorous) (Skill 4.6)

   A.   Local wars were ended

   B.   Living standards were raised

   C.   Demands for self-government and feelings of nationalism surfaced

   D.   Economic developments occurred

Answer: C – Demands for self-government and feelings of nationalism surfaced

Rationale: The nineteenth century imperialism by Western European nations had some very serious and far-reaching effects. The most important and lasting effect on events of the twentieth century were the demands for self-government and the rise of nationalism. Both World War I and World War II were caused to a large degree by the rise of nationalist sentiment across Europe and Asia. Nationalism has also fueled numerous liberation movements and revolutionary movements across the globe from Central and South America to the South Pacific to Africa and Asia.

59. **Which of the following did not contribute to the Stock Market Cash in 1929?**
(Average) (Skill 5.1)

   A.   Uneven distribution of wealth

   B.   Speculative investments

   C.   Buying on Margin

   D.   World War I

Answer: D – World War I

Rationale: (D) World War I did not contribute to the Stock Market Crash. The Crash occurred because of problems in the economy. There was (A) an uneven distribution of wealth and this led to (B) speculative investments in stocks with a lot of (C) margin buying. The market was very unstable because of this, and once the slide began, it couldn't be halted.

60. **The New Deal involved:**
(Rigorous) (Skill 5.2)

A.   Financing stock market speculation

B.   Programs to relieve the suffering of the Depression and to stimulate the economy

C.   A new monetary system

D.   A new pact with England

Answer: B – Programs to relieve the suffering of the Depression and to stimulate the economy.

Rationale: The New Deal was the name given to the programs that were implemented to try to pull the economy out of the Great depression.

61. **Which of the following was not a New Deal program?**
(Rigorous) (Skill 5.2)

A.   Public Works Administration

B.   Bretton Woods System

C.   National Recovery Administration

D.   Works Progress Administration

Answer: B – Bretton Woods System

Rationale: The purpose of the New Deal was to pull the economy out of the Great Depression. There were various publics works programs to provide jobs such as (A) the Public Works Administration and the (D) Works Progress Administration. The (C) National Recovery Administration was a serious of programs with various goals to achieve these purposes. The (B) Bretton Woods System was not a part of the New Deal. It was the new monetary system that was implemented at the end of World War II.

62. **Which of the following was not a leadiong figure during World War II? (Easy) (Skill 5.3)**

    A.   Hitler

    B.   Stalin

    C.   Tojo

    D.   Castro

Answer: D – Castro

Rationale: (A) Adolf Hitler (1889-1945), the Nazi leader of Germany, and (C) Hideki Tojo (1884-1948), the Japanese General and Prime Minister, were well known World War II figures who led Axis forces into war on a quest of spreading fascism. (B) Joseph Stalin (1879-1953) was the Communist Russian head of state during World War II. Although all three were repressive in their actions, it was (D) Fidel Castro is the Socialist dictator of Cuba who came into power during the 1959 revolution.

63. **Which of the following was not a leading figure during World War II? (Easy) (Skill 5.3)**

    A.   Hitler

    B.   Stalin

    C.   Tojo

    D.   Castro

    Answer: D - Castro

64.   Of all the major causes of World Wars I and II, the most significant one is considered to be:
       (Rigorous) (Skill 5.3)

       A.   Extreme nationalism

       B.   Military buildup and aggression

       C.   Political unrest

       D.   Agreements and alliances

Answer: A – Extreme nationalism

Rationale: Although military buildup and aggression, political unrest, and agreements and alliances were all characteristic of the world climate before and during World War I and World War II, the most significant cause of both wars was extreme nationalism. Nationalism is the idea that the interests and needs of a particular nation are of the utmost and primary importance above all else. Some nationalist movements could be liberation movements while others were oppressive regimes, much depends on their degree of nationalism. The nationalism that sparked WWI included a rejection of German, Austro-Hungarian, and Ottoman imperialism by Serbs, Slavs and others culminating in the assassination of Archduke Ferdinand by a Serb nationalist in 1914. Following WWI and the Treaty of Versailles, many Germans and others in the Central Alliance Nations, malcontent at the concessions and reparations of the treaty started a new form of nationalism. Adolf Hitler and the Nazi regime led this extreme nationalism. Hitler's ideas were an example of extreme, oppressive nationalism combined with political, social and economic scapegoating and was the primary cause of WWII.

65.   Who is not associated with World War II?
       (Average) (Skill 5.4)

       A.   Hitler

       B.   Tojo

       C.   Queen Victoria

       D.   Stalin

Answer: C – Queen Victoria

Rationale: (A) Hitler was the leader of Germany in WWII; (B) Tojo was the Japanese premier during the war and (D) Stalin was the leader of Russia. (C) Queen Victoria had died quite a few years earlier.

66. **The international organization established to work for world peace at the end of the Second World War is the:**
    (Average) (Skill 5.4)

    A. League of Nations

    B. United Federation of Nations

    C. United Nations

    D. United World League

    Answer: C – United Nations

    Rationale: The international organization established to work for world peace at the end of the Second World War was the United Nations. From the ashes of the failed League of Nations, established following World War I, the United Nations continues to be a major player in world affairs today.

67. **Which one of the following would not be considered a result of World War II?**
    (Average) (Skill 5.5)

    A. Economic depressions and slow resumption of trade and financial aid

    B. Western Europe was no longer the center of world power

    C. The beginnings of new power struggles not only in Europe but in Asia as well

    D. Territorial and boundary changes for many nations, especially in Europe

    Answer: A – Economic depressions and slow resumption of trade and financial aid.

    Rationale: Following World War II, the economy was vibrant and flourished from the stimulant of war and an increased dependence of the world on United States industries. Therefore, World War II didn't result in economic depressions and slow resumption of trade and financial aid. Western Europe was no longer the center of world power. New power struggles arose in Europe and Asia and many European nations underwent changing territories and boundaries.

68. **The U.S. doctrine that sought to keep communism from spreading was:**
(Average) (Skill 5.6)

   A.   The Cold War

   B.   Roll-back

   C.   Containment

   D.   Détente

Answer: C – Containment

Rationale: The doctrine that sought to keep communism from spreading was called (C) containment. Containment was the creation of the Truman Administration following World War II and spawned the creation of the North Atlantic Treaty Organization, or NATO, in 1949. (A) The Cold War was the escalation of the threat of war between the United States and the Soviet Union following World War II up to the collapse of the Berlin Wall in 1989 and the full collapse of Communism in Eastern Europe in 1991. The Cold War was a nonviolent state of extreme tension in which fears ran high and threats were made but not carried out. The idea of (B) rollback is probably a reference to policy used at some point in the Vietnam War to scale back the intensity of fighting and pull US troops out of Vietnam.

69. **The study of the ways in which different societies around the world deal with the problems of limited resources and unlimited needs and wants is in the area of:**
(Easy) (Skill 6.1)

   A.   Economics

   B.   Sociology

   C.   Anthropology

   D.   Political Science

Answer: A – Economics

Rationale: The study of the ways in which different societies around the world deal with the problems of limited resources and unlimited needs and wants is a study of Economics. Economists consider the law of supply and demand as fundamental to the study of the economy. However, Sociology and Political Science also consider the study of economics and its importance in understanding social and political systems.

70. **After World War II, the United States:**
(Average) (Skill 6.3)

    A.   Limited its involvement in European affairs

    B.   Shifted foreign policy emphasis from Europe to Asia

    C.   Passed significant legislation pertaining to aid to farmers and tariffs on imports

    D.   Entered the greatest period of economic growth in its history

Answer: D – Entered the greatest period of economic growth in its history

Rationale: After World War II, the United States did not limit or shift its involvement in European affairs. In fact, it escalated the Cold War with the Soviet Union at a swift pace and attempted to contain Communism to prevent its spread across Europe. There was no significant legislation pertaining to aid to farmers and tariffs on imports. In fact, since World War II, trade has become more liberal than ever. Free trade, no matter how risky or harmful to the people of the United States or other countries, has become the economic policy of the United States called neo-liberalism. Due to this, the United States after World War II entered the greatest period of economic growth in its history and remains a world superpower.

71. **Who did not influence U.S. major political developments after 1960?**
(Average) (Skill 6.3)

    A.   John F. Kennedy

    B.   Gerald Ford

    C.   Harry S. Truman

    D.   Lyndon B. Johnson

Answer: C – Harry S. Truman

Rationale: (A) Kennedy, (B) Ford) and (D) Johnson were all American Presidents serving after 1960. (C) Truman is the only President in the list that served prior to 1960.

72. **During the 1920s, the United States almost completely stopped all immigration. One of the reasons was:**
   (Rigorous) (Skill 6.4)

   A.   Plentiful cheap unskilled labor was no longer needed by industrialists

   B.   War debts from World War I made it difficult to render financial assistance

   C.   European nations were reluctant to allow people to leave since there was a need to rebuild populations and economic stability

   D.   The United States did not become a member of the League of Nations

   Answer: A – Plentiful cheap, unskilled labor was no longer needed by industrialists

   Rationale: The primary reason that the United States almost completely stopped all immigration during the 1920s was because their once, much needed, cheap, unskilled labor jobs, made available by the once booming industrial economy, were no longer needed. This has much to do with the increased use of machines to do the work once done by cheap, unskilled laborers.

73. The only Central American country with no standing army, a freely elected government, and considered the oldest democracy in the region is:
(Rigorous) (Skill 7.1)

A. Costa Rica

B. Belize

C. Honduras

D. Guatemala

Answer: A – Costa Rica

Rationale: Belize, Guatemala, and Honduras have all struggled over the past few hundred years. Efforts for independence from colonial powers such as Spain and Great Britain proved difficult and brought up many difficult issues such as the violent border disputes between Guatemala and Belize as late as the 1980s and 1990s that created strong tensions and almost all out war. Honduras experienced many bloody civil wars since its quest for independence began in the early nineteenth century. Even today, Honduras struggles as one of the poorest nations in the world and has continued to experience serious exploitation and abuses of workers by first world multinational corporations. Since the late eighteenth century, Costa Rica on the other hand, has experienced longstanding democracy and stability. They have no army and despite a couple of breakdowns in the political system, most notably in 1917 and 1948, it is considered the longest standing democracy in Central America.

74. **One South American country quickly and easily gained independence in the nineteenth century from European control; was noted for the uniqueness of its political stability and gradual orderly changes. This most unusual Latin American country is:**
(Rigorous) (Skill 7.1, 7.2)

A. Chile

B. Argentina

C. Venezuela

D. Brazil

Answer: D – Brazil

Rationale: While Chile, Argentina, and Venezuela all have had histories marred by civil wars, dictatorships, and numerous violent coups during their quests for independence, Brazil experienced a more rapid independence. Independence was gained quickly and more easily than the other countries due to a bloodless revolution in 1889 that officially made Brazil a republic and the economic stability they had in place from a strong coffee and rubber based economy.

75. **The principle of zero in mathematics is the discovery of the ancient civilization found in:**
(Rigorous) (Skill 7.2)

A. Egypt

B. Persia

C. Mayan

D. Babylon

Answer: C – Mayan

Rationale: The Mayan were a very advanced culture in science, astronomy and mathematics. They had made a calendar that managed to calculate with incredible accuracy, the duration of a solar year. They also had invented the numeral zero.

76. **Which political and social system contained the capital known as the richest capital in the new world?**
(Rigorous) (Skill 7.2)

    A.   The Mayans

    B.   The Atacamas

    C.   The Incas

    D.   The Tarapacas

Answer: C – The Incas

Rationale: The Incas of Peru had an extensive knowledge of surgery and medicine as well as principles of irrigation, fertilization, and terrace farming. These were unique achievements for an ancient civilization. They were also considered to have the richest capital in the new world.

77. **What was not a factor in the move for Latin American independence?**
(Rigorous) (Skill 7.3)

    A.   The American Revolution

    B.   A war with Germany

    C.   The French Revolution

    D.   Napoleon's invasion of France

Answer: B – A war with Germany

Rationale: The movement for independence in Latin America was stimulated by (A) the American Revolution, (C) the French Revolution and (D) Napoleon's invasion of France. There was no (B) war with Germany at the time.

78.   The United Provinces of Central America did not include:
       (Rigorous) (Skill 7.3)

       A.   Mexico

       B.   El Salvado

       C.   Honduras

       D.   Nicaragua

Answer: A – Mexico

Rationale: The United Provinces of Central America consisted of the areas of Guatemala, El Salvador, Honduras and Nicaragua under the rule of Braulio Carrillo. (A) Mexico is a part of North America, not Central America.

79.   "First Nations" refers to:
       (Rigorous) (Skill 8.2)

       A.   Mexican Indian tribes

       B.   American Indian tribes

       C.   Canadian Indian tribes

       D.   Honduran Indian tribes

Answer: C – Canadian Indian tribes

Rationale: "First Nations" are the Native peoples who are entitled to official recognition as part of an Indian tribe or nation. Many members of the First Nations live on reserves throughout Canada and concentrated in the provinces of British Columbia and Ontario. There are currently over 600 recognized First Nations bands or nations.

80. **Soil erosion is most likely to occur in large amounts in:**
(Rigorous) (Skill 8.6)

    A.   Mountain ranges

    B.   Deserts

    C.   Tropical rainforests

    D.   River valleys

Answer: C – Tropical rainforests

Rationale: Soil erosion is most likely to occur in tropical rainforests as the large amount of constant rainfall moves the soil at a greater rate across a greater area. Mountain ranges and river valleys experience some soil erosion but don't have the levels of precipitation found in a tropical rainforest. Deserts have virtually no soil erosion due to their climate.

81. **Which French Renaissance writer made contributions in the area of literature and philosophy?**
(Rigorous) (Skill 9.3)

    A.   Francois Rabelais

    B.   Desiderius Erasmus

    C.   Michel de Montaigne

    D.   Sir Francis Bacon

Answer: C – Michel de Montaigne

Rationale: (A) Francois Rabelais (1490-1553) was a French writer and physician who was both a practicing monk (first Franciscan then later Benedictine) and a respected humanist thinker of the Renaissance. (B) Desiderius Erasmus (1466-1536) was a Dutch humanist who was very critical of the Catholic Church but was equally conflicted with Luther's Protestant Reformation. Although Luther had once considered him an ally, Erasmus opposed Luther's break from the church and favored a more internal reform to corruption, he never left the Catholic Church. (D) Sir Francis Bacon (1561-1626) was an English philosopher and writer who pushed the idea that knowledge must come from thorough scientific knowledge and experiment, and insufficient data must not be used in reaching conclusions. (C) Michel de Montaigne (1533-1592), a French essayist from a mixed background, half Catholic and half Jewish, did write some about the dangers of absolute powers, primarily monarchs but also of the Church. His attitude changed as his examination of his own life developed into a study of mankind and nature.

82. **The changing focus during the Renaissance when artists and scholars were less concerned with religion but centered their efforts on a better understanding of people and the world was called:**
    (Easy) (Skill 9.3)

    A.   Realism

    B.   Humanism

    C.   Individualism

    D.   Intellectualism

    Answer: B – Humanism

    Rationale: Realism is a medieval philosophy that contemplated independence of existence of the body, the mind, and God. The idea of individualism is usually either a reference to an economic or political theory. Intellectualism is the placing of great importance and devotion to the exploring of the intellect. Therefore, the changing focus during the Renaissance when artists and scholars were less concerned with religion but centered their efforts on a better understanding of people and the world was called humanism.

83. **Who made important contributions in the area of anatomy during the Renaissance?**
    (Rigorous) (Skill 9.3)

    A.   Vesalius

    B.   Servetus

    C.   Galen

    D.   Harvey

    Answer: A – Vesalius

    Rationale: Andreas Vesalius (1514-1564) is considered to be the "father of anatomy" as a result of his revolutionary work on the human anatomy based on dissections of human cadavers. Prior to Vesalius, men such as Galen, (130-200) had done work in the field of anatomy, but they had based the majority of their work on animal studies.

84. **In Western Europe, the achievements of the Renaissance were unsurpassed and made these countries outstanding cultural centers on the continent. All of the following were accomplishments except: (Rigorous) (Skill 9.3)**

    A.   Investment of the printing press

    B.   A rekindling of interest in the learning of classical Greece and Rome

    C.   Growth in literature, philosophy and art

    D.   Better military tactics

Answer: D – Better military tactics

Rationale: The Renaissance in Western Europe produced many important achievements that helped push immense progress among European civilization. Some of the most important developments during the Renaissance were Gutenberg's invention of the printing press in Germany and a reexamination of the ideas and philosophies of classical Greece and Rome that eventually helped Renaissance thinkers to approach more modern ideas. Also important during the Renaissance was the growth in literature (Petrarch, Boccaccio, Erasmus), philosophy (Machiavelli, More, Bacon) and art (Van Eyck, Giotto, da Vinci). Therefore, improved military tactics is the only possible answer as it was clearly not a characteristic of the Renaissance in Western Europe.

85. **Studies in astronomy, skills in mapping, and other contributions to geographic knowledge came from:**
(Rigorous) (Skill 9.3)

    A.   Galileo

    B.   Columbus

    C.   Eratosthenes

    D.   Ptolemy

Answer: D – Ptolemy

Rationale: Ptolemy (2nd century AD) was important in the fields of astronomy and geography. His theory stated that the earth was the center of the universe and all the other planets rotated around it, a theory that was later proven false. Ptolemy, however, was important for his contributions to the fields of mapping, mathematics, and geography. Galileo (1564-1642) was also important in the field of astronomy but did not make the mapping and geographic contributions of Ptolemy. He invented and used the world's first telescope and advanced Copernicus' theory that the earth revolved around the sun, much to the dismay of the Church.

86. **The Age of Exploration begun in the 1400s was led by:**
(Average) (Skill 9.3)

    A.   The Portuguese

    B.   The Spanish

    C.   The English

    D.   The Dutch

Answer: A – The Portuguese

Rationale: Although the Age of Exploration had many important players among them, the Dutch, Spanish and English, it was the Portuguese who sent the first explorers to the New World.

87. **The ideas and innovations of the period of the Renaissance were spread throughout Europe mainly because of:**
(Rigorous) (Skill 9.3)

   A.   Extensive exploration

   B.   Craft workers and their guilds

   C.   The invention of the printing press

   D.   Increased travel and trade

   Answer: C – The invention of the printing press

   Rationale: The ideas and innovations of the Renaissance were spread throughout Europe for a number of reasons. While exploration, increased travel, and spread of craft may have aided the spread of the Renaissance to small degrees, nothing was as important to the spread of ideas as Gutenberg's invention of the printing press in Germany.

88. **Who is considered to be the most important figure in the spread of Protestantism across Switzerland?**
(Rigorous) (Skill 9.3)

   A.   Calvin

   B.   Zwingli

   C.   Munzer

   D.   Leyden

   Answer: A – Calvin

   Rationale: While Huldreich Zwingli (1484-1531) was the first to spread the Protestant Reformation in Switzerland around 1519, it was John Calvin (1509-1564), who's less radical approach to Protestantism who really made the most impact in Switzerland. Calvin's ideas separated from the Lutherans over the "Lord's Supper" debate over the sacrament, and his branch of Protestants became known as Calvinism. Calvin certainly built on Zwingli's early influence but really made the religion widespread throughout Switzerland. Thomas Munzer (1489-1525) was a German Protestant reformer who's radical and revolutionary ideas about God's will to overthrow the ruling classes and his siding with the peasantry got him beheaded. Munzer has since been studied and admired by Marxists for his views on class. Leyden (or Leiden) was a founder of the University of Leyden, a Protestant place for study in the Netherlands.

89.   **The Protestant Reformation began in:**
        (Average) (Skill 9.3)

        A.   Italy

        B.   Germany

        C.   England

        D.   Ireland

Answer: B – Germany

Rationale: The Protestant Reformation began when German Monk Martin Luther revolted in Germany. He was opposed to the abuses that he saw taking place in the Church.

90.   **Which one of the following did not contribute to early medieval European civilization?**
        (Average) (Skill 9.3)

        A.   The heritage from the classical cultures

        B.   The Christian religion

        C.   The influence of the German Barbarians

        D.   The spread of ideas through trade and commerce

Answer: D – The spread of ideas through trade and commerce

Rationale: The heritage of the classical cultures such as Greece, the Christian religion which became dominant, and the influence of the Germanic Barbarians (Visigoths, Saxons, Ostrogoths, Vandals and Franks) were all contributions to early medieval Europe and its plunge into feudalism. During this period, lives were often difficult and lived out on one single manor, with very little travel or spread of ideas through trade or commerce. Civilization seems to have halted progress during these years.

91. **The European Union does not include:**
    (Rigorous) (Skill 9.6)

    A.   A Parliamentary System

    B.   Common currency

    C.   Dictatorship

    D.   Uniform economic policies

    Answer: C – Dictatorship

    Rationale: The European Union refers to the economic and political arrangement between the European countries. There are twenty seven countries that belong to the European Union. They have, among other things, (A) a Parliamentary System, (B) common currency and (D) uniform economic policies. (C) Dictatorship is not a part of the picture.

92. **One difference between a presidential and a parliamentary system is a parliamentary system:**
    (Rigorous) (Skill 9.6)

    A.   The Prime Minister is head of government, while a president or monarch is head of state

    B.   The President is head of government and the Vice-President is head of state

    C.   The President, pro-tempore of the Senate is head of state while the prime minister is head of government

    D.   The President appoints the head of state

    Answer: A – The Prime Minister is head of government, while a president or monarch is head of state.

    Rationale: In a parliamentary system, the Prime Minister is the head of the government and the president or monarch is the head of state. In a presidential system, the President is the head of government and the head of state.

93. **Which of the following countries was not a part of the former Eastern Europe?**
(Easy) (Skill 9.7)

   A.   Romania

   B.   Bulgaria

   C.   France

   D.   Albania

   Answer: C – France

   Rationale: (A) Romania, (B) Bulgaria and (D) Albania were all a part of the Soviet bloc or what was referred to as Eastern Europe. France is a part of Western Europe.

94. **The drought stricken region of Africa south of the Sahara and extending east and west from Senegal to Somalia is:**
(Average) (Skill 10.1)

   A.   The Kalahari

   B.   The Namib

   C.   The Great Rift Valley

   D.   The Sahel

   Answer: D – The Sahel

   Rationale: The (A) Kalahari is located between the Orange and Zambezi Rivers and has an annual rainfall of about 5 to 20 inches. The (B) Namib is a desert, rocky plateau along the coast of Namibia in Southwest Africa that receives less than .5 inches of rainfall annually. The (C) Great Rift Valley is a fault system that runs 3000 miles from Syria to Mozambique and has great variations in elevation. Therefore, it is the (D) Sahel, the region of Africa South of the Sahara and extending East and West from Senegal to Somalia. The Sahel experienced a serious drought in the 1960s and then again in the 1980s and 1990s. International relief efforts have been focused there in an effort to keep the region alive.

95. **Which of the following was not a group from Africa?**
(Easy) (Skill 10.2)

   A. Inca

   B. Kushites

   C. Bantu

   D. Ibu

Answer: A – Inca

Rationale: (B) The Kushites are a group from East Africa that engage in farming. The (C) Bantu are the largest groups in East and Equatorial Africa. (D) The Ibu are a West African group. (A) The Inca were an Indian group in Peru.

96. **Where was the Slave Coast located?**
(Rigorous) (Skill 10.3)

   A. Libya

   B. Ivory Coast

   C. Mali

   D. Dahomey

Answer: D – Dahomey

Rationale: The Slave Coast was a kingdom in (D) Dahomey which was known for its cultural and unique traditions, like a female army and human sacrifices.

97. **The Nile River:**
(Easy) (Skill 11.1)

   A. Is the longest river in the world

   B. Flows through Europe

   C. Flows through Canada

   D. Flows through Mexico and the U.S.

Answer: A – Is the longest river in the world.

Rationale: The Nile River flows from Central Africa, north to the Mediterranean Sea. The Nile River Delta is in Egypt.

98. **Which was not a religion of the Middle East?**
     (Easy) (Skill 11.3)

     A.   Christianity

     B.   Hinduism

     C.   Islam

     D.   Judaism

Answer: B – Hinduism

Rationale: The three religions that are represented in the Middle East are (A) Christianity, (C) Islam and (D) Judaism. (B) Hinduism is the religion of India.

99. **The first ancient civilization to introduce and practice monotheism**
     was the:
     (Rigorous) (Skill 11.3)

     A.   Sumerians

     B.   Minoans

     C.   Phoenicians

     D.   Hebrews

Answer: D – Hebrews

Rationale: The (A) Sumerians and (C) Phoenicians both practiced religions in which many gods and goddesses were worshipped. Often these Gods/Goddesses were based on a feature of nature such as a sun, moon, weather, rocks, water, etc. The (B) Minoan culture shared many religious practices with the Ancient Egyptians. It seems that the king was somewhat of a god figure and the queen, a goddess. Much of the Minoan art points to the worship of multiple gods. Therefore, only the (D) Hebrews introduced and fully practiced monotheism, or the belief in one god.

100. **Which one of the following is not an important legacy of the Byzantine Empire?**
(Rigorous) (Skill 11.3)

    A.   It protected Western Europe from various attacks from the East by such groups as the Persians, Ottoman Turks, and Barbarians

    B.   Its center was at Constantinople

    C.   Its military organization was the foundation for modern armies

    D.   It had been a center for Christianity

Answer: C – Its military organization was the foundation for modern armies

Rationale: The Byzantine Empire (1353-1453) was the successor to the Roman Empire in the East and protected Western Europe from invaders such as the Persians and Ottomans. The Byzantine Empire was a Christian incorporation of Greek philosophy, language, and literature along with Roman government and law. Therefore, although regarded as having a strong infantry, cavalry, and Engineering corps along with excellent morale amongst its soldiers, the Byzantine Empire is not particularly considered a foundation for modern armies.

101. **The Ottoman Empire resulted in:**
(Rigorous) (Skill 11.3)

    A.   Free rule for the Middle East

    B.   A free Israel

    C.   Colonization of much of the Middle East

    D.   Colonization of the Middle East by the British

Answer: C – Colonization of much of the Middle East

Rationale: The Turks and their Ottoman Empire resulted in the (C) colonization of much of the Middle East. They did not have free rule and Israel was not I existence yet. World War I brought the Ottoman Empire to an end.

102. **The most populated continent is:**
(Easy) (Skill 12.1)

    A.   South America

    B.   Asia

    C.   Australia

    D.   Europe

Answer: B – Asia

Rationale: The most populated continent is Asia. It is also the largest continent.

103. **The world religion which includes a caste system is:**
(Average) (Skill 12.3)

    A.   Buddhism

    B.   Hinduism

    C.   Sikhism

    D.   Jainism

Answer: B – Hinduism

Rationale: Buddhism, Sikhism, and Jainism all rose out of protest against Hinduism and its practices of sacrifice and the caste system. The caste system, in which people were born into castes, would determine their class for life including who they could marry, what jobs they could perform, and their overall quality of life.

104. **The term Oceania refers to all except:**
(Average) (Skill 13.1)

    A.   Indonesia

    B.   New Zealand

    C.   Papua New Guinea

    D.   Hawaii

Answer: D – Hawaii

Rationale: (A) Indonesia, (B) New Zealand and (C) Papua New Guinea are all a part of a group of islands known as Oceania. (D) Hawaii, an island, if one of the fifty states.

105. **Which of the following geographic regions is not a part of the geography of Georgia?**
(Average) (Skill 14.1)

A.   The Atlantic Coastal Plain

B.   The Panhandle

C.   The Piedmont

D.   The Blue Ridge

Answer: B – The Panhandle

Rationale: (A) The **Atlantic Coastal Plain** makes up the eastern part of the lower half of the state, bordering on the Atlantic Ocean. (C) The **Piedmont** is a hilly region that cuts across the middle part of Georgia. It extends from the foot of the mountainous regions in the north to the edge of the coastal plains where the elevation drops rapidly, creating rapids and waterfalls where it is crossed by rivers. (D) The **Blue Ridge** mountain system extends into the northeastern corner of the state. (B) The panhandle is not a part of Georgia. Florida, Texas, and Oklahoma have panhandles which derive their name from the shape of the area.

106. **Which tribes were part of the Native American cultures of the Southeastern U.S.?**
(Rigorous) (Skill 14.2)

A.   Cherokee and Cree

B.   Inca and Mayan

C.   Hopi and Cherokee

D.   Navajo and Hopi

Answer: A – Cherokee and Cree

Rationale: The Incan and Mayan were Central American tribes. The Hopi and Navajo are Southwest American tribes. The Cherokee and Cree are Southeastern American tribes.

107. **The only colony not founded and settled for religious, political or business reasons was:**
(Average) (Skill 14.3)

   A.   Delaware

   B.   Virginia

   C.   Georgia

   D.   New York

Answer: C – Georgia

Rationale: The Swedish and the Dutch established Delaware and New York as Middle Colonies. They were established with the intention of growth by economic prosperity from farming across the countryside. The English, with the intention of generating a strong farming economy settled Virginia, a Southern Colony. Georgia was the only one of these colonies not settled for religious, political or business reasons as it was started as a place for debtors from English prisons.

108. **Who received a charter to form Georgia?**
(Rigorous) (Skill 14.3)

   A.   Vasco da Gama

   B.   King George II

   C.   James Oglethorpe

   D.   John Cabot

Answer: C – James Oglethorpe

Rationale: (A) Vasco da Gama and (D) John Cabot were early explorers. (B) King George II was the King of England when (C) James Oglethorpe, who was active in prisoner reform, requested a charter to establish Georgia as a colony for debtors.

109. **The first ten amendments to the Constitution are called the:**
     (Easy) (Skill 14.4)

     A.   Bill of Petition

     B.   Petition of Rights

     C.   Rights of Man

     D.   Bill of Rights

     Answer: D – Bill of Rights

     Rationale: The Bill of Rights is the first ten amendments to the Constitution. They were added to the Constitution within the first two years of ratification and applied only to the federal government. Since then, the passage of the Fourteenth Amendment in 1868 afforded most of the Bill of Rights to the states as well.

110. **Georgia ratified the U.S. Constitution in:**
     (Rigorous) (Skill 14.4)

     A.   1776

     B.   1788

     C.   1792

     D.   1783

     Answer: B – 1788

     Rationale: Georgia did not ratify the United States Constitution until 1788.

111. **The First Great Awakening refers to:**
(Average) (Skill 14.5)

    A.   The role of Catholicism in Georgia

    B.   A Protestant religious movement

    C.   The realization that slavery was wrong

    D.   The existence of the Ku Klux Klan

Answer: B – A Protestant religious movement

Rationale: Baptists have been present in Georgia since the first colonists arrived in 1733. At about that time, the Methodist denomination was developing in England and the American colonies during what is called the First Great Awakening. This protestant religious movement in the colonies emphasized a personal involvement in one's church and personal responsibility for sin and salvation. In Georgia, as elsewhere, protestant denominations gained in membership throughout the eighteenth century.

112. **Georgia's first constitution was adopted in:**
(Average) (Skill 14.4)

    A.   1776

    B.   1784

    C.   1779

    D.   1777

Answer: D – 1777

Rationale: Georgia adopted its first Constitution in 1777, the year after the Declaration of Independence. They were one of the first states to do so.

113. **The New South refers to:**
(Average) (Skill 14.7)

   A.   A new housing development

   B.   The South after the Civil War

   C.   The South before the Civil War

   D.   The South after World War I

Answer: B – The South after the Civil War

Rationale: The New South refers to the post Civil War South with the end of slavery and the plantation system and the growth of industry.

114. **In the post World War II years, Georgia experienced all but the following:**
(Easy) (Skill 14.9)

   A.   Elimination of the poll tax

   B.   The re-establishment of the plantation system

   C.   The development of industry

   D.   Growth of cities

Answer: B – The re-establishment of the plantation system

Rationale: The post World War II years saw (A) the elimination of the poll tax, (C) the development of industry and the (D) growth of cities. (B) The plantation system which existed prior to the Civil War was not re-established.

115. **In the post World War II years, Georgia experienced all but the following:**
(Easy) (Skill 14.9)

    A.   Elimination of the poll tax

    B.   The re-establishment of the plantation system

    C.   The development of industry

    D.   Growth of cities

Answer: A – Elimination of the poll tax

116. **Which of the following was not a Georgian?**
(Easy) (Skill 14.9)

    A.   Martin Luther King, Jr.

    B.   Rose Parks

    C.   Governor Eugene Talmadge

    D.   Senator Strom Thurmond

Answer: D – Senator Strom Thurmond

Rationale: (A) Martin Luther King, Jr. was the civil rights leader who was from Atlanta. (B) Rosa Park was the Atlanta woman who refused to move to the back of the bus which sparked the civil rights movement. (C) Governor Eugene Talmadge was a governor of Georgia. (D) Senator Strom Thurmond was from South Carolina.

117. **An obligation identified with citizenship is:**
(Easy) (Skill 15.2)

      A.   Belonging to a political party

      B.   Educating oneself

      C.   Running political office

      D.   Voting

Answer: D – Voting

Rationale: (A) Although belonging to a political party and (B) educating oneself are often done in preparation for voting, and (C) running for political office is the right of citizens who feel that they could serve their constituency well, only (D) voting is considered to be an obligation identified with citizenship.

118. **The Bill of Rights in the Georgia Constitution does not guarantee its citizens the right to:**
(Easy) (Skill 15.2)

      A.   Life, liberty and the pursuit of happiness

      B.   Freedom of Worship

      C.   To bear arms

      D.   To be free of taxation

Answer: D – To be free of taxation

Rationale: (A) Life, liberty and the pursuit of happiness, (B) Freedom of Worship and (C) the right to bear arms are all guarantees of the Georgia Constitution. There is no such thing as the rights to (D) be free of taxation.

119. **According to the Georgia Constitution, the Senate can consist of no more than:**
   (Rigorous) (Skill 15.4)

   A.   56 members

   B.   93 members

   C.   100 members

   D.   38 members

   Answer: A – 56 members

   Rationale: The Georgia State Constitution provides that the Senate shall consist of no more than 56 members and the State House of Representatives will consist of not less than 180 delegates.

120. **In the State of Georgia, a bill can be introduced by:**
   (Average) (Skill 15.6)

   A.   The Governor only

   B.   A Senator only

   C.   A House member only

   D.   Any member of the General Assembly

   Answer: D – Any member of the General Assembly

   Rationale: The General Assembly as the legislative branch of Georgia government is responsible for the enactment of laws for the State. Any member of the General Assembly may introduce a bill or a resolution to change or amend State law. Bills may have a sponsor or multiple cosponsors.

121. Which one of the following are called meridians?
(Average) (Skill 17.2)

    A.   Elevation or altitude

    B.   Ocean currents

    C.   Latitude

    D.   Longitude

Answer: D – Longitude

Rationale: Latitude is the primary influence of earth climate as it determines the climatic region in which an area lies. Elevation or altitude and ocean currents are considered to be secondary influences on climate. Longitude is considered to have no important influence over climate.

122. **Meridians, or lines of longitude, not only help in pinpointing locations but are also used for:**
(Easy) (Skill 17.2)

    A.   Measuring distance from the Poles

    B.   Determining direction of ocean currents

    C.   Determining exact locations

    D.   Measuring distance on the equator

Answer: C – Determining the time around the world

Rationale: Meridians, or lines of longitude, are the determining factor in separating time zones and determining time around the world.

123. **In which of the following disciplines would the study of physical mapping, modern or ancient, and the plotting of points and boundaries be least useful?**
(Easy) (Skill 17.2)

    A.   Sociology

    B.   Geography

    C.   Archaeology

    D.   History

Answer: A – Sociology

Rationale: In geography, archaeology, and history, the study of maps and plotting of points and boundaries is very important as all three of these disciplines hold value in understanding the spatial relations and regional characteristics of people and places. Sociology, however, mostly focuses on the social interactions of people and while location is important, the physical location is not as important as the social location such as the differences between studying people in groups or as individuals.

124. **The study of "spatial relationships and interaction" would be done by people in the field of:**
(Average) (Skill 17.2)

   A.   Political Science

   B.   Anthropology

   C.   Geography

   D.   Sociology

Answer: C – Geography

Rationale: Geography is the discipline within Social Science that most concerns itself with the study of "spatial relationships and interaction".

125. **The name for those who make maps is:**
(Rigorous) (Skill 17.2)

   A.   Haberdasher

   B.   Geographer

   C.   Cartographer

   D.   Demographer

Answer: C – Cartographer

Rationale: (A) Haberdasher is a "British dealer in men's furnishings" according to the dictionary. (B) Geographers study mostly locations, conditions, and spatial relations. (C) Cartographers are people who make maps. (D) Demographers would be most concerned with the study of human populations.

XAMonline, INC. 21 Orient Ave. Melrose, MA 02176

Toll Free number 800-509-4128

TO ORDER Fax 781-662-9268 OR www.XAMonline.com

GEORGIA ASSESSMENTS FOR THE CERTIFICATION OF EDUCATORS -GACE - 2008

PO#   Store/School:

Address 1:

Address 2 (Ship to other):

City, State Zip

Credit card number_____-_____-_____-_____   expiration_____

EMAIL _____

PHONE   **FAX**

13# ISBN 2007	TITLE	Qty	Retail	Total
978-1-58197-257-3	Basic Skills 200, 201, 202		$59.95	
978-1-58197-528-4	Biology 026, 027		$59.95	
978-1-58197-529-1	Science 024, 025		$59.95	
978-1-58197-341-9	English 020, 021		$59.95	
978-1-58197-569-7	Physics 030, 031		$59.95	
978-1-58197-531-4	Art Education Sample Test 109, 110		$15.00	
978-1-58197-545-1	History 034, 035		$59.95	
978-1-58197-527-7	Health and Physical Education 115, 116		$59.95	
978-1-58197-540-6	Chemistry 028, 029		$59.95	
978-1-58197-534-5	Reading 117, 118		$59.95	
978-1-58197-547-5	Media Specialist 101, 102		$59.95	
978-1-58197-535-2	Middle Grades Reading 012		$59.95	
978-1-58197-545-1	Middle Grades Science 014		$59.95	
978-1-58197-345-7	Middle Grades Mathematics 013		$59.95	
978-1-58197-546-8	Middle Grades Social Science 015		$59.95	
978-158-197-573-4	Middle Grades Language Arts 011		$59.95	
978-1-58197-346-4	Mathematics 022, 023		$59.95	
978-1-58197-549-9	Political Science 032, 033		$59.95	
978-1-58197-544-4	Paraprofessional Assessment 177		$59.95	
978-1-58197-542-0	Professional Pedagogy Assessment 171, 172		$59.95	
978-1-58197-259-7	Early Childhood Education 001, 002		$59.95	
978-1-58197-548-2	School Counseling 103, 104		$59.95	
978-1-58197-541-3	Spanish 141, 142		$59.95	
978-1-58197-610-6	Special Education General Curriculum 081, 082		$73.50	
978-1-58197-530-7	French Sample Test 143, 144		$15.00	
			SUBTOTAL	
FOR PRODUCT PRICES GO TO WWW.XAMONLINE.COM			Ship	$8.25
			TOTAL	

LaVergne, TN USA
27 December 2010
210196LV00001B/2/P